CASTLES OF IRELAND

Frontispiece.]

ADARE CASTLE.

Castles of Ireland

Some Fortress Histories and Legends

BY

C. L. ADAMS

ILLUSTRATED BY REV. CANON LUCIUS O'BRIEN

Fredonia Books
Amsterdam, The Netherlands

Castles of Ireland:
Some Fortress Histories and Legends

by
C. L. Adams

ISBN: 1-4101-0300-5

Copyright © 2003 by Fredonia Books

Reprinted from the 1904 edition

Fredonia Books
Amsterdam, The Netherlands
http://www.fredoniabooks.com

All rights reserved, including the right to reproduce this book, or portions thereof, in any form.

In order to make original editions of historical works available to scholars at an economical price, this facsimile of the original edition of 1904 is reproduced from the best available copy and has been digitally enhanced to improve legibility, but the text remains unaltered to retain historical authenticity.

INTRODUCTION

THE Castles of Ireland are far too numerous for any single volume to contain their separate histories, and all that I claim for the present work is that it includes epitomised accounts of those of chief interest, as well as some regarding which I had special facilities for collecting information. It is, I also believe, the first collection of such records, and therefore I hope but the forerunner of similar works which may be issued in the future, so that the time will yet come when all these interesting relics of a troubled and stormy past may be classified and chronicled, and the present obscurity in which the history of so many of them is shrouded be entirely cleared away.

The number of ruined castles in Ireland is always a matter of surprise to visitors from the Sister Isle, and perhaps they help us, of less stirring days, to realise more fully the continual state of warfare in which our ancestors must have lived than printed records can ever do.

These castles range in dimensions from the few blocks of protruding masonry on the green sward, which mark the foundation of a ruined peel tower, or the scarcely traceable line of wall which was once a fortified bawn, to the majestic ruins of castles like Adare with its three distinct and separate fortifications one within the other, or royal Trim, deemed strong enough to be a prison for English princes.

Yet in the majority of cases little or nothing is known locally about the builders, owners or destroyers who have left us these picturesque, if somewhat sad, mementoes of their warfaring existence. Three items of information will in all probability be supplied to the enquirer—that they were built by King John, occupied by the Geraldines, and demolished by Cromwell in person, and indeed if the hill from which the bombardment was carried out is not shown to the stranger his informant is lacking in the general art of story-telling. In some cases the origin of the castles is boldly attributed by tradition to the Danes, thereby unconsciously introducing the much wider controversy as to whether such stone fortresses were known in Ireland before the landing of the Normans at Wexford in 1169. Be this as it may, it was only subsequent to this date that they were built in any number. Both invaders and invaded relied chiefly on these strongholds for obtaining supremacy in their constant struggles. Grants of land were generally given with the condition of erecting a fortified residence. It was only when the introduction of gunpowder rendered such buildings untenable in war, that they were very generally deserted for more comfortable dwellings, and jackdaws alone keep watch to-day from many a crumbling battlement that once echoed a sentinel's tread, and bovine heads protrude from the doorways from which mailed knights rode forth to battle.

I regret to say that space forbids my mentioning by name all those owners of castles and others who have so generously assisted me in compiling the following accounts, but perhaps I may be allowed to specially acknowledge the valuable help I received from the Librarian and Assistant Librarians of the National Library, Dublin, Lord Walter Fitzgerald, and Mr. Herbert Wood, of the Public Record Office.

C. L. ADAMS.

LONDON, 1904.

CONTENTS

	PAGE
INTRODUCTION	v
LEGEND OF KILKEA CASTLE	xi
ADARE CASTLE	1
ANTRIM CASTLE	9
ARKLOW CASTLE	15
ARTANE CASTLE	18
ATHLONE CASTLE	22
BALLYMOTE CASTLE	27
BALLYSHANNON CASTLE	31
BALLYTEIGUE CASTLE	37
BARBERSTOWN CASTLE	39
BARGY CASTLE	42
BARRYSCOURT CASTLE	45
BIRR CASTLE	48
BLACK CASTLE, WICKLOW	54
BLARNEY CASTLE	57
BUNRATTY CASTLE	65
CARLOW CASTLE	71
CARRICKFERGUS CASTLE	77
CARRICK-ON-SUIR CASTLE	85
CARRIGOGUNNEL CASTLE	90
CASTLE BARNARD	97
CASTLE BORO	101
CASTLE DONOVAN	104
CASTLE KEVIN, COUNTY CORK	107
CASTLE KEVIN, COUNTY WICKLOW	109
CASTLE SALEM	114
CLOGHAN CASTLE	116
CROM CASTLE	121
DOE CASTLE	126
DRIMNAGH CASTLE	133
DUBLIN CASTLE	137
DUNDANIEL CASTLE	142

CONTENTS

	PAGE
DUNDRUM CASTLE, COUNTY DOWN	148
DUNDRUM CASTLE, COUNTY DUBLIN	152
DUNLUCE CASTLE	157
DUNSOGHLY CASTLE	165
ENNISCORTHY CASTLE	168
ENNISKILLEN CASTLE	172
FERNS CASTLE	177
FERRYCARRIG AND SHANA COURT CASTLES	182
GEASHILL CASTLE	185
GLENARM CASTLE	191
GLIN CASTLE	193
GREENCASTLE, COUNTY DONEGAL	198
GREENCASTLE, COUNTY DOWN	202
HOWTH CASTLE	209
KILBARRON CASTLE	214
KILBRITTAIN CASTLE	217
KILKEA CASTLE	220
KILKENNY CASTLE	228
KILLIANE CASTLE	235
KILLYLEAGH CASTLE	239
KING JOHN'S CASTLE, CARLINGFORD	244
KING JOHN'S CASTLE, LIMERICK	250
LEA CASTLE	257
LEAP CASTLE	264
LEIXLIP CASTLE	272
LISMORE CASTLE	280
LOHORT CASTLE	285
LOUGH CUTRA CASTLE	287
MACROOM CASTLE	289
MALAHIDE CASTLE	292
MALLOW CASTLE	297
MAYNOOTH CASTLE	305
MONGEVLIN CASTLE	311
MONKSTOWN CASTLE, COUNTY CORK	313
PORTUMNA CASTLE	316
ROSCOMMON CASTLE	318
ROSS CASTLE	325
ROSSCLOGHER CASTLE	330
SHANES CASTLE	336
SWORDS CASTLE	344
TILLYRA CASTLE	350
TIMON CASTLE	351
TRALEE CASTLE	353
TRIM CASTLE	359

LIST OF ILLUSTRATIONS

	PAGE
ADARE CASTLE	*Frontispiece*
ANTRIM CASTLE	8
BIRR CASTLE	49
BLACK CASTLE, WICKLOW	55
BLARNEY CASTLE	59
BUNRATTY CASTLE	64
CARLOW CASTLE	72
CARRICKFERGUS CASTLE	79
CARRICK-ON-SUIR CASTLE	84
CARRIGOGUNNEL CASTLE	91
CASTLE DONOVAN	105
CROM CASTLE	120
DRIMNAGH CASTLE	132
DUBLIN CASTLE	136
DUNDRUM CASTLE, COUNTY DOWN	149
DUNLUCE CASTLE	156
DUNSOGHLY CASTLE	164
ENNISKILLEN CASTLE	173
GLENARM CASTLE	190
GREENCASTLE, COUNTY DONEGAL	199
GREENCASTLE, COUNTY DOWN	203
HOWTH CASTLE	208
KILBARRON CASTLE	215
KILKEA CASTLE	221
KILKENNY CASTLE	229
KILLYLEAGH CASTLE	238
KING JOHN'S CASTLE, CARLINGFORD	245
KING JOHN'S CASTLE, LIMERICK	251

LIST OF ILLUSTRATIONS

	PAGE
LEA CASTLE (INTERIOR)	258
LEA CASTLE (EXTERIOR)	262
LEAP CASTLE	265
LEIXLIP CASTLE	273
LISMORE CASTLE	282
MALLOW CASTLE	298
MAYNOOTH CASTLE	304
ROSS CASTLE	324
SHANE'S CASTLE	337
SWORDS CASTLE	345
TRIM CASTLE	361

CASTLES OF IRELAND

THE LEGEND OF KILKEA CASTLE.

IT is seven years since they last awoke
   From their death-like sleep in Mullaghmast,
And the ghostly troop, with its snow-white horse,
   On the Curragh plain to Kilkea rode past.
For the Lord of Kildare goes forth to-night,
   And has left his rest in the lonely rath.
Oh, roughen the road for the silver shoes,
   That they wear full soon on his homeward path.

So thus to his own he may come again,
   With a trumpet blast and his warriors bold,
And the spell that was by his lady cast
   Will pass away as a tale once told.
For dearly she loved her noble lord,
   And she wished that no secret from her he kept,
So she longed to know why in chamber small
   He watched and toiled while the household slept.

But the Wizard Earl would not tell to her
   The secret dark of his vaulted cell,
"For fear," he said, "in the human frame,
   Lets loose the power of furthest hell."
But she feared for naught save his waning love,
   And at length to her wish he bent an ear,
So flood, and serpent, and ghost gave place,
   For the lady's heart had shown no fear.

Then her lord to a bird was soon transformed,
   That rested its wing on her shoulder fair;
But the lady screamed and swooned away
   When a cat sprang forth from the empty air.
For a woman must fear for the one she loves,
   And a woman's heart will break in twain,
When she knows that her hand has struck the blow
   To the man she had died to save from pain.

And thus the Earl must sleep as dead
   Till the silver shoes of his steed are worn,
By which every seven years, they say,
   To Kilkea and back to the rath he's born.
And swiftly they pass, that phantom band,
   With the Earl on his charger gleaming white,
So we think 'tis the shade of a cloud goes by,
   With a shifting beam of the moon's pale light.

PEERS HERVEY

ADARE CASTLE

> "Peaceful it stands, the mighty pile
> By many a heart's blood once defended,
> Yet silent now as cloistered aisle,
> Where rung the sounds of banquet splendid."
> GERALD GRIFFIN.

THIS name is a corruption of Athdare, or Ath-daar, signifying "The ford of oaks." The present village is situated on the west bank of the River Maig, nine miles south-south-west of Limerick.

Desmond Castle, on the east bank, commands the river pass, and near the northern entrance to the castle were formerly the remains of a gateway and wall, traditionally supposed to have belonged to the ancient town of Adare.

The ruins of the fortress are extensive. They consist of an outer and inner ward, separated by a moat, which in former times was crossed by a drawbridge.

There are three entrances to the outer ward, the chief being a square gate tower in the west wall which was defended by a portcullis. There is another entrance on the north, as well as a doorway opening on the river.

The chief buildings are situated near the water's edge. They consist of the great hall which is 75 feet long by 37 feet in breadth. It is lighted by three windows of rough masonry in its south wall and by one on the west, with fifteenth-century "ogee" heads inserted in the older workmanship.

The doorway on the east opens to the river. The chief

entrance and porch were on the north side. The base of one of the sandstone jambs remains, showing it to have been of thirteenth century date. The walls are 3 feet thick, and the roof, which had a very high gable, was supported by four pillars.

At the eastern end are the buttery and smaller offices, while separated from them by a passage is the ruined kitchen (45 feet by 19 feet), which contains the remains of an oven and also a small well of river water. A curtain wall running west, connects these building with a fine oblong, two-storey structure, 56 feet by 31 feet, which is remarkable, inasmuch as the walls of the top storey are thicker than those below, the extra width being supported by projecting stones. The top room, which has loops splayed for archery, was reached by an exterior stone stair. The floor was supported on beams, and the lower room seems to have been used as a stable.

Adjoining the building is a small square tower, which projects into the river that flows under it through an archway in the basement. A wall connects this tower with the gateway.

The inner ward is now reached by a small wooden bridge. The gate tower is connected with the S.E. angle of the keep by a thick curved curtain with an embrasured and looped parapet. A turret protected the juncture of the outer and inner walls. A semicircular tower also projects from the boundary wall on the left of the inner court. It was loopholed, and divided into two storeys.

The keep, which is in the inner court, is about 40 feet square and 67 feet high. Only the north wall and the portions adjoining it remain at their original height. The side next the river is entirely broken down, tradition saying it was destroyed with cannon in Cromwell's time from the opposite hill. The angles of the remaining wall are crowned with turrets.

The doorway leading to the vaults being of later date

ADARE CASTLE

than the rest it is supposed they were of more recent insertion. One of the dungeons seems to have been used as a prison. It is lighted by a loop of peculiar construction.

A staircase leads to the chief apartments, and a well of river water is within the walls. The height of the keep seems to have had a third added to it after its original construction as is shown by the old weather-tabling of the roof. The present building was divided into three storeys above the ground floor, which was vaulted. The stairway was in the thickness of the west wall. Small cells occupy the projecting portions at the angles.

From the objects that have been found in the moat which surrounds the keep, it has been thought likely that it occupies the site of a rath, as some of the relics are of much anterior date to the Norman Conquest. The fortress is supposed to have been formerly a stronghold of the O'Donovans until they were dispossessed by the invaders.

The architecture of one of the windows seems to be that in vogue during the close of the twelfth century.

Lenihan states that Adare was famous for its castle and church in the reign of Henry II.

Geoffrey de Mariscis, Justiciary of Ireland, was granted permission to hold a fair in his manor of Adare in 1226, but according to the Spanish historian, Lopez, it had passed into the hands of the "Earls" of Kildare in 1227, when (still according to him) the Earl of March came from Scotland to Adare on shipping business, and the "Earls" of Kildare, not deeming the accommodation at the inn fit for his rank, insisted that he should come to their castle. During the visit he spoke in such praise of the Trinitarian order that the Earl's father said he would found a priory at Adare. The story is probably inaccurate. In the first place the Earldom of Kildare was not created until 1316, and Lopez speaks of "Earls" in the plural. It is also hard to imagine what shipping business could have been transacted in an inland town. Yet no doubt there is some foundation for the record, as in 1279, 1315, and 1464 other abbeys were founded at Adare by the Kildare Geraldines.

In 1290 the manor of Adare was in the possession of Maurice FitzGerald, 5th Baron of Offaly, and his wife, Lady Agnes de Valence, cousin of the King. Their claim being disputed, a charter was issued in 1299 confirming the grant.

The castle was rebuilt in 1326 by the 2nd Earl of Kildare.

Edward III. granted the lands of Adare to the Earl's stepfather, Sir John Darcy, during the Earl's minority in 1329, and it was probably at this time that the inquisition was held in the report of which we find the first authenticated mention of the castle. It is described as having a hall, a chapel with stone walls and covered with thatch, a tower covered with planks, a kitchen covered with slates, and a chamber near the stone part covered with thatch.

Turlough O'Brien burned it sometime during the fifteenth century.

The estate was forfeited by Gerald, 8th Earl of Kildare, for his adherence to the cause of Perkin Warbeck, but it was shortly afterwards restored.

When the 9th Earl of Kildare was summoned to London to answer the charge of allowing the Earl of Desmond to evade arrest, it is likely that he set out from Adare, as he was in that part of the country. It was during this trial in 1526 that Cardinal Wolsey cried out, "The Earl, nay, the King of Kildare—for, when you are disposed, you reign more like than rule the land."

Upon the confiscation of the estate after the rebellion of "The Silken Thomas," in 1536, the Earl of Desmond became possessed of Adare, which he leased the following year from the Crown. He seems to have done so with the intention of restoring the lands to his kinsman, the young Gerald, then in hiding from the Government.

ADARE CASTLE

The castle remained in the Earl of Desmond's possession (with intermissions) until his death in 1583, when it reverted to the Kildare branch of the Geraldines. His name still clings to the ruins, no doubt because of the stormy scenes that occurred at Adare during his short ownership.

Here in 1570 the celebrated Leverus, Bishop of Kildare, sought shelter with the Earl of Desmond. He had been tutor to the young heir to the Earldom of Kildare, when a price was set upon his head after the rebellion of the Lord Thomas. Leverus had saved his pupil, who was ill with smallpox, by putting him in a basket, wrapped in blankets, and taking him from Kildare to Thomond.

In 1578 the castle was taken by Sir Nicholas Malby after a siege of eleven days, and garrisoned by English under Captain Carew.

Sir John Desmond, the Earl's brother, shortly afterwards assaulted it in vain. The following year saw continual warfare round the town of Adare between the two parties, and a garrison of English was placed there by the Lord Deputy, who was accompanied by the Earl of Kildare.

Desmond made every effort to recover the castle in 1580. He resorted to several stratagems, one of which was to send a beautiful young woman to the constable, by whose means he hoped the castle might be betrayed. But upon hearing from whence she came, the officer tied a stone round her neck and threw her into the river.

The following year, however, Colonel Zouch, having disbanded part of his forces, the Earl gained possession of the castle, and put the garrison to the sword. Fresh forces arriving from Cork, Zouch marched on Adare, only to find it deserted; but he pursued the Irish to Lisconnel, where he defeated them in an engagement.

Captain Mynce was recommended as custodian in 1585, and in 1598 Mr. Marshal's castles of Bruff and Adare were reported to have been taken.

In 1600 the Sugan Earl of Desmond occupied Adare,

but upon the approach of Sir George Carew, in July, the Irish burnt the castle and fled. He reports it as "a manor-house belonging to the Earls of Kildare, wholly ruined by Pierce Lacy."

This Lacy was one of the Earl of Desmond's supporters. Insurgents seized the stronghold in 1641, but were driven out by the Earl of Castlehaven, and the castle is said to have been dismantled in 1657 by Cromwell's orders.

The lands remained in the possession of the Earls of Kildare until 1721, when they were purchased by the Quin family, now represented by the Earl of Dunraven.

Authorities Consulted.

J. Dowd, "The County of Limerick."
The Countess and Earl of Dunraven, "Memorials of Adare."
Marquis of Kildare, "The Earls of Kildare."
M. Lenihan, "Limerick : Its History and Antiquities."
J. Ferrar, "History of Limerick."
Parliamentary Gazetteer.
Calendar of State Documents.
Calendar of Carew MSS.

ANTRIM CASTLE.

ANTRIM CASTLE

> "Brown in the rust of time—it stands sublime
> With overhanging battlements and towers,
> And works of old defence—a massy pile,
> And the broad river winds around its base
> In bright, unruffled course."

ANTRIM town is situated in the county of the same name, on the right bank of Six-Mile-Water just before it enters Lough Neagh, a little more than thirteen miles north-west of Belfast.

The castle, sometimes erroneously called Massereene Castle, was erected in the reign of James I. by Sir Hugh Clotworthy, a gentleman of Somersetshire.

Hugh and Lewis Clotworthy were amongst those who accompanied the Earl of Essex in his expedition to Ulster in 1573, and in 1603 Captain Hugh Clotworthy was doing garrison duty at Carrickfergus under Sir Arthur Chichester. In 1605 he received a grant of the confiscated lands of "Massarine," and erected a residence on the site of the present building. This consisted of a moated courtyard flanked by towers.

Shortly afterwards he was knighted, and married the beautiful Marion Langford "of the flowing tresses."

In 1610 Sir Hugh Clotworthy commenced to erect a castle according to the undertaking of the grant, and it was completed in three years. It consisted of a quadrangular pile, three storeys in height, which enclosed a small courtyard, and was flanked at the angles by square towers. The walls measured 6 feet in thickness. A short flight of granite steps led to the entrance hall, which contained a great open fireplace. On the right of the hall was the "buttery," where at about 3 feet from the floor was a small square door through which food was distributed to the poor. The townspeople had the privilege of passing through the hall by the buttery to a pathway leading to the lake.

The river protected the castle on the west, while on the other sides it was surrounded by a moat. The "Mount" to the east of the castle was furnished with ordnance. Two bastions commanded respectively the town on the south and the lake on the north. The whole fortress covered more than five acres of ground.

Extensive alterations were made in the castle in 1813 by Chichester, fourth Earl of Massereene. At present it consists of a square embattled building of three storeys with a long wing at the same elevation running northward, flanked by two castellated towers near the end. At its extremity rises a very high tower in Italian style, which gives a most picturesque appearance to the stables when viewed from the lough.

The grand entrance hall is square, and the wall which once divided it from the centre courtyard has been replaced by oak pillars leading to an inner vestibule and staircase which occupies the site of the former open space. From this a passage extends the whole length of the castle to the Italian tower. The oak room is a magnificent apartment, wainscotted in dark Irish oak, relieved with lighter shades and exquisitely carved. The panels are painted with armorial bearings. There is a beautiful carved chimney-piece at the lower end of the apartment set with the grate in one frame. Upon touching a secret spring this all swings out and discloses a recess large enough to hide in. The furniture of the room is also

ANTRIM CASTLE

Irish oak. Here is preserved the "Speaker's Chair" of the Irish House of Commons.

The drawing-room and library are both very handsome rooms, and with the oak room, breakfast-room, parlour, and dining-room, form a splendid suite of rooms, opening one off the other. There is a very valuable collection of family portraits in the castle.

The Italian tower contains the chapel, record-room, and a small study. The first of these is in Gothic style and beautifully proportioned. Among the treasures to be seen here are Cranmer's New Testament and Queen Mary's Bible.

Over the front entrance is a stone screen slightly raised from the wall and ending in a pointed arch under the parapet wall. It is about 8 feet in width, and is handsomely sculptured with arms, mottoes, and events connected with the castle and its owners. At the top is a carved head representing Charles I., supposed to have been placed there by the first Viscount when he added to the fortress in 1662. Lower down are the arms of the founder and his wife, with the date of erection (1613), &c. Immediately over the hall door is a carved shell supported by mermaids, which represents the Skeffyngton crest.

The two ancient bastions have been formed into terrace gardens, and the grounds of the whole castle are most beautifully laid out. A splendid view is obtained from the old "Mount," the summit of which is reached by a winding path.

The demesne is entered from the town through a castellated entrance, surmounted by a turretted warder's lodge, which upon state occasions in modern times has been sentinelled with warders garbed in antique costume, battle-axe in hand.

Near the gatehouse upon the angle of the southern bastion is the carved stone figure of "Lady Marion's Wolfdog," representing that splendid Irish breed now extinct. At one time this statue surmounted a turret of the castle, where the great animal appeared to be keeping a "look out" over the lough. Local superstition said that it had appeared there without human agency on the night after the incident occurred with which the legend connects it, and that as long as it keeps watch over the castle and grounds so long will the race of Lady Marion Clotworthy continue to live and thrive.

The story is as follows:—The lovely bride of Sir Hugh Clotworthy wandered one day in his absence outside the bawn walls along the shores of Lough Neagh. Hearing behind her a low growl, she turned round to find a wolf preparing to spring. In her terror she fell to the ground, and with the force of the animal's leap he passed beyond her. Before he had time to return to his victim a large wolf-hound had seized him in mortal combat. The lady fainted at the sight, and when she recovered consciousness the dog was licking her hands, while the wolf lay dead. She bound up the noble animal's wounds, and he followed her home, being her constant companion for many a day, until he suddenly disappeared and no trace of him could be found.

Shortly after this the castle was built, and one wild, stormy night the deep baying of a wolf-hound was heard passing round and round the walls of the fortress. The warders, scared by the unusual sound, kindled the beacon on the mount, and by its light discoverd a band of natives making preparation for an attack. A few shots dispersed them, but before they left a howl of pain was heard near the entrance gate, where a few flattened bullets were found the next morning. Then upon the castle tower the affrighted warders perceived the stone figure of the dog.

It is probable that Sir Hugh had the figure carved to please his lady, and after the attack considered its mysterious appearance on the fortress the best protection against a superstitious enemy, who had most likely destroyed the beautiful original, which had come from the Abbey of Massarine to warn its former kind friend of danger.

Sir Hugh Clotworthy was succeeded by his son, Sir John, afterwards first Viscount Massereene. He sat in both the Irish and English Houses of Commons, and was one of Stafford's chief accusers. He was in London when the rebellion of 1641 broke out. The insurrection was in part prevented by a retainer of his, one Owen O'Conally, called "the great informer."

Sir John's brother, James, secured the castle in his absence from attack, and the owner returned to it at the end of the year, and took command of the forces in the district. He was imprisoned in 1647 for three years for censuring (with other Members of Parliament) the seizing of the King. During this time his mother, the Lady Marion, occupied the castle. O'Conally commanded Sir John's regiment in his absence, and in 1649 it was joined to General Monk's forces. Oliver Cromwell made O'Conally commander of the regiment then at Antrim Castle, and Monro marched against it and killed its leader, but the castle still remained in possession of the troops.

Sir John was raised to the peerage by Charles II. in 1660 as Viscount Massereene. He had no son, and was succeeded in the title and estates by his son-in-law, Sir John Skeffyngton, and henceforward his surname was added to the family name of Clotworthy.

James II. conferred several honourable appointments on him, nevertheless the "Antrim Association" was formed in the castle upon the beginning of the revolution, and the Viscount's eldest son, Colonel Clotworthy Skeffyngton, was appointed Commander-in-Chief.

The Jacobite General, Hamilton, pushed on to Antrim after his success at Dromore, and Lord Massereene fled from the castle at his approach. The family plate, valued at £3,000, which was hidden before the family left, was shown to the newcomers by a servant, and was seized by them.

Colonel Gordon O'Neill, son of the great Sir Phelim, occupied the fortress in 1688–89, but Lord Massereene recovered his property when William came to the throne.

His grandson was created an earl in 1756, but this title expired in 1816, when Harriet Viscountess of Massereene succeeded to the estates, and through her they passed to the present Viscount.

The last time that the castle figured in history was during the battle of Antrim in 1798. The yeomanry bravely held the castle gardens against all comers, while the great gun of the mount, " Roaring Tatty," was drawn from its position and fired on the town. One, Ezekiel Vance, gave the signal to the military outside the town to advance by waving a woman's red cloak from one of the towers of the fortress.

The present Lord Massereene is the 11th Viscount.

Authorities Consulted.

C. O'Neill, " Antrim Castle."
O'Laverty, " Diocese of Down and Connor."
Smith, " Memoirs of '98," in *Ulster Journal of Archæology*.
Parliamentary Gazetteer.

ARKLOW CASTLE

THE town of Arklow is thirty-nine miles and a half south by east of Dublin, in the County Wicklow.

Joyce thinks the name may have a Danish origin, but others believe it comes from the Irish word *Ardchoch*.

The ruins of the castle are situated on high ground on the south side of the Ovoca River, and consist of a ruined and now ivy-clad round tower, which protected the northern angle. This building is broken on the riverside to about 12 feet in height, but on the south side it measures some 46 feet.

About 10 feet from the ground is a pointed doorway, which leads to a stone floor formed by the arch of the lower chamber. Thirty-four stone steps in the thickness of the wall give access to the top of the tower from this platform.

This building is one of similar flanking towers which defended the walls still running south and west, the remains of some of the other turrets having only disappeared during the last century.

A barrack for two companies of soldiers was built near the former site of the castle, and the walls of the latter were incorporated with those enclosing the yard of the new building.

A monastery was founded at Arklow by Theobald FitzWalter, hereditary Lord Butler of Ireland, who also built the castle.

Lord Theobald Walter le Botiller died in the castle in

1285, and was buried in the convent of the Friars Preachers in Arklow, beneath a tomb ornamented with his effigy.

In 1331 the castle was attacked by the O'Tooles, but Lord de Bermingham came to its relief with a small party, and drove the enemy off with considerable loss. The same year, however, the Irish got possession of it by treachery.

The Lord Chief Justice again re-captured it in 1332, with the help of Dublin citizens and the English settlers in Wicklow, so that it was once more in the King's hands, and at this time it was partly rebuilt.

In 1522-24 Sir Piers Butler was accused of being in league with the O'Mores, and of using the castle of Arklow to rob both by land and sea.

The following year the Earl of Kildare made a series of charges against the Earl of Ormond through Lord Leonard Grey, amongst which was that of keeping a ward of evil persons in Arklow Castle to rob the surrounding neighbourhood.

A few years later (1532) the Earl of Ossory and Ormond complained to Thomas Cromwell that the Earl of Kildare was trying to get some of his castles into his possession (amongst which he mentioned Arklow), under the plea of holding them by lease from the Earl of Wiltshire. He states these fortresses "bee the veray keyes of the cuntrey," and that the King ought to prevent Kildare becoming too powerful. Sir Thomas Bullen had then been created Earl of Ormond and Wiltshire by Henry VIII.

During the rebellion of "the Silken Thomas" in 1536 the King had to send "an army royal" to get the castle of Arklow and others into his possession.

The following year the manor was re-granted to Peter Butler, Earl of Ossory and Ormond.

In 1578, when forming the county of "Wicklo or Arcklo," the castle of the latter is mentioned as the chief

ARKLOW CASTLE

place, and belonging to the Earl of Ormond, who was also Lord of Arcklow.

The Lord Deputy placed a garrison there in 1581.

In March, 1589, Feagh M'Hugh O'Byrne seized the wife of Hugh Duff O'Donnell, uncle to Sir Hugh O'Donnell, who was a tenant of the Earl of Ormond in Arklow Castle. In the autumn of the same year O'Byrne tried to force an entrance into the castle "to execute his malice" upon Hugh O'Donnell.

The land was laid waste round the fortress in 1600, but the castle was held for the Queen by the Earl of Ormond at his own expense.

In the rebellion of 1641 the Irish surprised the fortress and killed the garrison. It remained in their possession until 1649, when it was captured by Cromwell's forces, of which the following is the account:—

"The army marched through almost a desolate country until it came to a passage of the River Doro, about a mile above the Castle of Arklow, which was the first seat and honour of the Marquis of Ormond's family, which he had strongly fortified; but it was upon the approach of the army quitted, wherein he (Cromwell) left another company of foot."

AUTHORITIES CONSULTED.

MS. Ordnance Survey.
Brewer, "Beauties of Ireland."
Grose, "Antiquities of Ireland."
Bagwell, "Ireland Under the Tudors."
Joyce, "Irish Names of Places."
Carew MSS.
State Papers.
Marquis of Kildare, "Earls of Kildare."
Griffiths, "Chronicles of County Wexford."
Murphy, "Cromwell in Ireland."
Parliamentary Gazetteer.

ARTANE CASTLE

THE name was originally Tartain, and is probably derived from Tortan, meaning a diminutive *tor*, being a small knoll or high turf-bank. The site of the former castle is situated on the southern border of the Barony of Coolock, in the County of Dublin, about three miles from the city.

The Artane Industrial School now occupies the castle grounds, and the manor house is used as the residence of the Christian Brothers. Lewis states that this house was built of stones from the old castle, but, at any rate, the present dining-room is supported by beams taken from the fortress.

A hen-run belonging to the school is now on the site of the former stronghold not far from the present house.

The manor of Artane was acquired by the family of Hollywood, or "de Sacro Bosco," in the fourteenth century, by Robert de Hollywood, one of the Remembrancers, and afterwards Baron of the Exchequer.

In 1416 and 1420 the King committed the custody of the lands to Philip Charles and Richard FitzEustace during the minority of Robert Hollywood, the King's ward, son of the late Christopher Hollywood.

On the 27th of July, 1534, the rash Lord Offaly rose in rebellion, and threw the Sword of State on the Council table in Dublin, upon the rumour of his father, the Earl of Kildare, having been murdered in London. He left the presence of the assembly with armed men to muster fresh forces for the rising, and Dublin was at once seized with panic.

John Allen, Archbishop of Dublin, was then in Dublin Castle, and having been as bitter and relentless a foe of the Geraldines as his patron Wolsey, he decided to fly when news of the outbreak reached him. He had with him a trusted servant named Bartholomew FitzGerald, who urged him to sail to England, and offered to pilot him across. The Archbishop seems to have had implicit faith in his follower, although a Geraldine, and it has never been actually proved that it was misplaced.

The Prelate and his attendants embarked in the evening at Dames Gate, but owing, some say to adverse winds, and others to the design of the pilot, the little vessel stranded at Clontarf.

The Archbishop at once made his way to the house of his late friend, Thomas Hollywood, at Artane, whose hospitality he had commemorated in his "Repertorium Viride."

At this time the wardship of the heir, Nicholas Hollywood, was in the hands of Richard Delahide and Thomas Howth.

It seems hardly possible that the Lord Thomas FitzGerald could have heard of the mishap so quickly unless treachery had been employed. Be that as it may, he and a band of armed followers arrived at Artane in the early morning, being the 28th of July, and surrounded the castle while the Archbishop still slept.

Among the party were the young Vice-Deputy's uncles, Sir James and Oliver FitzGerald, James Delahide, and about forty men.

He sent two Dublin yeomen, John Teeling and Nicholas Wafer, into the house to bring out the Archbishop. They dragged him out of bed, and brought him before the Lord Thomas "feeble for age and sickness, kneeling in his shirt and mantle, bequeathing his soul to

God, his body to the traitor's mercy." He "besought him not to remember former injuries, but to consider his present calamity, and whatever malice he might bear to his person to respect his calling."

It seems that the "Silken Thomas" was touched by the appeal of his helpless foe, and turning his head aside, he said, "*Beir uaim an bodach*," meaning, "Take the churl away from me," and, no doubt, as he afterwards said, he only intended them to imprison him. His followers, however, put a different interpretation upon his order, and immediately murdered the Archbishop, who was in the fifty-eighth year of his age.

Some say he was dragged within the castle hall, and there put to death, while others say that the spot on which he was slain was hedged in and shunned as an unholy place for many years.

Lord Thomas could not have been ignorant of what had occurred, as he sent Robert Reilly the same day to Maynooth with a casket which had belonged to the murdered prelate.

Lord Offaly was excommunicated for the crime in St. Patrick's Cathedral with great solemnity.

Shortly after this Thomas Howth, *alias* St. Laurence, one of young Hollywood's guardians, went to live at Artane.

This Nicholas Hollywood also died while his son Christopher was a minor, and in 1570 the wardship and marriage of the boy was granted to John Bathe, of Drumcondra. In 1585 a Charles Hollywood is referred to as being of Tartaine.

Nicholas Hollywood possessed the manor and lands of Artane in 1587. They contained one castle, six messuages, and one hundred and ninety acres of land held of the King, *in capite* by knight's service. He died in 1629.

During the rebellion of 1641 Lord Netterville's son, Luke, possessed himself of the castle, and established a

ARTANE CASTLE

body of Royalist troops in the stronghold. He met with no opposition, as one of the Hollywood family named Christopher was a partisan, who afterwards sat in the Council of Confederate Catholics at Kilkenny.

Nicholas Hollywood forfeited the estate at this time, and John Hollywood, one of the signers of the Roman Catholic Remonstrance, came into possession.

In 1680 the King granted the estate for one thousand years to Sir Arthur Forbes, one of the Commissioners of the Court of Claims.

Lewis says the old Castle was pulled down in 1825 by Mathew Boyle, Esq., who erected the present manor house with the material. He also says it belonged to the Callaghan family in 1837, while D'Alton states Lord Maryborough owned it in 1838. The Butler family resided there at a later date.

A tomb of Elizabeth, daughter of John Talbot of Malahide, and wife of Christopher Hollywood, is in the old churchyard adjacent. She died in 1711, and her husband in 1718.

AUTHORITIES CONSULTED.

Marquis of Kildare, "The Earls of Kildare."
J. D'Alton, "History of County Dublin."
J. D'Alton, "Memoirs of the Archbishops of Dublin."
S. Lewis, "Topographical Dictionary of Ireland."
Parliamentary Gazetteer.
Fiants of Elizabeth.

ATHLONE CASTLE

THE castle of Athlone is situated on the Connaught side of the river Shannon in the Barony of Athlone, County Roscommon, sixty miles west-by-north of Dublin.

The name is derived from *ath*, "a ford," and *luain*, "the moon," and signifies "the ford of the moon," to which it is supposed to have been dedicated in pagan times. Some gold lunettes and crescents found in a neighbouring bog seem to bear out the statement.

The castle commands the bridge, and is built upon a spur of the hill upon which the town on the Connaught side is built. It is overlooked by the houses of the town, while on the river side it is supported by a great buttress of masonry.

The entrance is on the road which leads from the bridge up to the town, and is by a modern drawbridge.

The fortress consists of a strong curtain wall having circular towers mounted with cannon at irregular intervals. Most of them have been restored with fresh blue limestone.

The Connaught tower, which stands isolated in the courtyard, is considered the oldest part of the fortress, and usually supposed to have formed the keep of the first Norman castle built in King John's reign. It is decagonal in form, but owing to having been pebble-dashed and whitened of late years, it does not retain an appearance of antiquity.

The English stronghold was erected on the site of an

ATHLONE CASTLE

old Celtic fortress of the O'Connors. It is recorded that the castle and bridge of Athlone were built in 1129 by Turloch O'Connor, "in the summer of the drought."

The following year they were demolished by Murogh O'Mleghlin and Feirnan O'Rorke, and in 1153 the castle was burned.

Between 1210 and 1213 the Norman fortress was erected by John de Grey, Bishop of Norwich, in his capacity of Lord Justiciary of Ireland. During its building a tower fell and killed Lord Richard Tuit, who founded the Cistercian Abbey of Granard, County Longford.

Athlone Castle was built on abbey land, and in 1214 King John commanded Henry, Archbishop of Dublin, to give the monks a tenth of the expenses of the castle in lieu of the land used, in accordance with the conditions agreed to by the Bishop of Norwich when he was fortifying it. After this there are several references in the State Documents to the tithes and other compensation due to the monks.

In 1221 the King instituted a fair to be held at the castle.

The fortress being situated on the border of Irish territory, its early history has an exceedingly stormy record. In 1226 Geoffrey de Marisco, who was then Justiciary of Ireland, complained that as the King of Connaught refused to come to Dublin, he had appointed to meet him at Athlone, although the castle was fortified against the Crown.

In 1232 an order was issued to Hubert de Burgh to deliver the castle to Peter de Rivall, and the next year one to Richard de Burgh, who was to surrender it to Maurice FitzGerald, Justiciary of Ireland.

Walter de Lacy received twenty marks for the custody of the fortress in 1240, and eleven years later a tax was levied for its repair.

It was granted to Prince Edward, the King's son, in 1254; and during the years 1276–77 it was repaired.

Richard de Verdon was besieged in the castle in 1288 by Richard de Burgo, and the same year John, Archbishop of Dublin, took up residence there to oversee its better fortification, and to try and make terms with the Irish.

In 1305 Richard de Burgh, Earl of Ulster, was constable.

The castle was "obtained" for the King in 1537, having been in the hands of the Irish for many years. It contained only one piece of broken ordnance, and there is a request that another piece should be sent.

During Queen Elizabeth's reign it was the residence of the President of Connaught, and also the Chief Justice and Attorney-General for Connaught.

Tradition states that the Earl of Essex frequently stayed in the castle, and some of his letters to the Queen are dated from Athlone.

The O'Conor Don was imprisoned in the fortress in 1570 while Sir E. Fitton was constable, as a hostage for the good behaviour of his sept. Some of his followers, however, brought a "cot" under the castle walls, into which the captive stepped, and so escaped.

In 1585–86 it is described as being a fitter residence for the Chief Commissioner of Connaught than the Lord Deputy in the following words:—"That the castle is conveniently furnished with buildings and other necessaries fit for the said Commissioner, but far too mean for the Lord Deputy and the train that must follow the state."

It was ordered to be garrisoned in 1599, and the following year it was to be entrusted to none but a "sound Englishman." In 1606 it was repaired and added to.

Two years later it was seized by the Earls Tyrone and Tyrconnell. It passed again to the Crown, and the Earl of Clanricard was constable in 1610.

Thirteen years later it was repaired, and a curious tax is

mentioned with regard to the operations, which is, that the sept of Kellyes was bound to supply three hundred labourers yearly for work in the fortress.

The Court of Claims sat in the castle during the Commonwealth.

In 1682 Sir H. Piers writes of it:—" In the centre of the castle is a high raised tower which overlooketh the walls and country round about. On the side that faceth the river are rooms and apartments which served always for the habitation of the Lord President of Connaught and Governor of the castle, the middle castle being the storehouse for ammunition and warlike provisions of all sorts."

After the battle of the Boyne in 1690, Lieut.-General Douglas, with ten regiments of infantry, three of horse, two of dragoons, twelve field-pieces, and two small mortars, endeavoured to take possession of Athlone. The bridge across the Shannon was broken, and he erected his batteries on the Leinster side of the river.

He continued the cannonading for eight days, but his powder running short he was obliged to retire. In his despatch he stated he had done his best, and that it was his opinion Athlone Castle was "of the greatest importance of any in Ireland."

Colonel Richard Grace held the fortress for King James.

The following year the main division of William's army, under de Genckell, laid siege to the town. At once seizing that portion of it that is in Leinster, he began to play his batteries on the north-east side of the castle on June 22nd. By seven in the evening he had made a large breach in the walls.

Firing continued all night, and by five in the morning the side of the castle next the river was completely broken down, and the garrison was obliged to go in and out by a hole made in the wall on the western side.

The following evening the castle garrison raised two

batteries above the castle, and some others, but the firing had little effect. The bridge was slowly and surely gained by the besieging troops, and their guns played constantly on the fortress, wrecking the Connaught tower and walls.

Two officers deserting from the town informed William's troops that the best regiments had been withdrawn by St. Ruth, and thereupon a concerted and sudden attack was made on the 30th of June, which carried the bridge, castle, and town by storm.

Repairs were at once begun by the victors on July 3rd, and in 1697 the castle was the chief depôt of military stores in the west.

It is now used as a barrack, and officers' quarters and other buildings have been erected inside the walls.

Authorities Consulted.

Weld, "Statistical Survey of Co. Roscommon."
Joly, "Old Bridge of Athlone."
Parliamentary Gazetteer.
State Documents.
State Papers.
Carew MSS.
O'Donovan, "Annals of the Four Masters."
D'Alton, "History of Drogheda."
Proceedings of Royal Society of Antiquaries of Ireland.
In Journal of same, Langrishe, "Walls of Athlone," and "Sieges of Athlone."

BALLYMOTE CASTLE

THIS fine old ruin is situated in the Barony of Corran, County Sligo, about twelve miles north-west of Boyle.

The name signifies the "town of the moat," and was not used before the building of the Norman fortress. Some think "mote" is derived from "mound," but it is more likely to refer to the ditch which surrounded the castle until the close of the seventeenth century. The place was formerly called Athcliath-in-Chorainn, or "the hurdleford of Corran."

The castle fell to ruin after the rebellion of 1688. The curtain walls, which are 9 feet thick, were flanked by six round towers, one of them still being about 60 feet in height. The courtyard which was thus enclosed contained 150 square feet.

A passage about 3 feet wide ran round in the thickness of the walls, and communicated with the towers and defences. The state-rooms were on the north side of the courtyard, and some of them were fine apartments. The Survey of 1633 calls this part "the Court." A few traces of outworks remain.

About twenty years ago the present Rector of Ballymote was told by an old man that an underground passage was locally supposed to lead from the castle to the abbey, a distance of about 200 yards. Upon further investigation Canon Walker discovered two arches, one in the vestry of the abbey and the other within the castle, apparently leading in the same direction. Both are now choked with rubbish. The entrance in the castle is exceedingly narrow, and was reached from the castle yard by descending steps.

Ballymote was erected by Richard de Burgo, "the Red Earl," in 1300. It was dismantled in 1318, and twenty-two years later it was in the possession of Turlough O'Conor, King of Connaught, who was besieged in it by MacDermot. Peace was afterwards concluded.

In 1346 it was restored and garrisoned by John de Kerrew.

Two years later it is referred to as belonging to Rory O'Conor, and it was by that family entrusted to the MacDonoughs to hold against the Burkes. These MacDonoughs seized the castle of Ballylahan in 1381, and taking its gate to Ballymote, there erected it.

In 1470 Brian MacDonough, who was lord of Ballymote, was slain by Teige MacDonough, who took possession of the castle. It was still in this family's possession in 1522 when the famous parchment "Book of Ballimote" was sold by the MacDonough of the time to Hugh Oge O'Donnell for the large price of 140 milch cows, he having first obtained the consent of his family to the transaction.

The MacDermots laid siege to the castle in 1561, and Cathal and Owen MacDermot were both slain before the walls. Five years later the castle was taken by the English and Hugh and Comac MacDonough imprisoned. Almost immediately, however, the fortress was surprised by Tomaltach and Duagal MacDonough.

Sir Richard Bingham recovered Ballymote in 1584 and placed his brother George in charge with seven warders, while he also carried off MacDonough as hostage. At this time sixteen quarters of the best land were set aside for the castle's maintenance, which seems to have given rise to a great deal of jealousy regarding its custody. The year after its capture Sir Richard applied to be made constable, with a lease of the fortress for sixty years.

BALLYMOTE CASTLE

In 1587, writing to Mr. Treasurer Wallop, he states he is willing to give up Ballymote if he is refunded the money he has laid out upon it. The following year George Goodman and Thomas Wood seem to have been constables.

The Irish burnt the town and drove the garrison back to the castle in 1593, and two years later O'Conor Sligo petitioned the Government for the fortress. The next year there was an unsuccessful attempt to surprise it, and this year O'Conor Sligo occupied it upon his return from England.

Bingham managed to victual the castle across the Curlew mountains in 1595, but with the loss of many of his best soldiers, and in 1598 it was betrayed to the MacDonoughs by two men the constable trusted. The captors immediately put the fortress up to auction. There seems to have been sharp bidding between Sir Conyers Clifford and Red Hugh O'Donnell, but it was finally purchased by the latter for £400 and 300 cows.

O'Donnell remained in it until Christmas, and he continued to occupy it at different times until 1601, being six months in residence after his victory of the Yellow Ford. It was from here he set out for his disastrous march to Kinsale.

He left Owen O'Gallagher as Governor, who handed the keys to Roderick O'Donnell in 1602.

Two years after it was granted to Sir James Fullerton by James I., and when he left Ireland to be tutor to Duke Charles (afterwards Charles I.), the castle passed to Sir William Taaffe.

It was surrendered to Sir Charles Coote upon articles in 1652, which are still preserved.

The chief conditions were that the garrison was to march away with bag and baggage, and twenty days were to be allowed for the removal of goods, during which time Major-General Taaffe and his family might remain at the castle. After this he was to have a free pass to the

Continent, and Lady Taaffe was to be allowed to live at Ballymote, on condition she did not use it against the State, and that the Parliamentary forces might garrison it at any time.

In 1689 the castle was held for King James by Captain M'Donough. A party under Captain Cooper was sent to reconnoitre the district, and pursued M'Donough's men to the drawbridge of the fortress.

Two years later Lord Granard summoned the castle, but the governor, named O'Conor, refused to surrender. Thereupon he despatched Baldearg O'Donnell and a thousand men to lay siege to the place. They brought with them one 12-pounder and two small field-pieces, and as soon as O'Conor saw the guns he surrendered, upon condition the garrison might march out with their belongings and proceed to Sligo.

After this period the castle was dismantled, and the land subsequently passed to the Gore Booths. Of late there has been some talk of erecting a modern institution within the old walls.

Authorities Consulted.

Wood-Martin, "History of Sligo."
O'Rorke, "History of Sligo."
State Papers.
Atkinson, "Book of Ballimote."
Parliamentary Gazetteer.
Bagwell, "Ireland under the Tudors."

BALLYSHANNON CASTLE

THE name used by the early annalists to denote Ballyshannon, was Athseanaigh, which signified the "Ford of Seanach," who was ancestor of the Princes of Tirconnell. "Bel" stands for mouth, and the modern designation is a corruption of the Celtic name meaning "the entrance to Seanach's ford."

The town is situated on both sides of the river Erne, about eleven miles south-south-west of the town of Donegal, to the extreme south of the county.

The castle was on the north bank of the river, and commanded the principal ford. For this reason its possession was of immense strategical importance, it being the key to the province of Tirconnell. Of the great fortress of the O'Donnells only a small portion of one of the walls remains. This is on the north side of the market yard, part of it being incorporated with a grain store and part with a butter shed. It is 10 feet high and 5 feet thick.

The fortress originally occupied the whole of the market square, and it is most likely that its stones were used in the erection of a cavalry barracks, which subsequently occupied the present market enclosure, but which has now been removed.

Round the castle stretched a beautiful park, the name being still preserved in some old leases. This extended almost to the summit of the hill on the north. Quantities of human bones have been found in the neighbourhood,

The castle was erected in 1423 by Niall, son of Turlough O'Donnell. In 1435 Naghtan O'Donnell gave it to Brian Oge O'Neill for promising him assistance against the O'Neill. Brian, however, went treacherously to his chief without O'Donnell's knowledge, leaving his warders in the castle. O'Neill, not approving of such double dealing, took him and his two sons prisoners, cutting off a hand and a foot from each, under which treatment one of the sons died.

The fortress was taken from O'Donnell's warders in 1496 by his son Hugh. His brother Con, with the assistance of Maguire, laid siege to the castle and dislodged him. O'Neill possessed himself of the stronghold in 1522, and slew the warders. It seems to have remained in his possession until Sir Henry Sidney came north in 1566 and had it delivered to him, as well as the castles of Donegal, Beleek, Bundrowes, and Castle Sligo. All these fortresses he placed in the hands of O'Donnell and his allies, who were at this time in high favour with England.

The next year Shane O'Neill liberated Con O'Donnell and his brother, who were at the time his prisoners, and the castles of Ballyshannon and Beleek were delivered to Con.

About this time the Government began to look with alarm on the growing power and popularity of the O'Donnells, and the State Papers of the period contain notes regarding the advisability of garrisoning Ballyshannon and the other fortresses of Tirconnell.

The regular military force under O'Donnell consisted of 1,500 foot and 300 horse, out of which the garrison of Ballyshannon numbered 200 foot soldiers and 40 mounted men.

In 1584, Lord Deputy Perrot recommended the erection of a castle and bridge at Ballyshannon, no doubt to counteract the power of the O'Donnells' fortress, which

BALLYSHANNON CASTLE

could hold the main ford against all comers. Four years later the Lord Deputy dates a letter from Ballyshannon, and about this time young Hugh O'Donnell was kidnapped and imprisoned in Dublin Castle.

In 1592, Mr. Ralph Lane applied to Burghley, asking for the custodianship and fee-farm of the castle and lands of Ballyshannon, &c. The successful escape of Red Hugh, however, from Dublin Castle seems to have placed the possibility of the Government's disposing of his ancestral home quite out of the question, and in 1592 the greatest of the O'Donnells received a most royal welcome from his father's dependents in the north.

Arriving at Ballyshannon, where the O'Donnell warders still guarded the fortress, the whole country flocked to meet him and offer their congratulations on his escape.

The neighbourhood was in the most fearful state, being entirely overrun by freebooters, against whom even the English were powerless—the castles of Ballyshannon and Donegal alone remaining in the hands of the O'Donnells.

After a most successful campaign against the marauders, Hugh O'Donnell returned to Ballyshannon to undergo medical treatment for his feet, which had been fearfully injured by travelling from Dublin to Glenmalure in his house-shoes over the mountains and in bitter cold. He did not recover entirely until the end of the year, as both his great toes had to be amputated.

In 1594 Sir Ralph Lane, writing to Burghley, mentions that Hugh Roe O'Donnell would have broken down Ballyshannon but that his mother dissuaded him from it, assuring him that it might be defended with his own forces. Yet this very year it was evidently in the hands of the O'Donnells, and remained so until its capture in 1602.

The State Papers of this period are full of letters requesting money and forces sufficient to take it, alleging that the fortress was the "key of the province," and no peace could be hoped for in the north until it was garrisoned by English.

In the meantime the O'Donnells lived in royal state, and with lavish hospitality entertained the surrounding chiefs, while their flag floated from the battlements.

Sir George Carew observes of the Prince of Tirconnell: "O'Donnell is the best lorde of fishe in Ireland, and exchangeth fishe allwayes with foreign merchants for wyne, by which his call in other countryes is the kinge of fishe."

It was during a great assemblage of chiefs at Ballyshannon to organise a raid on the English border, that the great Shane O'Neill became madly enamoured of O'Donnell's lovely daughter, Helen. He went to her father and demanded her hand, but was informed that the lady was already betrothed to Maguire, the young chieftain of Fermanagh, who held his lands under suzerainty of O'Donnell. This young man had been educated at the Spanish court, and was all that a maiden could wish in a suitor.

One evening the lovers left the castle together, for a stroll by the river side, towards Belleek. Here, while Helen was singing to her harp, O'Neill, who had followed them, broke in upon their happiness. Maguire drew his sword to defend the lady, but he was no match for the great chief from whom he quickly received his death wound. O'Neill placed the fainting form of the fair Helen before him on his horse, and, with a few followers, rode to Dungannon Castle. Her father at once called his forces together, and followed to revenge the injury. The end of the story has several variations, but the most probable seems to be that O'Neill, finding the beautiful girl irreconcilable to the loss of her handsome lover, returned her to her father. The world had, however, lost its charm for her, and the rest of her short life was spent in seclusion.

BALLYSHANNON CASTLE

In 1597 the first determined attack was made on Ballyshannon. Sir Conyers Clifford, Governor of Connaught, with four thousand men, foot and horse, marched on the stronghold, accompanied by Donough, the son of Connor, Murragh, Baron of Inchiquin, and other Irish nobles. O'Donnell having all the fords guarded, they were obliged to cross the river about half a mile west of Belleek. Here the Baron of Inchiquin was shot through his armour, while his horse was standing in the deep water below the ford, where he was encouraging the soldiers and saving them from drowning.

The ordnance was landed by water and planted against the castle. The siege lasted three days, but when the little garrison were thinking of surrendering, help arrived from Tyrone, and the English were driven off with great loss. The defenders of the castle numbered only eighty men, and were commanded by a Scotchman named Owen Crawford.

During Red Hugh's absence in Spain in 1602 the English took the opportunity to again attack the fortress. The warders, seeing no hope of relief, fled, after the walls had been battered by a big gun, and Captain Digges took "that long desired place."

Ballyshannon, with 1,000 acres, was reserved to the King in 1603, and five years later Sir Henry Folliot was appointed Governor. In this year the plot to seize the King's castle of Ballyshannon was one of the charges in the indictment against the Earls of Tyrone and Tirconnell. In 1610 the castle, lands, and fishings were granted to Sir H. Folliot for twenty-one years. He was raised to the peerage under the title of Baron Folliot of Ballyshannon, 1619.

During the Jacobite troubles the castle was still used as a military headquarters, and the town was for a time in the hands of the Royalists.

The land on which the ancient fortress stood is now

part of the Connolly estate, and was acquired by purchase from the Folliots.

AUTHORITIES CONSULTED.

Allingham, "Ballyshannon, its History and Antiquities."
Donovan, "Annals of the Four Masters."
Calendar of State Papers.
"The Donegal Highlands."
Parliamentary Gazetteer.

BALLYTEIGUE CASTLE

This castle is situated in the townland of the same name upon the shore of Ballyteigue Lough, in the County Wexford. The name signifies "O'Teige's town."

The old fortress forms part of a modern dwelling-house, and the keep has always been kept roofed and in good repair.

It was erected by Sir Walter de Whitty, one of the Norman settlers, the name being spelt variously—Whythay, Whythey, Wytteye, Whittey, Wythay, in old documents.

Sir Richard Whitty was summoned to Parliament as a baron by Edward III., and his son Richard held three carucates of land in Ballyteigue in 1335.

In 1408, as we learn from a MS. in the British Museum, the Castle of Ballyteigue was burnt by Art M'Murrough Kavanagh on Tuesday, the morning after the Feast of St. Barnabas.

Richard Whitty, of Ballyteigue, died in 1539, and his son Robert being only fourteen at his father's death, the custody of Ballyteigue was granted to John Devereux during his minority. The estate contained 3 manors, 3 carucates, and 523 acres.

The manor and castle of Ballyteigue were in the possession of Richard Whittie in 1624 and 1634.

The estate was forfeited in the time of the Commonwealth, and was granted to Colonel Brett. It afterwards passed into the hands of the Sweenys, and subsequently to the Colcloughs, a branch of the family of Tintern Abbey.

In 1798 the castle was the residence of John Colclough, one of the leaders of the Wexford insurgents. He was only twenty-nine when the rebellion broke out.

As soon as Bagnal Harvey heard that Lord Kingsborough's terms for the surrender of Wexford would not be ratified, he hastened to Ballyteigue, but Colclough and his wife and child had already fled to one of the Saltee Islands, about ten leagues from Wexford. He followed them, but the island was searched, and the fugitives taken in a cave. They were conveyed to Wexford, and Harvey and Colclough were immediately tried and hanged. Colclough's head is buried in St. Patrick's Cemetery, Wexford.

His little daughter and only child inherited Ballyteigue. She afterwards married Captain Young, and both lived in the castle until their death. Their only daughter sold the house to Mr. Edward Meadows, from whom it passed to Mr. Thomas Grant.

A legendary tale of " Sir Walter Whitty and his cat," published some years ago by the late M. J. Whitty, editor of the *Liverpool Post*, may have originated from the lion which is represented in the Whitty arms.

AUTHORITIES CONSULTED.

MS. Ordnance Survey.
Parliamentary Gazetteer.
Book of Inquisitions of Leinster.
R. Madden, " United Irishmen."
" Balliteigue Castle," in *The People*.
Joyce, " Irish Place Names."

BARBERSTOWN CASTLE

THIS castle is situated in the parish of Straffan, County Kildare, in the barony of North Salt, about a mile north of the village of Straffan.

The name is spelt variously Barberstowne, Barbeston, Barbieston, Barbiestowne, Barbiston, Barbitstowne, Barbyeston.

The present building consists of a battlemented rectangular keep considered by experts to be of thirteenth-century construction, and measuring at its greatest height 52 feet. It is divided into three floors. The lower room, which is vaulted to the height of 17 feet, is 18 feet long by $15\frac{1}{2}$ feet wide, and the walls are $4\frac{1}{2}$ feet in thickness.

The entrance is situated at the north-west angle, above which are two grooves of sufficient width to stand in, and evidently intended for the protection of the doorway.

The room above the vault is of slightly greater proportions than that below, owing to the walls being of less thickness.

Two small rectangular towers are joined to the main building on the south side's western angle, and west side's northern angle respectively. The latter contains a winding stone stair of fifty-three steps leading to the now slated roof. The original crenelated loops for musketry have here and there been enlarged to admit more light. The summit of the watch tower is reached from the roof by a short flight of nine steps.

A man is said to be interred between the top of the main

stair and the roof of the tower. His family having held the castle by a lease which expired when he was put underground, determined to evade relinquishing their hold on the property by keeping him always above the earth.

The southern tower consists of three storeys corresponding with those in the keep, and had formerly doors opening from the main rooms. Next the southern wall is a curious slit in each floor just wide enough to permit of a ladder giving access to the apartment above or below. The ground floor in this tower is of very small dimensions, being about 3 feet square.

The walls of the keep slope considerably at the outside base so as to prevent an enemy getting out of gun shot by closing up to the building. Large modern windows now light each floor, and the whole is in excellent preservation.

A flue runs in the thickness of the wall on the north side, which is crowned by a handsome brick chimney, evidently added when the Elizabethan dwelling-house which adjoins the castle was erected. A still more modern house has been added to the north of this building, so that at present three distinct periods are represented by the castle and houses, which are all joined together.

The remains of an old wall near the fortress points to its having once been of larger dimensions. Tradition states that an underground passage leads from the castle to a lodge near the roadway. Some fine old yews of great age adorn the lawn, similar to those which are to be seen near Maynooth Castle.

Locally it is believed that Barberstown was once the residence of the King of Leinster, but its architecture does not bear out the tradition.

In 1622 William Sutton, of Barberstown, is mentioned in an inquisition, and in 1630 it is stated that he held it as tenant of the Earl of Kildare.

Nicholas Sutton was in possession of the castle in 1641, and at a subsequent date it must have passed to the

BARBERSTOWN CASTLE

Crown, who granted it in 1666 to John King, first Lord Kingston.

His son Robert, the second Baron, was exempted from mercy by Tyrconnell's proclamation, and his estate sequestered in 1689.

Richard, Earl of Tyrconnell, then became possessed of the fortress, and, strange to say, that although he could only have retained it until he was attainted in 1692, yet it was known for many years as Tyrconnell Castle. Lady Tyrconnell retained some of her husband's lands in the neighbourhood to a much later date.

Bartholomew Vanhomrigh, Esq., of Dublin, father of the famous Vanessa, bought Barberstown from the Crown in 1703 for £1,300. James Young was the tenant at the time, and the property is thus described: "In the parish of Straffan, distant from Dublin ten miles, Naas 5, and Manooth 3; is Arable Medow and Pasture, on it 1 Castle in repair, with a large stone House adjoyning, and Orchard, also 8 Cabbins, with Gardens."

At the beginning of the next century it was occupied by a family named Douglas, and it was purchased by the Bartons, of Straffan, in 1826. They restored and re-castellated it, and it still remains in their possession.

Subsequently it was occupied by Admiral Robinson, and the present tenant is S. F. Symes, Esq.

A most extensive view is obtained from the summit.

AUTHORITIES CONSULTED.

A Book of Postings and Sale of the Forfeited and other Estates, &c.
Book of Survey and Distributions.
Book of Inquisitions, Province of Leinster.
S. Lee, "Dictionary of National Biography."

BARGY CASTLE

THIS castle takes its name from the Barony of Bargy, County Wexford, on the borders of which it is situated, about eight miles south-west of the town of Wexford, on the margin of Lake Tucumshane.

The fortress is in excellent preservation, having been several times restored. It consists of a square keep, to which two wings have been added at more recent dates, probably in the fifteenth and seventeenth centuries.

The chief entrance to the Castle was formerly by the central tower, where a stained-glass window bearing the Harvey Arms is now to be seen. On the outside of the embrasure is a stone carved with figures supposed to represent Queen Elizabeth and her court, and far above this slab may be seen a large machicolation, once used for hurling missiles for the defence of the door. The tower is ascended by a winding stone stair, off which are openings commonly known as "murdering holes." The keep, in which are several rooms, is separated from the rest of the mansion by a large door at the foot of the stairway. A beautiful view can be had from the battlements.

In the north wing of the castle is a small panelled room, and not far from it a carved oak partition bears with a cross and shamrock the following on the reverse side: "I.H.S. 1591. R.R. M.S."

A beautiful oak staircase leads from the chief apartments.

BARGY CASTLE

The castle grounds were formerly entered from the south, where the old piers and gateway still remain. At the back of the castle is part of the old moat or fosse, which now contains large cellars.

The fortress is usually supposed to have been erected by the Rossiter family at the beginning of the fifteenth century, though some authorities state it owes its origin to Hervey de Montmorency, one of the first Norman invaders.

William Rowcester, of Bridge of Bargie (Bargie Castle), was pardoned for felony in 1540. He is described as a "horseman," which, according to Hollinshead was a position next to that of captain or lord. About 1553 Nicholas Roche was granted the wardship and marriage of his son Richard.

The Most Rev. Michael Rossitter, Bishop of Ferns, is supposed by some to have been born in Bargy Castle, in 1648, but the Down Survey maps of 1657 describe the castle as being in ruins.

The last Rossiter to own Bargy was William Rositer, who took part in the defence of Wexford against Cromwell. His lands were confiscated in 1667, and Bargy Castle was granted to William Ivory, Esq.

After this it passed to the Harvey family, and here Beauchamp Bagnal Harvey was born, who commanded the Wexford insurgents in 1798.

Bargy was confiscated to the Crown, after the suppression of the rebellion; and Bagnal Harvey, who owned the castle, and Colclough were captured on the Saltee Islands and executed at Wexford.

Troops were quartered at Bargy from 1798 to 1808, when the property was restored to James Harvey, brother of the late owner.

It is said that when a detachment of soldiers was sent to take possession of the fortress in 1798 they indulged so freely in the contents of the great wine cellars, that some of them injudiciously disturbed the hives in the garden, whereupon the bees attacked their tormentors with such force that some of the soldiers died from the effects, and others were pursued by the irate insects to the very town of Wexford.

Mr. Harvey lived in London, and the castle gradually fell into dilapidation until his death, when it passed to Councillor John Harvey, who restored it. Major Harvey, who died in 1880, is entombed in a mausoleum before the hall door. The castle was afterwards let to Mr. Leared, who re-roofed and improved it.

Ghostly tappings are reported to be heard on the castle windows between 10 and 11 p.m., while a phantom carriage is said to be sometimes audible driving up the disused avenue, when the horses' hoofs cease before the old entrance in the keep, and a minute or two later the coach is again heard returning by the old drive.

AUTHORITIES CONSULTED.

Act of Settlement.
Down Survey Maps.
Fiants of Edward VI.
Doyle, "Notes and Gleanings of Co. Wexford."
Madden, "The United Irishmen."
Article and letter in *The People*.

BARRYSCOURT CASTLE

THE fine ruins of this fortress are situated about half a mile south of Carrigtohill, in the County Cork.

It consists of a rectangular structure about 70 feet in height, flanked by three towers, which open into the main building at each storey.

A small oblong shaft in the south-east angle of the keep runs from the upper to the lower rooms. A passage in the main north wall is now filled up.

The arches are of good workmanship and well preserved. In some of the smaller apartments the marks of the wattle frames used in the building are still easily traced on the ceilings, which show an early date of construction.

In the chamber above the chapel appears the date 1588, as well as an inscription stating the castle was erected by " D.B." and " E.R.," which initials stand for David Barry and his wife, Eliza Roche. In another room the date 1596 is inscribed.

The lands of the Barrys in Cork were confirmed to Philip Barry by King John in 1206, and he later became possessed of Barry's Court. The present castle is, however, supposed to have been built during the fourteenth century.

Tradition states it was erected upon the site of an older fortress belonging to the Lyons or Lehanes of Castle Lyons, and that during the excavations for the present foundations an inscribed stone was found stating that " O'Lehan hoc fecit MCIII.," but O'Donovan does not think the story probable.

Geraldus Cambrensis is credited with having written part of his history of the conquest in the earlier castle.

In 1490 the head of the Barry family was summoned to Parliament as Lord Barry of Barry's Court, and 1588 "James Barry of Barrescourt, Viscount Barrymore, otherwise James, called Barrymore and Barryroo," was in possession.

The Commissioners who were appointed to govern Munster while the Earl of Desmond was in prison, wrote, after arriving in Cork, in 1568: "Wood Kerne, under Gerot Bracke, one of the Earl of Desmond's near kinsmen, intercepted our letters, certain Kerne lay in ambush for us, but Lord Barrymore and John FitzEdmund, Dean of Cloyne, met us, and led us to Barry's Court."

In 1580 Sir Walter Raleigh started from Cork to make complaint to Lord Grey in Dublin that the Barrys and Condons were in league with the rebels. He received orders to besiege Barry's Court, but Lord Barry, hearing of his intention, set the castle on fire, while he and his friend, Fitzgerald, the seneschal of Imokilly, lay in wait for Sir Walter at the ford near the old abbey of Midleton.

In the encounter so little expected, Raleigh only saved his life by his somewhat foolhardy daring.

In the account of his doings in Ireland in 1583, Sir Henry Sydney writes: "I was well entertained at the Viscount Barrie's house, called Barrie's Court."

During the Desmond rebellion of 1585, David Lord Barry, whose initials are carved over the mantelpiece of the castle, was associated with the disaffected. He afterwards submitted and sat on the Council of Munster under Sir George Carew. He was present at the relief of Kinsale in 1602, and died at Barry's Court in 1617. He was the second son of James Barry, and his wife, Ellen Roche, was a daughter of Lord Fermoy.

Writing of him in 1606, Sir John Davys says: "From Youghall we went to Cork, and dined by the way with the

BARRYSCOURT CASTLE

Viscount Barrie, who, at his castle at Barriecourt, gave us civil and plentiful entertainment."

Barryscourt was regranted by James I. to his grandson David, who succeeded him.

The castle seems to have again been consumed by fire after James II.'s visit to Ireland, as it is stated that the velvet bed hung with gold brocade in which he slept at Sir James Cotter's, of Ballinsperrig, was then at Barryscourt, and so destroyed by the conflagration.

The castle was in possession of the Coppinger family for many years, William Coppinger being the owner in 1861.

It now belongs to Lord Barrymore.

A member of the Wakeham family informs me that it was in possession of her ancestors several centuries ago, and that the Lord Barrymore of that day gave the owners, John and William Wakeham, the estates of Springhill and Water-rock instead of it, which their descendants still possess.

AUTHORITIES CONSULTED.

Gibson's " History of Cork."
Carew MSS.
Patent and Close Rolls, Chancery, Ireland.
State Papers.
" Local Names" and "Notes and Queries" in *Journal of Cork Archæological Society*.

BIRR CASTLE

"Lords to whom great men submit,
Are the O'Carrolls of the plain of Birr."
O'HEERIN.

THIS fortress was one of the numerous strongholds of the O'Carrolls of Ely O'Carroll. The derivation of the name, formerly Biorra, is doubtful. *Bir* signifies "water," *birra*= "abounding in wells," or "fountains of water," *bir*="a spit," *bior*="the brink of a river," and the name may have originated from any of these words.

The town is situated on the right bank of the Little Brosna River at its juncture with the Birr rivulet. It is in the barony of Ballybrit, King's County, sixty-two and a half miles west-south-west of Dublin.

The O'Carroll's stronghold, called the "Black Castle," stood some sixty yards north-west of the present building on the high bank of the river. The principal tower was raised on an artificial mound, and in 1627 Sir Laurence Parsons added a watch tower, which stood on thirteen corbels, projecting on the outside, and was higher than all the other buildings. The dungeon of the stronghold was situated in the Black Castle, but this older fortress has long since been demolished.

In 1620–21 Sir Laurence Parsons made a great many additions to the castle. He erected a tower 46 feet long and 25 feet broad, at each end of which an arch of hewn stone gave entrance to the fortress. The present hall, which is reached by a flight of stone steps under a vaulted

BIRR CASTLE

vestibule, is the centre part of this tower, as it is also that of the present mansion.

In the following two years Sir Laurence also built a porter's lodge, known as the "Garden House," fitted up a drawing-room and made a garden and orchard.

In 1624 he built a new line of offices, which formed one side of the courtyard, and in which was a kitchen, &c. Another side of the enclosure was occupied by the stables, which extended along the river, south of the Black Castle.

BIRR CASTLE.

On the north was a double wall filled up with earth, and having a gateway in the centre.

Sir William Parsons threw all these buildings down in 1778.

The castle was enlarged and remodelled under the direction of Mr. J. Johnstone, architect, who altered the entrance to the back of the building, away from the town.

Sir Laurence Parsons had also added a "French Flanker" in 1627, but on what site is not known.

The Annals of Clonmacmoise record that Byrre Castle was besieged in 1207 by "Moriertagh Mac Bryen an Sleyve," who burnt the whole town.

Ely O'Carroll was granted to FitzWalter by Henry II., nevertheless King John re-granted it to William de Braosa in 1200, and FitzWalter had to buy it back to regain possession.

It shortly afterwards passed into the hands of Hugh de Hose or Hussey.

The English rebuilt and enlarged the stronghold in 1213.

In 1432 the Earl of Ormond went to war with O'Carroll of Ely, and demolished his two chief castles, which most likely were Birr and Leap, for in spite of Royal grants the stronghold remained in the possession of the O'Carrolls.

A dispute arose about the chieftainship of the sept in 1532, the senior branch of the family holding Birr Castle.

Ferganainm O'Carroll, the son of the late chief, enlisted the aid of the Earl of Kildare, whose daughter he had married, and together they laid siege to Birr. The Earl received a bullet in his side from the garrison. It is said that a soldier, hearing him cry out in agony, remonstrated with him, remarking he himself had been wounded three times and was none the worse, to which the Earl replied he was sorry he had not received the fourth bullet in his stead. The ball was extracted the following spring, but it is said to have hastened his end.

In 1537 Lord Leonard Grey took Birr Castle, and is reported to have received submission from O'Carroll, who was created Baron of Ely in 1552.

At the time of the plantation of Ely, Birr and its castle were granted to Sir Laurence Parsons in 1620, and the same year his steward arrived to make preparations. Shortly afterwards O'Carroll appealed in vain.

In 1641 Sir William Parsons was made Governor of Ely

BIRR CASTLE

O'Carroll and the Castle of Birr, which latter he garrisoned with his tenants.

He put the place at once in a state of defence. He raised a flanker behind the stables, and erected scaffolds inside the castle for the garrison to fight from.

After some skirmishing the fortress was closely besieged in 1642, and of the nine hundred people in town and castle many died of starvation, while others were reduced to eating dogs and cats.

At length the Earl of Ormond sent a detachment to its relief, but early the next year General Preston approached the stronghold with artillery and troops.

He reconnoitred the town from Drumbawn Hill, and after firing a few shots encamped in the neighbouring woods. On the second day of the siege he sent a messenger to the Governor to inquire if he held the castle for the King or the Parliament, and asking to be allowed to garrison it for his Majesty's use.

Sir William replied that he had not heard of any difference from his Majesty or from the Parliament, and that he held his commission as Governor of Ely O'Carroll.

At this reply Preston entrenched, and next day began to bombard the fortress in earnest. The following night a mine was commenced under the direction of a mason who had been employed in the castle. The garrison, hearing the noise, fired on the sappers, but the darkness prevented the shot taking effect, and in the morning they were underground.

Preston continued firing, and destroyed much of the wall and one of the flankers. He said he would break down the fortress about the Governor's ears. Some of the balls found in the masonry weighed 9 lbs. each.

Under cover of a parley the defenders of the mill were withdrawn, and the garrison held out for two days after they had been undermined. A conference was held and the besieged were granted honourable terms.

Lord Castlehaven conducted them to Athy. They numbered about eight hundred men, women, and children.

Preston seems to have retained possession of Birr until 1645, when for five years it was held by the Confederate Catholic forces.

It was taken from the Irish in 1650 by General Ireton, the enemy having burnt it before retreating. The Marquis of Clanrickarde tried to retake it in vain.

In 1688 Birr was so infested with robbers that Sir Laurence Parsons took some of his neighbours and tenants inside the castle and closed the gates. This act was magnified to the Government by his enemy, Colonel Oxburgh, who obtained an order from the Lord Lieutenant to put a garrison in the castle.

Oxburgh demanded admittance, and Sir Laurence refused until he should hear from Lord Tyrconnel. A siege then began, and when they attempted to undermine the fortress terms of capitulation were agreed upon.

Both terms of surrender (1643–1688) are preserved in the castle and have been published in the Report of the Historical MSS. Commission.

Sir Laurence and some of his tenants were imprisoned in the fortress. He was tried for high treason and several times reprieved. He was liberated after the Boyne, and appointed High Sheriff for the King's County.

In 1690 the castle garrison, being English, was summoned, but after a parley the enemy retired.

Later the same year it was attacked by Sarsfield, who fired all day on the stronghold. The marks of the shot are still to be seen upon the castle walls. The besieged, under Captain Curry, held out until reinforcements arrived.

The English army, passing through Birr in 1691, left four hundred wounded men in the castle for two months.

Sir Laurence Parsons died in 1698.

The second Earl of Rosse succeeded to the estates

in 1841. His experiments towards improving the reflecting telescope had been begun in 1827 at Birr Castle. He employed local workmen, and the tools, machinery, furnaces, ovens, &c., were all constructed on the spot, many of which are still to be seen.

At length, after many failures, two specula were cast in 1842–43. They each measured 6 feet in diameter, weighed 4 tons, and were of 54 feet focus.

The tube in which one was mounted is 58 feet long and 7 feet in diameter. It is slung on chains between two piers of masonry, and the telescope is moved and supported by a complex system of cast-iron platforms, triangles, and levers.

It is the largest telescope in the world, and cost about £20,000 to construct. Observations were commenced in February, 1845. There are several smaller telescopes at the castle as well.

The present Earl of Rosse is the third Earl, and, like his father, is an eminent scientist.

Authorities Consulted.

T. Cooke, "History of Birr," &c.
Cooke, "Picture of Parsonstown."
Brewer, "Beauties of Ireland."
Donovan, "Annals of the Four Masters."
S. Lee, "Dictionary of National Biography."
Parliamentary Gazetteer.
Report of Historical MSS. Commission.

BLACK CASTLE, WICKLOW

WICKLOW is situated about twenty-five miles south-southeast of Dublin, and the ruins of the Black Castle occupy an isolated rocky promontory east of the town, and on the south side of the Leitrim river. The name Wicklow is likely to have been of Norwegian origin, but the meaning is uncertain. The Irish name Kilmantan signified S. Mantan's Church. The castle followed the natural shape of the dark rock on which it was built, and from which, no doubt, the designation "Black" is taken. It was divided from the mainland by a chasm, which was probably bridged in former times. A few fragments of walls, with window openings, are all that remain.

The fortress can never have been of large dimensions if it was confined to the rock on which the ruins now stand.

In 1176, after Maurice FitzGerald had been recalled by Strongbow, he received a grant of the Castle of Wicklow, among other possessions, in lieu of his lands in Wexford, which King Henry wished to retain. From this it would appear to have been the site of an older fortification.

Maurice FitzGerald began to erect a Norman stronghold on the promontory, but he died before it was completed.

Soon after his death William FitzAdelm managed by falsehood to get possession of the Black Castle from his son Gerald, first Baron of Offaly, and surrendered him instead the unprotected Castle of Ferns.

The Earl of Ormond being arraigned for treason in

BLACK CASTLE, WICKLOW

1422, one of the charges against him was that he had retained William Edward, Constable of Arklow, in his service after he had assisted the O'Byrnes in seizing the King's Castle of Wicklow. They killed John Liverpoole, the constable, and sent his head to the O'Byrne. They also imprisoned a priest, whom they found in the fortress, to hold for ransom.

The O'Byrnes seem to have been in possession of the castle in the early part of the sixteenth century, but in

BLACK CASTLE, WICKLOW.

1534 it had again passed to the Crown, and Thomas Stevyns was appointed constable. In 1567 Sir Thomas Fytzwylliams began his suit for the fortress, which, in 1575, he offered to re-edify, though his doing so does not seem altogether to have worked in his favour.

It seems generally believed that the present ruins represent the stronghold he built, but in 1580 it was reported that Wicklow Castle was razed by the enemy.

Nineteen years later the terrible disaster took place in

June, 1599, in which the English troops were utterly routed between Rathdrum and Glenmalure by the combined Irish septs of the district. It was this that caused Essex such a sharp reprimand from Queen Elizabeth.

Sir Henry Harrington was in command, and his troops fell back upon Wicklow Castle in the wildest disorder, chased by the Irish within half a mile of the town.

Captain Adam Loftus seems to have been the only one who endeavoured to redeem the day. He was wounded in the leg and conveyed to the castle. A surgeon was sent for, though the wound was not considered dangerous at first; but he shortly afterwards succumbed to the effects.

In 1610 Sir William Usher, Knight, was made constable of the fortress, and in 1641 Luke O'Toole and a band of insurgents laid siege to the town and castle, but retreated upon the approach of Sir Charles Coote with some English troops.

Authorities Consulted.

Gilbert, "History of Viceroys of Ireland."
Marquis of Kildare, "Earls of Kildare."
O'Toole, "History of the Clan O'Toole."
Brewer, "Beauties of Ireland."
Joyce, "Irish Names of Places."
Parliamentary Gazetteer.
State Papers.
Book of Howth. Carew MSS.

BLARNEY CASTLE

"There is a stone there whoever kisses,
  Oh, he never misses to grow eloquent,
'Tis he may clamber to a lady's chamber
  Or become a member of Parliament.
A clever spouter, he'll sure turn out, or
  An 'out an' outer' to be let alone,
Don't hope to hinder him or bewilder him,
  Sure he's a pilgrim to the Blarney Stone!"

FATHER PROUT.

APPROPRIATELY built on an isolated limestone rock, the castle of the Blarney (Blarna meaning "little field") was the chief stronghold of the chiefs of the sept Carty, from Cartheigh, "an inhabitant of the rock." It is situated some three and a half miles north-west of Cork, near the junction of the Comane (*i.e.* crooked stream) and the Awmartin River. The present ruins show three distinct periods of construction, of which the oldest is a slender tower, or peel, situated at the north-west corner of the larger block of masonry that was built to it, the whole being the great keep of the fortress.

A stone bearing the inscription "Cormac M'Carthy, Fortis Me Fieri Facit, A.D. 1446," forms the sill of one of the machicolations on the south side of the tower, and being damaged during the siege in Cromwell's time, has been supported with iron.

The keep is gnomon in shape, the later rectangular tower being 60 feet by 36 feet, while the peel, which is half built into the north-west corner, forms a projection of 18 feet by 12 feet. The tower is about 120 feet high. The original entrance to the peel, which was 10 feet above the ground, is now built up, and access is gained by the large newel stair in the later building. What are called "the back stairs," were the original flight belonging to the first tower. Here is situated the "Earl's bedroom," with a more modern bay window, and remnants of the tapestry which once covered the walls may still be seen. In the very top storey is situated a kitchen with two great fireplaces, and one of the now floorless rooms in this tower was probably the chapel.

In the later portion of the keep is the store-room and guard chamber near the entrance, which is a low-pointed doorway once defended from above. The apartment in the third floor was most likely used as a reception room, above which the great banqueting hall is situated, with an elaborately-worked chimney, and a fireplace 12 feet wide. The tower on the south and east is finished by machicolated parapets, resting on fourteen corbels, and having a corresponding number of opens or crenelles above.

The keep represents the fifteenth-century masonry, except where it is surmounted by the ogee parapet of brick work, which was seemingly added at the time the now ruined mansion to the east of the tower was built. This dwelling, erected by the Jeffreys family, was unroofed and its timber sold in 1821.

What are locally called "the dungeons" are merely divisions in the well cavern, which was at one time connected with the castle by a covered passage now filled up.

There seems to be great uncertainty as to the identity of the famous kissing stone, said to give a persuasive tongue to whoever touches it with his lips. The power of conferring this accomplishment appears to have been unknown in the early part of the nineteenth century.

The inscribed stone already mentioned is generally supposed to be the true "Blarney stone," chiefly, it seems because it has been carefully propped, and most likely had the mystic reputation conferred upon it when a slightly water-worn hollow stone situated on the parapet of the east side of the turret disappeared more than a quarter of a century ago.

Again a stone bearing the date 1703, on the highest part of the north-east angle, and another engraved with a shamrock in relief have each been asserted to be the original stone.

BLARNEY CASTLE.

The origin of "Blarney," meaning flattery, is said to have been from an exclamation of Queen Elizabeth upon receiving a very plausible letter from M'Carty, to the effect that it was all "Blarney" and he did not intend to carry out his promises.

The castle at one time covered eight acres. In a quarry near a large number of human bones have been found.

Cormac MacCarty, surnamed Laider, or the Strong, came

into the lordship of Muskerry three years after he had built Blarney Castle, and such was his power that English settlers paid him a yearly tribute of £40 to protect them against the attacks of the Irish. He was fourth lord, and direct descendant of the former Kings of Desmond and Cork. He died in 1494.

Teige MacCormac Carty signed an indenture of allegiance to the English laws in 1542, and this was faithfully adhered to by his descendants, who, unlike the other great Irish septs, never went eagerly into rebellion. At this time the clan could raise three thousand fighting men. His son Dermod was knighted in 1558.

The Manor of Blarney, Twhoneblarney, the entire country of Muskerry, with all its lordships and possessions, were granted to M'Dermod to hold by military service in 1589.

His cousin Charles, however, was page to Sir Walter Raleigh, and through his interest procured from the Privy Council a sequestration of the rents.

In 1596 Cormack M'Dermot M'Carthy asked for a new grant of the Manor of Blarney with a release of all conditions.

When war broke out, although Lord Muskerry remained with the English forces, he was seized as a traitor (1600) because his brother had joined the rebels, and a relative informed the Council that he himself was plotting against them.

Tyrone at this time encamped with all his forces near Blarney, which is described as one of the strongest castles in the province of Munster, "for it is four piles joined in one, seated upon a main rock, so as it is free from mining, the wall 18 feet thick, and flanked at each corner to the best advantage."

Sir Charles Wilmot and Captain Roger Harvey endeavoured to surprise the garrison after the arrest of Lord Muskerry, but the warders, suspecting their motive, made them partake of the food they asked for, outside the castle walls.

When Lord Muskerry was put upon his trial he indignantly denied the charges made against him. The President replied that he had better either confess his guilt and ask pardon, or deliver up Blarney Castle until the accusations were proved false. This Lord Muskerry hesitated to do, and so was committed to prison. At length he consented to give up Blarney to Captain Taafe, on condition that it would be restored to him unaltered.

Shortly after this he escaped, in 1602, but seeing the struggle against the Crown was hopeless, he asked leave to make submission to Sir George Carew, which was granted.

In 1628 he was created Baron of Blarney and Viscount Cartie of Muskerie, and as such went to Parliament.

Charles I. appointed him President of Munster, but in 1646 Lord Broghill, afterwards Earl of Orrery, took the castle of Blarney and made it his headquarters. Lord Muskerry was the last Royalist in Ireland to lay down arms, and he was tried for his life by Ludlow and others. He was permitted to pass to Spain, while his wife was allowed to receive his income from the estate, except £1,000 a year granted to Lord Broghill for his services (1656).

Two years later Lord Muskerry was recalled, after the Restoration, and created Viscount Muskerry and Earl of Clancarty. His property was given back to him, except the portion allowed to Lord Broghill, who was now a supporter of the King.

When James landed at Kinsale, Blarney Castle was used as one of the prisons for the Protestants of Cork, the fourth Earl of Clancarty being one of the King's chief supporters.

Upon the succession of King William the Clancarty estate, worth about £150,000, was confiscated and sold, a pension of £300 being allowed to the Earl, who died at Hamburg, 1734.

The Rev. Dean Davies, of Cork, was tenant of the castle for some years after the Hollow-Sword-Blade Company of

London bought it. Upon leaving he took away many of the oak beams of the castle for his new residence at Dawstown.

Chief Justice Pyne then purchased it, and held it for a short time, but in 1703 Sir James Jeffreys bought the castle and lands, and from him the present owner, Sir George Colthurst, is descended.

There is in the possession of The O'Donovan, at Liss Ard, Skibbereen, a dadagh, or Irish skean, with which an O'Donovan killed M'Carty Reagh about the middle of the sixteenth century. The dispute arose about some plundered cattle which M'Carty wished to drive into the bawn of Blarney without division. Being opposed by O'Donovan, he attacked him and threw him down, but O'Donovan, although on the ground, snatched the dadagh from him, and slew him with his own weapon.

About a quarter of a mile south-west of the castle, in the park is the lake, where it is supposed the plate chest of the last Earl of Clancarty was thrown before the castle was surrendered to William's forces, and a legend says that the Earl rises from the lake every seven years, and walks two or three miles in the hope that some one will speak to him, so that he may tell them where it lies. Another version says that as soon as the estate is restored to the MacCartys the chest will be discovered. A little silver ring has been found in the lake.

Authorities Consulted.

Calendar of State Papers.
Carew MSS.
Parliamentary Gazetteer.
Joyce, "Irish Names of Places."
Croker, "Fairy Legends," and "Researches in the South of Ireland."
Savage, "Picturesque Ireland."
Windele, "Notices of the City of Cork and Vicinity."
Smith, "History of Cork."
C. C. Woods, "Blarney Castle" (*Journal of the Cork Archæological Society*).
Proceedings of Archæological Association of Ireland.

BUNRATTY CASTLE.

BUNRATTY CASTLE

THE village of Bunratty is situated in the Barony of Lower Bunratty, County Clare, and the castle stands on the banks of the Ougarnee River, a little above its juncture with the Shannon on its northern bank, about six miles below Limerick.

The former name of the river was Ratty, and the name, therefore, signifies the end or mouth of the Ratty.

The fortress is still in a very fair state of preservation and shows many signs of alterations during its existence.

It consists of an oblong structure, flanked by four square towers built into the angles, which are joined at the head by depressed arches.

The north-east tower contains an oratory. It has a piscina, and the ceiling is a handsome specimen of richly moulded seventeenth-century stucco work, probably executed when the "great Earl" of Thomond restored the castle in 1610. Out-offices and servants' quarters formerly surrounded the main building, but were removed by the late Mr. Studdert to supply material for the modern manor house.

An inscribed stone at the summit of the castle states that the present building was erected by O'Brien in 1397. There are marks of shot still visible on the walls.

The cantred of Tradee was granted in fee farm to the Norman Robert de Muscegros, at a yearly rent of £30.

Henry III. remitted him two years' rent in 1251 to enable him to fortify Bunratty Castle, which he had built.

Shortly after he surrendered it to the King on condition he was allowed for the repairing, provisioning, and defending of it. It was taken by the Irish in 1257.

De Muscegros exchanged his lands of Tradee, in Thomond, with Sir Richard de Clare in 1275 for property in England, and the following year Bunratty Castle was taken for the King by Geoffry de Gyamul, Lord Justice.

The same year King Brian the Red granted to de Clare the district he had acquired by exchange, and he at once began to repair the castle. It is recorded he built "a defensive thick-walled castle of lime and stone, which was a sheltered, impregnable fortress, and a wide white-washed mansion which he founded in the clear-harboured Bunratty," and that he resided here with English retainers whom he purchased "for love or money."

Torlough O'Brien invaded Thomond, and its King, Brian, fled to Bunratty. Among those who opposed the invaders was de Clare's brother-in-law, Patrick FitzMaurice, who was slain in the conflict. When news of his death reached Bunratty there was great lamentation, and his sister, de Clare's wife, denounced King Brien, who was then at dinner, as the cause of the disaster.

He was thereupon dragged from the table, bound to wild horses, and literary torn to pieces. This act of treachery was rendered even more horrible from the fact that he and de Clare had sworn friendship with the most solemn rites.

Among the State Documents of 1298 is an entry for expenses and wages of horse and foot soldiers in an expedition to relieve Bunratty, which was besieged by Turlough O'Brien. This attack probably took place at an earlier date.

The castle was besieged again in 1305 by Coveha MacConmara and the outworks burnt, which is thus picturesquely described: "Yea, at this bout, the open-spaced Bunratty, when it was gutted, fed the flames; and

BUNRATTY CASTLE

by the Wolf-dog's pertinacity, not once, but twice, were many of the lime-white towers burnt."

The fortress was not taken, and Lord Burke persuaded MacConmara to raise the siege.

At this time Maurice de Rochford was custodian.

The Earl of Ulster marched into Clare with a great army in 1311 to besiege Bunratty. Richard de Clare sallied out to meet him on the hill behind the fortress, but was obliged to retreat. William de Burgo, pressing too far in pursuit, was taken prisoner, as well as John, son of Walter de Lacy.

In 1313, de Clare was about to hang O'Brien's son, who was hostage for the tribe of Coileau, but his wife, with the clergy and nobility, interceded for him.

De Clare and his son Thomas were killed in 1318 in the battle of Dysert O'Dea, and upon his wife, Lady Johan de Clare, hearing of the disaster, she set fire to the castle and sailed for England.

The following year it was spoiled by King Mortogh.

It was immediately repaired, and the Government assigned it to Matilda, wife of Robert de Wills, and Margaret, wife of Bartholomew de Badlesmere, sisters to Richard de Clare, and appointed Robert Sutton constable.

In 1326 it was held for the Crown by James de bello Fago, and in 1332 it was besieged and taken by the Macnamaras.

There is an order dated 1356 to liberate Thomas, the son of John FitzMaurice, who had been imprisoned as accessory to the loss of the castle.

The Lord Deputy recovered the fortress in 1558 by firing across the river until the garrison of Donnell O'Brien surrendered it.

The Earl of Thomond was proclaimed rebel in 1570, and fled to sea; the Earl of Ormond meantime garrisoned Bunratty with his own men, but in 1585 the castle was confirmed to the Earl of Thomond.

The "Great Earl" of Thomond restored it in 1617.

Some authorities say Lord Forbes seized the castle in 1642 in a buccaneering expedition.

When the rebellion broke out in 1641 the Earl of Thomond of the time found himself in a difficult position, for by religion he might have been supposed to side with the Government, while at the same time he was closely related to many of the prominent Confederates, being uncle to Lord Muskerry who commanded their troops in the south. He, therefore, remained quietly at Bunratty taking neither side, but he was too powerful to be allowed to presevere in neutrality.

The Supreme Council of the Confederates entrusted the seizure of both the castle and Earl to his relatives, the O'Briens, but in the meantime the Earl of Ormond had entered into a treaty with the Earl of Thomond whereby the latter was to surrender the castle of Bunratty to a governor they mutually agreed upon.

The choice fell upon Colonel Adams, "a stout officer," who, with upwards of six hundred men, took possession of the stronghold in 1645. The governor was a Scotchman whose family name was Adam, but upon settling in Ireland he seems to have been called Adams, and sometimes MacAdam. He was married to the Hon. Catherine Magennis, granddaughter of Hugh, Earl of Tyrone, therefore his wife was first cousin to Owen Roe O'Neill, which, no doubt, guided his selection as commander of Bunratty garrison.

Before the castle was surrendered the Earl of Thomond built all his plate and money into the walls to the amount of £2,000, and had the place plastered and rough cast. Some of the servants betrayed the fact to the soldiers, and they seized the Earl and threatened to kill him unless he showed them the treasure, whereupon they took it before his face. He afterwards tried to recover it as a debt from the Government in vain.

BUNRATTY CASTLE

The castle was provisioned at the cost of £1,200 by John Davies.

The Earl of Thomond left his fortress in the hands of the soldiers and sailed for England. Colonel Adams at once set to work to put the place in a state of defence by raising earthworks and fortifying outlying positions, as well as mounting cannon in the garden. He was much helped in his operations by the marshy character of the surrounding country.

The Confederates sent an army to besiege the castle, which encamped in the park. They were shortly afterwards joined by Lord Muskerry, who seems to have been only half-hearted in attacking his uncle's property, and it required the persuasion and presence of the Nuncio to push the siege to a victorious issue.

Cardinal Rinuncini must have been much impressed by the beauty of the spot, as later he had scenes of the siege painted on the walls of his Italian palace.

After some weeks a dam about half a mile from the castle was captured, but only held a few hours when deserted by its guards, who were hanged for the offence.

Two pieces of cannon were then directed upon a small outlying castle, and at the end of two days' firing Colonel Adams repaired to the place to see if it could be held any longer. A chance shot at the upper window mortally wounded him, and being carried out he died that night.

When Muskerry heard this he decided to attack in force, " knowing how much discouraged they were at the loss of so valiant a person."

The Irish gradually gained position, and at length the garrison capitulated for their lives, and the officers their swords, and returned to Cork by water. This was in 1646.

In 1712 Henry, 8th Earl of Thomond, disposed of his estate, and the castle passed to the Studdert family, who lived there until the neighbouring mansion was built.

For some years afterwards it was partly used for a police barrack, and now it is in the hands of a caretaker.

AUTHORITIES CONSULTED.

MS. Ordnance Survey.
Frost, "History of the County Clare."
White, "History of Clare."
O'Donoghue, "Memoirs of the O'Briens."
B. Adams and M. Adams, "History of the Adams Family."
Murphy, "Cromwell in Ireland."
Dwyer, "Diocese of Killaloe."
Joyce, "Irish Names of Places."
Gilbert, "Affairs in Ireland, 1641–52" (Apporismical Discovery of Treasonable Faction).
Gilbert, "History of the Irish Confederation by Richard Bellings."
Parliamentary Gazetteer.
State Documents.
State Papers.
Proceedings of Royal Society of Antiquaries, Ireland.
Westropp, "Normans in Thomond;" Macnamara, "Inchiquin, Co. Clare;" Shirley and O'Brien, "Extracts from the Journal of Thomas Dineley," all in *Journal of the Royal Society of Antiquaries, Ireland*.
Westropp, "On the Churches of County Clare," in Proceedings of R.I.A.
"Bunratty," *Dublin Saturday Magazine*.

CARLOW CASTLE

THE town of Carlow, Catherlough or Catherlogh, is situated on the banks of the Barrow, five and a half miles south-by-west of Castledermot near the junction of the above river with the Burren. The name signifies "the city on the lake," but the sheet of water from which it derived its name has disappeared.

The castle stands on a slight eminence to the west of the town on the east bank of the river, where it commanded the ford.

The present ruins consist of two round towers, and the western wall, which measures about 105 feet in length and some 70 feet in height. One of the towers is joined to this structure, and a small portion of the north and south walls adhere to both turrets respectively.

The doors were remarkably low and narrow, and light was admitted almost entirely by loopholes.

In Thomas Dineley's quaint diary he states that the fortress was built of freestone, and a picture in the same work represents it with gables and a high-pitched roof. It is flanked by round towers and has many tall chimneys. It appears to be surrounded by a low battlemented wall, and to have numerous little out-houses.

Like so many castles in Ireland, local tradition ascribes its erection to King John, but Eva, Strongbow's wife, Isabel, their daughter, Hugh le Bigod, 4th Earl of Norfolk, and Bellingham, Lord Deputy of Ireland, have been mentioned by other authorities. Ryan, in his history of Carlow, deals with the likelihood of each claim, and thinks that it was most probably built by Hugh de Lacy. He is said to have erected it about 1180, but the architecture is rather that of the beginning of the thirteenth century.

The castle is mentioned in the charter of William, Earl Marshal.

In 1283 we find the repairing of the old hall, kitchen, and tower among the accounts of Roger le Bigod, Earl of Norfolk, in whose possession it then was. Among the

CARLOW CASTLE.

items of expenditure are 700 nails and canvas, which were probably for the roofing of the great hall, which was covered with wooden shingles, and seems to have been difficult to keep in repair.

Carlow Castle was at this time the centre of government. The courts were held in the hall mentioned, and the Exchequer House was probably situated in one of the towers. The income of the lordship was £750 a year.

After all this expenditure, however, when the Earl's

possessions passed to the Crown in 1306, the castle and hall were so ruined that no value was placed upon them.

J. de Bonevill, of his Majesty's Castle of Carlow, was appointed seneschal of Carlow and Kildare in 1310 to put down the robberies and outrages in the country.

It is stated that the castle was seized in 1397 by Donald MacArt Kavanagh, the MacMorrough, but the authority is not considered very reliable.

In 1494 James Fitzgerald, brother to the Earl of Kildare, having gone into rebellion, seized the castle and hoisted his standard on its battlements. Sir Edward Poynings marched to Carlow, and after a siege of ten days recovered the fortress.

Carlow Castle was in the hands of Thomas, 10th Earl of Kildare, better known as the "Silken Thomas," during his rebellion in 1535. After his imprisonment in 1537 Lord (James) Butler, eldest son of the Earl of Ossory, appealed to the Crown for compensation for having defended the Castles of Carlow and Kilkea, "standing on the marches," close to Irish territory. He was granted his expenses, and appointed constable of both castles.

At the same time the Deputy wrote to the Lord Privy Seal advising him to let the King keep the "manors of Carlagh, Kylea, and Castledermont" in his hands to prevent Lord Ossory and his son from becoming too powerful.

Sir Robert Hartpole applied for the custodianship of the fortress in 1567, it being at that time in possession of Frances Randall, widow of its late keeper.

Rory Oge O'More, Chieftain of Leix, burned the town and Sir Robert Hartpole made a sally from the castle with fifty men and released Harrington and Cosby, who were his prisoners, but O'More escaped in the dark.

Queen Elizabeth desired the Lord Deputy to exchange some of the crown lands with Henry, Earl of Kildare, for the castle and lands of Carlow in 1589. During the unfortunate Essex's rule in Ireland, in 1598 to 1600 the Queen's warders held the fortress, but the Kavanaghs laid the surrounding country waste.

By the State Papers of 1604 the manor of Carlow was granted to Donagh, Earl of Thomond, with the exception of the castle, of which, however, he and his son were made constables. The following is taken from a document setting forth the conditions of the grant:—

"In all works made within the castle, the inhabitants of Carlow are to find six workmen or labourers daily, during the said work, at their own expense; also each tenant and cottager to weed the demesne corn yearly for three days, and a woman out of every house in Carlow to bind the sheaves for one day; each tenant and cottager to cut wood for the use of the castle for three days in summer, and each of them having a draught horse to draw the wood to the castle for three days, also to draw the corn out of the fields to the area of the said castle for three days; to give one cartload of wood, and one truss of straw at Christmas and Easter."

Shortly after this the castle and bawn was granted to Sir Charles Wilmot.

Five hundred English were besieged in the castle in 1642, and were in a starving condition when relieved by Sir Patrick Wemys, who had been despatched to their relief by the Earl of Ormond. The rebels burned the town and fled at his approach.

In 1647 the King's garrison was so hard pressed that the Earl of Ormond borrowed £60 for its relief, and forwarded it by Major Harman, but the fifty men who came to reinforce the garrison could not get in, as the stronghold was closely invested. The siege lasted about a month, and then the castle surrendered.

In Dr. Jones' diary he states that the Cromwellian army arrived before the castle on the 18th of March, 1649. That the garrison of two hundred men refused to surrender it until the battery played on the place, and preparations were made for storming.

The next day the castle was surrendered, and two companies left to garrison it. The officers in command being Colonel Hewson, Sir T. Jones, and Colonel Shelburn.

Again we learn that Ireton arrived to take the castle on July 2, 1650, and that he spent the whole day in preparing for the attack. The troops encamped on the Queen's County side of the river, the field still being pointed out. They had to erect a temporary bridge of ropes, hurdles and straw to cross the river, and the soldiers passed over one by one.

In Edmund Ludlow's "Memoirs" he describes the place as "a small castle, with a river running under its walls," and ascribes its importance to the fact of the neighbourhood being in sympathy with the garrison.

Just before sunset Ireton sent a letter to the governor offering terms to the defenders if they surrendered. The officer he sent returned to say Ireton should have an answer the next morning.

Accordingly, Captain Bellew sent a courteous reply to him asking for a truce of three days, so that he might communicate with the Bishop of Dromore. This was granted, and Ireton went on to Waterford, leaving Sir Hardress Waller in command.

After a short cannonade he took the town, and the castle surrendered upon articles. The garrison received a safe convoy to Lea Castle, and a pass of ten days to reach Athlone.

In Carte's "Life of Ormond," he attributes the castle's loss to treachery, but except in a local tradition this does not appear.

It is said that the garrison running short of water sent an old woman to the river to fetch some, but that she was taken prisoner by some of the soldiers, and brought to the hostile camp. She was promised her life and a reward if on the following night she would show by a torch on the battlements the position of the stairway where the walls were thinnest. The legend runs she fulfilled the conditions and that, the cannonade at once beginning, she was the first to lose her life through her own treachery.

The manor passed from the Earl of Thomond's family, on account of an unredeemed mortgage, to a Mr. Hamilton, M.P., who, in 1729, brought his case before Parliament for having been deprived of the castle yard during the time of privilege.

The castle was leased in 1814 to a Dr. Middleton. This gentleman intended to convert it into a lunatic asylum, and endeavoured to enlarge the windows and lessen the thickness of the walls by the then little known process of blasting. The results were disastrous. One morning, at about nine o'clock, while the workmen were fortunately at breakfast, the huge pile began slowly to totter to its fall.

An eye-witness who had time to escape from the threatened destruction said: "After viewing the portentous and amazing nodding of the towers, the immense pile gradually disparted into vast masses, which broke with difficulty into fragments less mighty."

AUTHORITIES CONSULTED.

J. Ryan, "History of County Carlow."
Brewer, "Beauties of Ireland."
State Documents.
State Papers.
Book of Howth, Carew MSS.
Parliamentary Gazetteer.
Lord Walter Fitzgerald, "Kilkea Castle," in *Journal of Kildare Archæological Society*.
R. Malcomson, "Cromwell at Carlow"; J. O'Meagher, "Diary of Dr. Jones"; E. Shirley, "Extracts from Journal of Thomas Dineley"; and J. Mills, "Accounts of the Earl of Norfolk's Estates in Ireland": all in *Journal of Royal Society of Antiquaries of Ireland*.
MS. Ordnance Survey of Ireland.

CARRICKFERGUS CASTLE

IT is popularly believed that Carrickfergus derived its name from a king called Fergus having been lost there in a storm about 320 B.C., whose body was washed up on the rocky peninsular where the castle stands. The name is, however, more likely to be a corruption of *Carraig na Fairge*, signifying "rock of the sea." It is often erroneously called Knockfergus in ancient documents. The town is situated on the northern shore of Belfast Lough, about ten miles distant from that city.

The castle occupies the whole of a tongue of rock at the south end of the town, which was at one time surrounded on three sides by water.

The entrance to the fortress on the north, or landward direction, was by a drawbridge across a dry moat. This was protected by two semicircular towers, and a portcullis which still exists. Above the entrance is an aperture, from which missiles and lead could be poured upon besiegers.

From the gate towers a high curtain follows the formation of the rock that gradually rises to about 30 feet in height towards the south. The wall is at present mounted with ordnance used by the militia. The enclosed space is divided into two yards. The outer one, which is entered immediately from the gateway, contains a number of buildings and offices erected in 1802, at which time the castle was used as a barrack. There are also vaults, which were supposed to be bomb proof. In the line of wall is situated a small projecting tower known as the

"Lion's Den." The inner yard is approached through a round arched gateway, and contains storehouses and keep. This latter is 90 feet high, and divided into five storeys. Its western side forms part of the outer wall. It was formerly entered by a doorway on the second floor, and a winding stone staircase in the wall of the west angle led to the top. Loopholes admitted light and air, and there was a small door at each storey. At present the ascent is made partly by wooden stairs inside. There are two towers at the summit of the keep, one on the south-east corner covering the top of the stairway, and the other at the south-west corner, which was intended for a sentry-box.

On the third storey is the large room known as "Fergus's Dining-room," being 40 feet long by 38 feet broad and over 25 feet high. It was made into a barrack in 1793, but is now employed as an armoury. Over the chimneypiece was once a stone inscribed in Irish, which was removed in 1793.

The former draw-well of the castle, 37 feet deep, was situated in the keep. It was famous for medicinal qualities. The lower portion of the building is now used as a magazine. The walls of the tower are 9 feet thick, and the corner stones, or quoins, are of yellowish limestone, which was probably quarried in the County Down on the opposite shore of the Lough.

The building of the castle is generally ascribed to John de Courcy, and, although there is no direct proof that this was the case, many facts tend to support the supposition. In the first place, as De Courcy settled a colony in Carrickfergus shortly after his conquest of Ulster, it is most likely that he would provide some means for its protection. Again, it was for a long time the hereditary property of the Earls of Ulster, who were descended from De Courcy. The ancient seal of the mayor of the town bears a spread-eagle, which was the De Courcy crest, and several coins of Henry II.'s time have been found near the building. In a preface to State Papers the editors say that "the oldest fort in Ulster is Carrickfergus, built in the days of De Courcy, and never out of the possession of the English."

In 1605, the Lord Deputy applying for means to have it restored, remarks it was "founded by his Majesty's ancestors, and much needing repair."

It is likely King John stayed in the castle during his visit to Carrickfergus in 1210, and an order is preserved to

CARRICKFERGUS CASTLE
(From an Engraving made in 1838.)

the Bishop of Norwich to buy supplies for it that year. It appears to have passed into the hands of Hugh de Lacy when King John granted him Ulster, but in 1223 a garrison was to be placed in the castle lest it should be attacked by De Lacy, who was then plotting against the King.

The following year a band of knights and soldiers were despatched by the Earl of Pembroke for its further defence.

Although it was being besieged by Hugh they managed to get into the fortress safely, and the siege was then raised.

Two years afterwards the custody of the castle was granted to Hugh de Lacy's brother Walter.

In 1245 an order was issued for its repair, and later (1253) it was assigned by the King as part of the dowry of Eleanor, Queen Consort.

In 1315 the castle was besieged by Edward Bruce, and Lord Mandeville, who endeavoured to relieve it, failed to do so. The gallant little garrison held out for more than a year, and it is said they were reduced to eating eight Scotch prisoners who had died within the walls. Upon the arrival of King Robert Bruce to aid his brother, the fortress was surrendered. After the death of Edward Bruce the castle passed again into the hands of the English, and it appears to have been the only place in Antrim not in the possession of the O'Neills after the assassination of the Earl of Ulster, 1333.

In 1337 the King appointed a constable to the castle under the belief that he was the owner of the stronghold, instead of holding it only during the minority of the Earl of Ulster, and as there was a constable already in office, compensation had to be found for the disappointed custodian. From this time there was a long list of constables, the last being Stewart Banks, Esq., of Belfast, who used merely to attend annually to see the Mayor sworn in the outer yard of the castle. In 1461 an Act of Parliament decreed that none but Englishmen should hold the office of Governor. The position is now a mere sinecure.

In 1390, in an order for repair, the castle is described as being "totally destitute and desolate of defence," and sixteen years later its state does not seem to have been much improved.

For the next two years it was kept for nothing by Sir James Whyte, who then (1408) petitioned the Crown to give him aid against the threatened attack of O'Donnell and his Scots.

CARRICKFERGUS CASTLE

After the order for English custodians, James, Earl of Douglas, was appointed Governor of Carrickfergus Castle in 1463.

At the beginning of the next century Clannaboy Niall, son of Con of Belfast, was prisoner in the castle on account of a row between his servants and some soldiers (1507). He exchanged his freedom for sixteen hostages, but no sooner was he liberated than he returned with his followers and took the castle and the Mayor, and rescued his pledges. In 1552 Sorley Boy MacDonnell surprised Carrickfergus and carried off Walter Floody, the constable of the castle. In consequence of these disturbances the Earl of Sussex marched to relieve the town in 1555. Two years later Hugh O'Neill Oge and some other prisoners in the castle escaped to join James M'Donnell. In 1559 the fortress was walled in and repaired. The building seems to have been much dilapidated in 1567, and upon Sir Henry Sidney coming north the following year, he had the keep roofed and restored. When the Earl of Essex arrived by sea in 1573, he reports that he discharged the ward of the castle, for it "doth not serve of any use, having in it very few rooms, and none of those covered, so as I have no apt place to employ her Majesty's munition and other store but in wet vaults."

From 1583 to 1598 Carrickfergus was the only town held by the Queen in the district, and in the latter year the castle was but poorly provisioned.

General Monroe, with four thousand Scotch auxiliaries, landed and took the castle in 1642, but four years later he was surprised by General Monk, who occupied the stronghold for the Parliament, being made Governor of it shortly afterwards.

The next year, but small resistance was offered to Lord Inchiquin, who then held it for the King for a few months, and it was retaken by Sir Charles Coote, who appointed a Governor for the Commonwealth.

In 1666, while the Duke of Ormond was at the head of affairs, so great was the dissatisfaction that the castle was seized by mutinous soldiers, and a strong force was required to quell the disturbance.

Eight years later the fortress was ordered to be furnished with twenty cannon.

The adherents of James II. sustained here a siege for six days from the troops of the Duke of Schomberg in 1689, after which they surrendered. It was on the 14th of June in this year that King William III. landed at Carrickfergus from the yacht *Mary*.

In 1711 50 feet of the outer wall fell down, and the tower was roofed with lead.

The castle was taken by the French Commodore Thurôt with three ships of war in 1760, but his squadron was captured a few days later by the English fleet.

In 1797 the United Irishmen laid a plot to seize the castle, which was discovered by one of the garrison turning informer.

The year after the rebellion State prisoners were confined at Carrickfergus, having been sent from Belfast. At one time the fortress was used as a prison for all Antrim.

In 1814 a small square tower on the south side was taken down and rebuilt.

The castle is now in the possession of the Crown.

Authorities Consulted.

State Papers.
Russell and Prendergast, Preface to State Papers.
Parliamentary Gazetteer.
M. Haverty, "History of Ireland."
Belfast Naturalists' Field Club Guide.
S. M'Skimin, "History of Carrickfergus."
Calendar of Patent Rolls.
Sweetman, Calendar of Documents.
Carew MSS.
"Notes on a Plan of Carrickfergus."
J. Bell, "Origin of the Name of Carrickfergus" (*Ulster Journal of Archæology*).

CARRICK-ON-SUIR CASTLE.

CARRICK-ON-SUIR CASTLE

"The court of Carrick is a court well fortified,
A court to which numbers of the noble resort,
A court noted for politeness—a court replete with pleasures,
A court thronged with heroes,
A court without torchlight, yet a court illumed;
A court of the light of wax tapers!
A plentiful mansion—so artistically stuccoed
With sun-lit gables and embroidery-covered walls."
                    Translated from Irish by J. O'DALY.

NINETEEN miles south-by-west of Kilkenny, in the Barony of East Iffa and Offa, County Tipperary, stands the old town of Carrick on the left bank of the Suir. The name Carrick is derived from a rock in the Suir at the point where the town is built. The castle was erected by Edmond le Bottiller in 1309, he being created Earl of Carrick six years later. Upon his son receiving the title of Earl of Ormond the old title fell into disuse.

The present remains consist of two great towers of the Plantagenet castle, rising behind the Tudor mansion which was erected by Thomas, 10th Earl of Ormond, in the reign of Elizabeth. Although not now inhabited it is preserved from further decay.

The two quadrangular towers of the older fortress stand on the river bank, and are separated by a courtyard which was entered on the north by an arched gateway from the river front. In one of these towers is situated the chapel, which is connected with the banqueting hall by a narrow passage. A strong light from a double window falls upon the altar, round which is the remains of a carved stone canopy supported by the figures of angels.

The Tudor house which connects the older buildings is a many-gabled mansion, and said by O'Donovan to be the most perfect specimen of that period's architecture in Ireland.

The ceiling of the Great Hall is a beautiful example of stucco work. It is divided by richly-moulded ribs enclosing Tudor emblems, and arms and mottoes relating to the Ormond family. This apartment is 63 feet in length by 15 feet in breadth, and is lighted by mullioned windows, that on the north side being large and deeply recessed. It also contains several handsome chimney-pieces.

The walls were richly hung with tapestry, which was removed at the beginning of the nineteenth century, some of it being transferred to Kilkenny Castle.

Little is known of the history of the early feudal fortress. Several charters granted by the Ormonds as Lords Palatine of Tipperary are dated from Carrick, showing that the family were occasionally in residence.

There is a tradition that Anne Boleyn was born in the castle. Thomas, Earl of Carrick and Ormond, who died in 1515, had two daughters, one of whom married Sir William Boleyn, a London merchant, and she was grandmother to the future Queen. History is uncertain where Anne Boleyn was born, as several places are mentioned; it is, therefore, not impossible that at Carrick Elizabeth's mother first saw the light. Henry VIII. created Anne's father Earl of Ormond and Wiltshire, but the former title afterwards reverted to the Butlers.

In 1571 Perrott visited Carrick Castle during his campaign in Munster, and it was plundered by the seneschal in the Desmond rebellion of 1582.

In the time of Thomas, 10th Earl of Ormond, it became the chief residence of the family. Thomas Dubh, or the Black Earl, was the favourite of Queen Elizabeth, who

CARRICK-ON-SUIR CASTLE

used to call him her " black husband," to the annoyance of his rival the Earl of Leicester. He was a great statesman and chivalrous nobleman, and enjoyed the full confidence of his Sovereign during her long reign.

In the latter years of his life he lived almost entirely at Carrick. A glimpse of his loyal love for England is given by Sir John Davys in the following observations of his on a journey in Munster in 1606 :—

"And because I was to pass by the Carricke, a house of my Lord of Ormond, where his lordship hath lain ever since his last weakness, I went thither to visit his lordship and to rest there upon Easter Day ; but because the feast of St. George fell out in the Easter holidays, I was not suffered in any wise to depart until I had seen him do honour to that day. I found the Earl in his bed, for he was weaker at this time than he had been for many months before ; so that upon the day of St. George he was not able to sit up, but had his robes laid upon his bed, as the manner is. From thence I returned to Dublin at the end of Easter week."

Towards the end of his life, Earl Thomas was quite blind, and a quaint old MS., discovered at Brussels in 1822, gives a graphic account of a prophecy supposed to have been delivered by him at a Christmas family gathering in Carrick Castle shortly before his death, which took place in 1614.

Among those present at the feast were Sir Walter Butler, of Kilcash, brother to the Earl, and also his son and grandson, James. The latter was only four years old, and there being no room at the table, he was let play about, and " being a sprightly boy, entertained himself with a whipping of his gigg " (a kind of top) behind his great-uncle's chair. Black Thomas asked what the noise was, and being told, he took the child (afterwards the great Duke of Ormond) between his knees and said :—

" My family shall be much oppressed and brought very

low; but by this boy it shall be restored again, and in his time be in greater splendour than ever it has been."

Viscount Tullogh, who was the Earl's son-in-law and heir, pushed back his chair angrily from the table, and again the blind Earl asked who made the noise. Upon hearing, he said—

"Ah! he is a flower that will soon fade."

Shortly afterwards the Viscount died without children, and later events proved the strange truth of the prophecy. A long law suit, manipulated for political purposes, impoverished the earldom, but it was brought to a satisfactory termination by James Butler of Kilcash marrying Lady Elizabeth Preston, the other claimant to the estates through her mother's rights.

The young couple began their married life at Carrick, where Walter, Earl of Ormond, joined them, and died in the castle in 1632.

When civil war broke out in 1646, James, then Marquis of Ormond, was appointed Chief Governor and hastened from France. He landed at Cork, and proceeded to Carrick. Here a deputation from the Confederate Assembly of Kilkenny waited on him.

Three years later Cromwell's troops, under Colonel Reynolds, took the town of Carrick, and about a hundred of the garrison fled to the castle, but surrendered the following day. It was well provisioned with stores, and Cromwell, it is said, intended to winter there. Ormond, hearing of its capture, despatched Lord Inchiquin to retake it. He was, however, repulsed with great loss.

In the time of the Commonwealth Carrick Castle, with its demesne, deer park, and 16,000 acres, were granted to Sir John Reynolds, brother-in-law to Lord Henry Cromwell. Upon the Restoration it reverted to its former owner, who was created Duke of Ormond. He spent much time at Carrick, and did a great deal to improve the trade of the town.

CARRICK-ON-SUIR CASTLE

In 1816 Mr. Wogan was the tenant of the castle, and he carried out some restoration. After he left the place was dismantled, and for many years was allowed to go entirely to decay. It is now, however, better preserved.

In 1876, when the present Marquis married Lady Elizabeth Grosvenor, daughter of the Duke of Westminster, a great feast for the Ormond tenantry was held in the castle.

The fairy "Leather Apron" is said formerly to have haunted the kitchen department and chastised servants who did not do their work.

A local legend foretells the fall of the fortress upon the wisest man. An underground passage is said to connect the building with Edenderry Castle.

Authorities Consulted.

Mason, "Parochial Survey of Ireland."
Murphy, "Cromwell in Ireland."
Bagwell, "Ireland Under the Tudors."
State Papers.
Parliamentary Gazetteer.
In *Journal of Kilkenny Archæological Society*, "Panegyric on Thomas Butler, 10th Earl of Ormond." Graves, "Ancient Tapestry of Kilkenny Castle." Graves, "Anonymous account of the early life and marriage of James, 1st Duke of Ormond."
In *Journal of Waterford and South-East of Ireland Archæological Society*, Hurley, "Was Anna Boleyn born in the Castle of Carrick-on-Suir?"
In *Clonmel Chronicle*. "Carrick-on-Suir and its Ancient Castle."

CARRIGOGUNNEL CASTLE

> "A sort of strength, a strong and stately hold
> It was at first, though now it is full old.
> On rock alone full farre from other mount
> It stands, which shews it was of great account."
>
> THOMAS CHURCHYARD.

THIS fortress, sometimes called Carrickaquicy, is situated five miles west-south-west of Limerick City, in the same county, in the barony of Pubble Brien. It stands on an abrupt basaltic rock which has forced itself through the limestone, and is surrounded by low marshy ground called Corkass land which stretches away to the Shannon.

O'Donovan states that the name signifies "rock of the O'Connolls," but it is more popularly believed to mean "rock of the candle," and several versions of the following legend are related to account for the designation:—

The site of the castle was formerly supposed to be inhabited by a hag of gigantic form called Grana, and every evening she lighted a candle in her habitation, which from its elevated position was visible for miles round, and every one who saw its light died before morning.

The great Finn hearing of this scourge ordered a man called Ryan to go and extinguish the light, and presented him with a charmed cap to accomplish the mission. This covered his eyes until he had scaled the rock, seized the candle, and thrown it into the Shannon.

The witch in a fury was about to grasp him when he took a jump of two miles westward, and she was only able

CARRIGOGUNNEL CASTLE.

CARRIGOGUNNEL CASTLE

to vent her rage by hurling a rock after him, which is still pointed out with the marks of her fingers on it to indicate the "Hag's Throw."

The castle ruins comprise one or two towers and part of the ramparts. It was finally destroyed by gunpowder, and huge masses of masonry lie about in all directions, indicating its once extensive proportions.

A great ash-tree adorns the centre of the pile.

William de Braose had large estates in Ireland when he was driven into exile in 1210, his wife and son starved to death, and his Castle of Carrigogunnel granted to Donogh Cairbreach O'Brien for a yearly rent of 60 marks.

This O'Brien had done homage to King John at Waterford, but he seems to have been shortly afterwards deprived of his land.

In 1535 Lord Leonard Grey marched to Limerick and Mathew O'Brien surrendered him the Castle of Carrigogunnel on condition it should only be garrisoned by Englishmen. It was said at this time to have been in undisturbed possession of the O'Briens for over two hundred years.

The Deputy garrisoned it under the command of George Woodward, "an honest and a hardy man."

In the meantime the fortress was given by indenture to Donough O'Brien to hold for the King. He was son-in-law to the Earl of Ossory, and had long been fawning on the Government with offers to besiege the castle for them, if provided with a hundred men and a piece of ordnance.

The governor of the castle, no doubt regarding this arrangement as a violation of the conditions on which the castle had been obtained, handed it back to its former owner, Mathew O'Brien, which the State Papers describe as losing it "by treachery."

This was in 1536, and the same year Lord Butler appeared before it to regain it for his relative, Donough O'Brien.

It was garrisoned partly by followers of Desmond and partly by those of Mathew O'Brien.

A messenger was sent to them offering them their lives, but otherwise no quarter. They returned no answer, but imprisoned the bearer.

A breach was soon made with a battering piece, and after several attempts, the castle was carried by storm.

The besiegers lost thirty killed and wounded, while seventeen of the defenders were killed in the attack, and forty-six were afterwards put to death.

A few of the principal O'Briens were conveyed to Limerick, tried for high treason, and executed. Large ransoms were offered for these men but were refused.

The fortress was then committed to Lord Butler, and he transferred it to Donough O'Brien, who, it is stated, "became a scourge to the citizens of Limerick."

James of Desmond besieged Carrigogunnel in 1538, and the following year great complaints were lodged about the plundering of the neighbouring country by the castle garrison.

Towards the close of the year these charges became so serious that Donough O'Brien was deprived of his possession.

The castle was in the hands of Brien Duff O'Brien, chieftain of Pobblebrien, in 1590, and is described as being very strong and "a most dangerous place if the enemy were seized thereof."

Donough O'Brien is mentioned as of Carrigogunnel in 1607, yet Brien Duff O'Brien surrendered his possessions and the castle to the Queen and received a patent for the same. He was knighted, and died in 1615.

Daniel O'Brien forfeited the castle and lands for taking part in the rebellion of 1641. Charles II. granted Carrigogunnel and four plowlands to Michael Boyle, Lord Archbishop of Dublin,

CARRIGOGUNNEL CASTLE

In Thomas Dineley's Journal he states that it belonged to His Royal Highness, and was at the time rented by the Primate and Chancellor of Ireland.

Archdale says that it at one time belonged to the Knights Templars.

In 1691, during the second siege of Limerick, after the battle of Aughrim, it was garrisoned by a Jacobite ward of a hundred and fifty men. Baron Ginle sent a strong party and four guns, under the command of Major-General Scravemore, to summon the castle, which was relinquished without a blow. An historian of the time, commenting upon this, says: "Which seems to have been rather from want of instructions what to do than courage to defend it; for, to give the Irish their due, they can defend stone walls very handsomely."

The garrison were marched as prisoners of war to Clonmel, and the following month both the Castle of Carrigogunnel and Castle Connell were blown up. Dean Story received £160 to purchase gunpowder for their demolition.

During the Whiteboy disturbances frequent meetings were held amid the ruins.

Mr. and Mrs. Hall relate at length a sad tradition about the daughter of a Palatine who was in love with one of the conspirators, and whose father, having tracked her to the ruins, was only saved from being put to death by her lover, whom she shortly afterwards married against her parents' wish.

Upon returning to bid farewell to them before going into exile with her husband, who was obliged to fly for his life, her father detained her. Her husband was unable to come openly to the house, and so she never saw him again, but gradually pined away, and died under the ash-tree growing among the castle ruins, where she used to meet him before their marriage. Since then her ghost is said to frequent the spot after nightfall.

AUTHORITIES CONSULTED.

J. Frost, "The County of Clare."
Croker, "Researches in the South of Ireland."
Croker, "Fairy Legends."
Ferrar, "History of Limerick."
Lenihan, "History of Limerick."
Bagwell, "Ireland under the Tudors."
Hall, "Ireland."
State Papers.
Parliamentary Gazetteer.
Shirley (with note by O'Brien), "Extracts from the Journal of Thomas Dineley," in *Journal of Kilkenny Archæological Society*.

CASTLE BARNARD

"Where Castle Bernard sees with glad surprise,
At every wish successive beauties rise."

THE former name for this stronghold was Castle Mahon. It is situated on the River Bandon not far from the town. The present castle is said to occupy the site of the former royal rath of the O'Mahonys, Kings of Munster. It was called Rathleann, and the great Saint Fin Barr was born there. This was much anterior to the English invasion, although an inquisition held in 1584 states that the O'Mahonys came from Carbery in 1460, and seized the Crown lands, which had been forfeited by the Barry Oges in 1399.

They were, however, only returning to the country over which they had formerly ruled. The fortress is supposed to have been built by an O'Mahony.

Francis Bernard, who succeeded to the estate in 1660, threw down the ancient bawn walls, and enlarged the windows. His son, Judge Bernard, rebuilt the castle after it came into his possession in 1690.

A new brick front was added on the river side, the bricks having been made in the neighbourhood.

He was succeeded by his son Francis (usually known as Squire Bernard) in 1731, who added an eastern front to the fortress, and planted the great beech avenue. Smith, who collected his information in 1749, describes the castle as having two regular fronts of brick, with Corinthian pilasters and coignes and beltings of Portland stone.

In 1788 Francis Bernard, afterwards the 1st Earl of Bandon, pulled down the two fronts which had been added by his predecessors, and connected the old castle by a corridor (some 90 feet in length) with a mansion he erected a little to the east of the stronghold. This new part has large rooms, the library being a very handsome oval apartment.

This forms the present beautiful country seat of the Earl of Bandon. It is situated in a park about four miles in circumference, through which the Bandon River flows.

The O'Mahonys were not a powerful sept: their regular field force only numbered twenty-six horse, no gallowglasses, and a hundred and twenty kern.

In 1575 the O'Mahony paid his respects to Sir Henry Sidney during his visit to Cork, of whom Sir Henry writes that he was "a man of small force although a proper countrie."

Conoher O'Mahony, of Castle Mahon, threw in his lot with the Earl of Desmond during his rebellion, in which rising he was killed at the age of twenty-three.

In 1587, an inquisition held at Cork found that Conohor O'Mahownye, late of Castle Mahown, entered into rebellion with Gerald, late Earl of Desmond, and was slain therein and that he was seized of Castle Mahowne and of the barony or cantred of Kineallineaky.

The following year the castle and lands were conferred by patent on Phane Beecher, son of Alderman Henry Beecher, of London.

Mr. William Weever, in his "discourse" on the Munster rebellion of 1598, records that Mr. Beecher deserted Castle Mahon during the rising.

In 1611 it seems the grant to Phane Beecher was confirmed.

The first Bernard to settle in Ireland during Elizabeth's

reign had a son Francis, who was lord of the manor of Castle Mahon, where he lived before the rebellion in 1641. He had one son, Francis, who was in possession of the castle in 1690 when Bandon was surprised and taken by Colonel M'Carthy's men. After the town had fallen into their hands they proceeded to Castle Mahon and demanded the fortress and its stores to be given up to King James, and the garrison to surrender as prisoners.

Mr. Bernard had served many years with the Bandon Militia, and had been rewarded with a grant of land from Cromwell for military service, so that he was not likely to surrender without a struggle when the trumpeter appeared on the esplanade in front of the castle.

He had gathered his retainers and the neighbouring farmers into the stronghold, and flew the red flag from King John's Tower.

Having received a negative to their demand, the besiegers attempted to batter in the great gate, but a discharge of musketry killing some of their number they desisted. They shook the windows and doors to try and effect an entrance.

A line of sentries were posted in front of the castle with orders to shoot any one who appeared at the windows, but the deadly fire of the besieged killed them nearly all.

Seeing that their numbers were rapidly thinning they sought cover from the out-houses in the rear, and from there they carried on an ineffectual fusilade for some time.

Finding, however, this was of no avail they retreated to the river, crossing by the ford. A pike blade and some swords of this date were recently found in a pond which lay in their route.

The brave garrison had many killed and wounded, Mr. Bernard being among those who lost their lives.

The dead Irish were collected and covered with straw in a stable until the next day, when they were buried in a disused graveyard at Killountain.

Judge Bernard succeeded his father, having been born in the castle in 1663. He changed the name from Castle Mahon to Castle Barnard.

His son, "Squire Bernard," did much for the neighbourhood until a dispute with the townspeople about trees caused him to go and live in England.

In 1760 a sad accident took place which led to the death of little Robert Bernard, one of the sons of the house. He had climbed to the top of King John's Tower, and as the bats and swallows flew in and out he tried to strike them with his battledore, but overbalancing, he stepped back to recover himself and fell through the trapdoor which gives egress to the summit. He died of the injuries received.

Francis Bernard was created Earl of Bandon in 1800, and Castle Barnard is still the principal residence of the Earls of Bandon.

AUTHORITIES CONSULTED.

G. Bennett, "History of Bandon."
C. Smith, "County and City of Cork."
Calendar of State Papers.
Calendar of Carew MSS.

CASTLE BORO

LORD CAREW'S demesne of about a thousand acres is situated in the townland of Ballyboro, six miles west-south-west of Enniscorthy, and is bisected by the River Boro. The ancient name for this stream was Bel-atha-Borumha, and was derived from the Borumha, or cow tribute, which the Kings of Leinster had to pay to the High Kings of Ireland.

To the south-east of Castle Boro mansion, on the other side of the river, is the ivy-clad ruin, formerly known as Ballyboro Castle. It now stands in the farmyard, and is 42 feet long by 27 feet wide when measured from the outside. Two gables are still to be seen, and the windows are built of brick.

Local tradition states that it was formerly the residence of Brien Boroimhe, but the site is all that could possibly have belonged to a dwelling of his.

About the year 1628 Robert Carew, younger son of Carew of Haccombe in Devonshire, obtained through his kinsman, Sir George Carew, afterwards Earl of Totnes, a grant of lands in the County Wexford, which had formerly belonged to the Desmonds. Charles II. confirmed the grant in 1663 to his son. This Carew is generally supposed to have built the now ruined castle, which was occupied by the family until near the close of the eighteenth century. By others, however, the date of architecture is considered to be that of the beginning of the seventeenth century, and the castle believed to have been the residence of "James Hoar of Bellaborow, constable of the Barony of Bantry" in 1608, who is mentioned thus in the Carew MSS.

When James II. was fleeing to Duncannon, after the battle of the Boyne, he stopped to water and rest his horses at the ford of Aughnacopple, near the castle. The Carew of that time sent provisions to the fugitives, and the pair of gold sleeve links given by the fallen monarch as a mark of his gratitude are still preserved as an heirloom at Castle Boro. There is some doubt as to whether they were presented at the river bank or sent later from Duncannon.

Towards the close of the eighteenth century the head of the family wished to have a more modern house than the old fortress, but not deeming it worth while to go to the expense unless he had a son to succeed him, he delayed the commencement of the work until the very day when his son and heir was born.

The insurgents of 1798 attacked the residence, and a picture hangs in the hall of Castle Boro which has holes in it that were made by the rebels' pikes.

Mr. Robert Carew was raised to the peerage in 1834, and in 1840, during the absence of the family, the newly-erected house was burned down, the fire having originated in a chimney. The west wing containing the library was the only portion saved.

Building operations were at once commenced under the direction of Mr. Robertson. The present mansion is in Classic style, having a centre block four storeys in height with wings at either side of a storey less. The drawing-rooms are especially handsome apartments, and are being decorated by the present Lady Carew with embroidered panels of Early English design.

In the gardens are a number of trees which have been planted by distinguished visitors, amongst whom were the late Duke of Clarence, the present Prince of Wales, the

CASTLE BORO

Duke of Aosta, the Count of Turin, the Earl of Halsbury and the late Sir H. M. Stanley.

A very handsome granite gateway gives access to the grounds.

The present Lord Carew is the 3rd Baron.

Authorities Consulted.

W. Flood, "History of Enniscorthy."
MS. Ordnance Survey of Ireland.
Parliamentary Gazetteer.
Joyce, "Irish Place Names,"

CASTLE DONOVAN

THIS stronghold is situated in a wild romantic district among the mountains, to the north of the village of Drimoleague in the eastern division of West Carbery, about seven miles east of Bantry, County Cork.

Above it rises the hill of Mulraugh-Nesha. The country round is destitute of trees, and from its elevated position the castle is visible from a wide area.

The fortress consists of a tall, square keep with crenelated battlements and defences projecting from the angles. It is built on a rock, the rough surface of which forms the floor of the lower room in the castle.

There seems to have been no attempt to make the ground even, as great indentations, nearly two feet in depth, extend the whole length of the apartment.

The first floor is supported by a vault, and this state apartment measures about 26 feet by 20. The windows and loops are exceedingly small, the former being surrounded by label mouldings well cut in the dark freestone.

A spiral stair leads to the hall above the vault, and this is open to the heavens, but the high-pitched gables of the roof still remain. Great cracks in the masonry run down the centre and through the south-west angle.

It belongs to the earliest type of castle which succeeded

CASTLE DONOVAN

the peel tower. The outworks, of which little remain but the foundations, are situated close to the keep.

The O'Donovans were descended from a long line of Munster kings. Cahill, the son of Donovan, was killed in 1254, and from him the district round the stronghold took its name, and also the clan of which he was chief.

It is likely that he erected the fortress.

James I. granted the castle (then called Sowagh) to Donell O'Donovan, of Castle Donovan, Gent., and with it

CASTLE DONOVAN.

a large tract of country, part of which was created the manor of Castle Donovan, with 500 acres of demesne.

Donell O'Donovan died in 1639, and his son forfeited the estate in the rebellion of 1641.

Tradition states that the castle was reduced by Ireton during the Parliamentary wars.

Charles II. bestowed the lands of Castle Donovan by letters patent on Lieutenant Nathaniel Evanson in 1679.

There is a legend regarding a mysterious drip of water which apparently comes from the upper masonry of the tower, and which it is said will continue as long as there is an heir to the chieftainship of O'Donovan.

AUTHORITIES CONSULTED.

J. Windele, "Notices of City of Cork."
Parliamentary Gazetteer.
"Rides through the County Cork" (*Dublin Penny Journal*), 1828.

CASTLE KEVIN, COUNTY CORK

THIS name was formerly written Castle Kiffin, and the fortress is situated between Doneraile and the Blackwater in the County Cork.

The castle has been much altered and modernised since its first erection. It contains thirty-two rooms, though some of them are exceedingly small. There are 365 windows, one, therefore, for every day in the year. The hall of black and white marble is L shaped and much worn by age. From this a very handsome oak staircase leads to the first landing, which is lighted by a beautiful old stained-glass window upon which the Thornhill arms are emblazoned.

During repairs in 1810 a number of skeletons were discovered under the steps. They were supposed to be those of soldiers, and beside one a gold piece of James II. and a number of copper coins of various dates were found. These are now in the possession of Colonel Badham-Thornhill.

During a siege, of which the fortress stood many, the water supply was a serious inconvenience. Not only was the well some distance from the castle, but it was apt to run dry when largely drawn upon. It is situated in the limestone rock at a great depth, and when being cleaned in 1825 the key of the portcullis was found at the bottom and carefully preserved by E. Badham-Thornhill, who was then owner.

The castle originally belonged to the O'Keeffs, from

which, no doubt, the name is derived. Their territory being seized, was given to the Anglo-Norman family of de Rupe, or Roche, and in 1583 David and Maurice Fitz John Roch are mentioned as of Castlekevin.

Cromwell's troops besieged and took the castle for the Commonwealth, tradition stating that the soldiers placed the late owner's head on a lance over the "Bell Gate," near the present stables.

The castle was then granted to Sir Richard Thornhill, who also possessed considerable property in the neighbourhood by purchase, so that the estate was about 10,000 acres in extent in the counties of Cork and Limerick.

The Thornhills occupied the castle until 1853, when it was sold in the Encumbered Estates Court, and the building was purchased by Mr. E. Reeves.

AUTHORITIES CONSULTED.

C. Smith, "County and City of Cork."
Fiants of Elizabeth.
Colonel Badham-Thornhill MS.

CASTLE KEVIN, COUNTY WICKLOW

> "The halls where mirth and minstrelsy
> Than Fertire's winds rose louder,
> Were flung in masses lonely,
> And black with English powder."

IN 1216 King Henry III. granted the manor of Swords with increased privileges to Henry de Loundres, Archbishop of Dublin, on condition that he should build and maintain a castle on his manor of Castle Kevin. Nearly two centuries later, Swords was seized by the Commissioner of Forfeitures on the plea that this had not been done, but it was afterwards returned to the Archbishop of the time as having been unjustly taken.

The fortress was intended for protection in this direction against the invasions of the O'Byrnes and O'Tooles. The site was some three and a half miles north-east of Glendalough, the ancient cathedral city of that diocese. Its natural defences were the bog, on the edge of which it stood, and thick woods that stretched almost from Dublin to Glendalough. Quite close to it ran a stream, which joined the Avonmore about a quarter of a mile lower down, near the present village of Annamoe.

It appears to have been a square building, flanked by towers at each corner. The foundations, which still remain, measure some 120 feet each way. They are elevated about 20 feet, and are now covered with grass.

The castle was built of rubble stone and excellent

mortar, which is shown by the huge blocks of the walls which still lie round the foundations.

The Archbishops held courts and exercised jurisdiction here through their officers, and had their own gallows.

In 1277-78 the Treasurer's account for the year contains £60 to John de Saunford for the custody of the new castle of Mackinegan and Castle Keyvin. The stronghold was often used by the Archbishops as a hunting-lodge, the woods around being well stocked with deer. It was also strongly garrisoned.

At the beginning of the next century (1308) the Viceroy Wogan marched against the O'Tooles, but was defeated with the loss of several knights. Castle Kevin was captured and the garrison killed, while the towns near were sacked and plundered.

Later Piers de Gaveston successfully subdued the rising, and made a thanksgiving offering at the Church of St. Kevin, Glendalough. The following year he built New Castle in the O'Byrnes' country and repaired Castle Kevin, at the same time cutting a pass through the woods, from it to Glendalough.

Thirty years later Alexander de Bickner received royal orders to repair his fortifications at Castle Kevin, so that at this time it was still connected with the See of Dublin, but it subsequently passed into royal keeping.

It appears that Henry VIII. by letters patent "made grants to Arte O'Toole and heirs the manor of Castle Kevin and the Farrtree" (hence Vartry) "on conditions they used the English habit, language, education, hostings, aidings, and the like, and that he should keep Castle Kevin in repair as a bulwark against the rebels."

Phelim O'Toole was the representative of the family in 1591 when Hugh Roe O'Donnell escaped from one of the gate towers of Dublin Castle, where he had been confined as a hostage for over three years.

O'Toole having visited him in prison, as a friend, during

CASTLE KEVIN, COUNTY WICKLOW

this time, he naturally thought he was safe in seeking shelter at Castle Kevin.

Phelim's loyalty was not, however, above suspicion, and he was divided between his wish to help the young fugitive and fear for his own head. In this difficulty a woman's wit apparently solved the problem. His sister Rose, wife to the great O'Byrne of Ballinacor, was at Castle Kevin at the time, and she advised him to send a slow messenger to Dublin advising the Lord Deputy of O'Donnell's arrival, and a fast messenger to her husband in Glenmalure (who was in a state of open rebellion), telling him to come and carry off Hugh before the Government officials arrived.

Phelim followed the advice given, but the "wine-dark" Avonmore becoming flooded the party of rescuers, at once despatched by O'Byrne, could not cross the river, and the King's men arrived first upon the scene. Whereupon Hugh O'Donnell was escorted back to Dublin, and was confined in the Wardrobe Tower in irons, from which, however, he escaped the following year.

Captain Charles Montague, writing to the Lord Deputy in 1596, states that Feagh M'Hugh O'Byrne had threatened to besiege the castle with three hundred men, and that he had provisioned it for a month. The same year a ward was placed in it during the rebellion, while in 1599 a commander was appointed to the forts of Rathdrome, Castlekeavyn, and Wicklowe, at ten shillings a day.

No doubt the O'Tooles were implicated in the rebellion referred to, for in 1609 we find John Wakeman, who had received the confiscated estate of the O'Tooles, selling Castle Kevin back to Luke (or Feogh) O'Toole. In the deed recording the transaction it is remarked that the castle for some years past "hath been waste and in utter decay."

An inquisition of 1636 found that the son of Arte O'Toole, to whom the lands were first granted, had gone into rebellion and died, and that his son Feogh O'Toole who represented the family at the time of the inquiry, had bought back Castle Kevin from the man to whom it had been granted after the confiscation of the O'Toole property. Castle Kevin had at this time been uncovered for thirty years, and this was deemed sufficient for forfeiture, as it had been granted on condition that it should be kept in repair.

Accordingly in July of the same year an ordinance was issued by the King taking possession. The castle and lands were then granted to Sir John Coke, Knight, Secretary of State. Dr. Alane Cooke, writing to him from Dublin in August describing his new property, says:— "Castle Kevin, the town where the castle doth stand ; this hath a goodly wood, but no great timber and very fine young oaks ; " and again :—" Castle Kevin is the fittest place to build the manor, because of the strength. The bawn is very good, very near 20 feet high. All the castle is down and the bounds are very nearly 50 yards square, a fine small river running at the foot of the castle."

The grant of land consisted of 15,441 acres of all sorts, English measure, 12 miles from Dublin, with a castle called Kevin, and a fine river full of salmon and trout.

It does not appear, however, that Luke O'Toole was easily dislodged, and when Oliver Cromwell left Dublin to march to Wexford in 1649 he proved a source of constant annoyance to the troops. At this time he was encamped at Glenmalure with his four sons, one of whom managed to seize Cromwell's favourite steed. Its owner offered £100 to Luke for its return, "but for gold or silver he would not give him back, but preferred to keep him as a monument."

It is said that in revenge for this Cromwell ordered his cannon to level Castle Kevin. Local tradition supports this statement by pointing out a furze-covered rath from which the castle is supposed to have been shelled by Ludlow, while the blocks of adhering masonry round the foundations are unlike the crumbling of age alone.

CASTLE KEVIN, COUNTY WICKLOW 113

Against this it is remarked that Castle Kevin does not appear in the list of Leinster castles reduced by Cromwell. This, however, might be accounted for from the fact that (as it appears) only a part of the castle walls were standing at the time, and that its final destruction had no strategical value, but was merely private revenge for the theft of a horse, and so was not recorded.

Luke O'Toole was afterwards captured and executed.

The land upon which the remains of the castle stand is now in the possession of the Rev. Charles Frizell, who also owns the modern manor house of Castle Kevin, some quarter of a mile distant, on a hill above the ancient building.

AUTHORITIES CONSULTED.

D'Alton, "Archbishops of Dublin."
O'Toole, "Clan of O'Toole."
State Papers.
Carew MSS.
Murphy, "Cromwell in Ireland."
O'Clery, "Hugh Roe O'Donnell." Introduction by Murphy.
Gilbert, "History of the Viceroys."
Stokes, "Anglo-Norman Church."
Reeves, Pamphlet on Swords.
Rev. W. Stokes, Pamphlet on Derrylossory.

CASTLE SALEM

BENDUFF, signifying the black peak or gable, was the former name of this fortress, which was built on a rock in the centre of a small valley about a mile north-west of Ross, in East Carbery, Co. Cork.

The present ruins consist of the castle and a more modern dwelling-house, which was added to the back of the fortress and communicated with it by the ancient doorway of the keep, about 12 feet from the ground, and which gave access to the first landing of the more modern staircase. The castle had three arches, the walls being 11 feet thick, and containing passages and recesses. A stone stair led to the summit, which originally was reached at about 70 feet from the ground.

When in possession of the Morris family the old covering was replaced by a slated roof, the material for which was, no doubt, procured at the neighbouring slate quarry.

The situation is so enclosed by the surrounding hills that figs grew plentifully here in former days. The pleasure grounds were at one time laid out in the Dutch style; yew, beech, and laurel grew to great perfection, and in a grove of the latter a rookery was established. The remains of a deer-park wall are still to be seen.

The fortress is generally supposed to have been erected by the O'Donovans, but it is also ascribed to the Lady Catherine Fitzgerald, daughter of Thomas, 8th Earl of Desmond, and sister-in-law to the long-lived Countess. This would place its building at the later end of the

CASTLE SALEM

fifteenth century. There are various legends told about "the black lady" in connection with Benduff, and they may refer to the above Geraldine.

Later the castle belonged to the M'Carthys, and at the time of the Commonwealth confiscation it was in the possession of one Florence M'Carty.

The estate was granted to Major Apollo Morris, an officer in Cromwell's army, during the seventeenth century, and upon the restoration of Charles II. he retained his lands through the interest of the King's secretary, to whom he was related.

The grant was preserved in the castle until the middle of the nineteenth century, when Mr. William Morris sent it to a Cork bookseller for publication, and it was lost through the failure of the firm.

Major Morris was succeeded by William Morris, who was an intimate friend of the great William Penn.

On the right-hand side of the avenue is an old Quaker burial-ground, which was established by him, and to which "Friends'" funerals came from all parts of Cork. He was himself interred there, but against all the rules of the order a tomb was erected to his memory, which may still be seen, and after that the Quakers ceased to bring their dead to Benduff for interment.

The property passed from the possession of the Morris family into that of the Fitzgibbons.

Authorities Consulted.

D. Donovan, "Sketches in Carbery."
Smith, "County and City of Cork."
Townsend, "Statistical Survey of the County of Cork."
Book of Survey and Distribution,

CLOGHAN CASTLE

THIS fortress is situated between the Shannon and Little Brosna River, on the banks of the latter, about three miles south of Banagher, in the King's County. This part of the country was formerly joined to Galway.

Joyce gives the meaning of the name Cloghan as "stepping stones," but Cooke states that the full appellation is Cloghan-na-geaorach, or "the stony place of the sheep," Cloghan Hill being still famous for rearing these animals.

When a tennis-court was being made some years back a number of human bones and cannon shot were found, while inside the castle a hand was discovered in the wall covered by the plaster.

The castle is supposed to have been built in the reign of King John and to be one of the oldest inhabited castles in Ireland.

In 1249 we have a mention of "MacCoghlan of the castles" of which Cloghan was one, but it subsequently passed to the O'Maddens. The fortress was usually called "Cloghan O'Madden," but on Sir William Petty's map it is marked "Poghan."

It was destroyed in 1548 for fear it might fall into the hands of the English, but it must have been afterwards restored, as in 1595 Sir William Russell, Lord Deputy, laid siege to it. A quaint account of the taking of the castle is given in a journal of the time which is, no doubt, accurate in the main.

CLOGHAN CASTLE

It appears O'Madden was absent " in rebellion," but he had garrisoned the castle with his chief men.

The Lord Deputy arrived on Thursday, 11th of March, and upon his approach the garrison set alight three of their houses near the castle, and opened fire on the troops, wounding two soldiers and a boy.

When surrender was demanded they replied to Captain Lea that even if every soldier was a Deputy they would hold out.

Captain Izod was detailed to see none of them escaped by the bog. Sir William visited the watch at midnight, and hearing there were women in the castle sent the garrison word that he would begin the attack next morning with fire and sword, and told them to send the women away, but they refused.

In the morning one of the soldiers threw a fire brand on the thatched roof of the castle, which set it alight, and at the same time a bonfire was lighted at the door, which smothered many of the inmates. A breach was soon made in the walls, and those who had not been suffocated were hurled over the battlements.

Forty-six persons were killed, two women and a boy being alone saved by the Deputy's command. Most of the garrison were O'Maddens, but a Captain M'Coleghan and his two sons were also amongst the slain.

Some accounts give the number executed as 140.

The O'Madden's territory was forfeited after the rebellion of 1641, and in 1683 Cloghan was granted to Garrett Moore, who claimed to be descended from Rory Oge O'Moore, Chief of Leix.

His almanac, or diary, was found in the castle, dated 1699. It contains entries of lead got for repairing the fortress. It also records methods of making expanding bullets and noiseless powder, as well as other strange information.

After the battle of Aughrim troops from Birr took

possession of the castle, and it was garrisoned under the command of Lieutenant Archibald Armstrong.

In the middle of last century it was purchased by Dr. Graves, and is at present in the possession of his descendant, Robert Kennedy Crogan Graves, Esq.

AUTHORITIES CONSULTED.

Donovan, "Annals of the Four Masters."
Cooke, "History of Birr."
J. Wright, "King's County Directory."
Joyce, "Irish Names of Places."
Proceedings of Kilkenny Archæological Society.

OLD CROM CASTLE.

CROM CASTLE

This castle is situated in the parish of Galloon, Barony of Coole, County Fermanagh. It stands on the east bank of Lough Erne, about sixteen miles from Enniskillen.

The name Crom, or Crum, signifies "sloping" or "crooked."

The remains of the chief walls form a square of about 50 feet, which does not coincide with the measurements given in several inquisitions. Some of the stones have evidently been carried off for building purposes since the building was burnt in 1764.

The position of the castle was commanded by wooded hills, and it is built so near the shore that the waves dash against it in winter time. It seems to have had no outer ring of defences, and it is therefore even more wonderful how it should have been successfully defended in two sieges.

The marks of the cannonading are now covered by a heavy growth of ivy.

Michael Balfour, laird of Mountwhany in Fifeshire, began to erect the fortress in 1611, when granted the manor of Crum, under the plantation scheme of Ulster.

In 1616 he sold the property to Sir Stephen Butler, and in 1619 Nicholas Pynnar describes Crum as follows: "Upon this proportion there is a bawne of lime and stone, being 60 feet square, 12 feet high with two flankers. Within the bawne there is a house of lime and stone."

The Rev. George Hill states that the castle was built by Butler and Balfour at great expense, so it is likely to have been added to after it changed hands.

In 1629 another inquisition describes it as "One bawne of stone and lime, containing 61 feet every way and 15 feet in height; and within the same is one castle, or capital messuage, built in like manner of lime and stone containing 22 feet each way."

Crum was leased to Dr. James Spottiswood, Bishop of Clogher, in 1624.

It must for a short time after this have been possessed by the M'Manuses, who offered it for sale at £100 and 100 cows. Among the State Papers of 1646 is preserved Sir William Cole's petition to the Commissioners to be advanced £160, so that he might become the purchaser. He promises to return the money if unsuccessful, and says it is the only hold the rebels have in the country and "a place of good strength." The money appears to have been sent.

We find, however, in 1645, that it is mentioned in Bishop Spottiswood's will, and through his daughter marrying Colonel Abraham Creichton the leasehold passed to that family.

It was afterwards converted into a perpetuity, subject to a small head rent, which was bought out by the Earl of Erne in 1810 from Brinsley, 4th Earl of Lanesborough, a descendant of Francis Butler.

In the struggle for the Crown between James and William, Crum was twice unsuccessfully besieged.

It was a place of considerable importance, as it commanded the waterway between Enniskillen and Belturbet.

The first attempt was made in March, 1689.

Colonel Abraham Creichton, although an old man, had fortified the castle and garrisoned it with his tenants and retainers. Lord Galmoy arrived at Belturbet with a considerable force belonging to King James's army, but found the roads so boggy as to be impassable for cannon. He therefore decided to make some mock guns by which to frighten the garrison into submission.

CROM CASTLE

They were manufactured out of tin, measured about a yard long and 8 inches in the bore. They were bound together with fine cord twisted round them, and the whole covered with a kind of buckram to represent the colour of a real cannon.

To this sham artillery sixteen horses were harnessed and they were brought to Crum with a great show of difficulty and much apparent urging of the animals.

As soon as they were within ordinary range of the fortress Lord Galmoy demanded its surrender, and upon being refused he tried to fire one of his fraudulent guns with a wooden bullet, but it burst and nearly killed the gunner.

He then began a systematic siege and sent messengers to Enniskillen to demand that garrison's surrender too.

The governor of the town at once despatched two hundred firelocks to relieve the castle of Crum. Some were sent by water and some by land during the night, but daylight had arrived before they reached their destination.

The besiegers opposed their landing, but nevertheless they forced their way into the castle with the loss of only one boatman, while Lord Galmoy's party lost several.

A sally was at once made from the fortress, and the besiegers were driven from their trenches with a loss of thirty or forty men, and the garrison captured the mock guns and took two suits of armour and several other valuable things.

Lord Galmoy then retreated to Belturbet.

Colonel Creichton's son David, then a lad of eighteen, greatly distinguished himself during the conflict.

Although the castle was unprovided with cannon, great execution was done by the long fowling-pieces generally used for wild fowl on the lake.

Lord Galmoy was standing on a hill about an English mile distant from the castle, with a glass of wine in his hand, which he was about to drink to the confusion of the garrison, when a fowler from the fortress shattered the glass he was raising and killed the man beside him.

At this time a Captain MacGuire was prisoner at Crum, and Lord Galmoy proposed to Colonel Creichton to exchange Captain Dixey for him. This was agreed to, but when MacGuire was sent, Lord Galmoy, instead of returning Dixey, had him hanged with a cornet named Charleton.

Captain MacGuire was so disgusted with the treachery that he returned to Crum and threw up his commission in James's army.

Lord Galmoy also enticed Colonel Creichton to a parley, and would have put him to death, too, had not Lord Mountcashel rescued the old man and conducted him safely back to his castle.

The following year Crum was again besieged, and Colonel Creichton sent an urgent message to Enniskillen to say that the besiegers had brought cannon with them. The next day he sent another message saying that Lieutenant-General MacCarthy had begun to batter the fortress.

This was Monday, and Colonel Wolseley returned answer that they should be relieved on Wednesday, and in the meantime he despatched orders for reinforcements to Ballyshannon.

A strong detachment set out, therefore, from Enniskillen to the castle's relief, but upon their approach the enemy withdrew to Newtownbutler, where a great engagement was fought that shattered the cause of James II. in the north of Ireland. The garrison of Crum Castle greatly distinguished themselves in this engagement.

The David Creichton, who was eighteen at the time of the siege, finally succeeded his nephew in the estate. He left an only son, who was created Lord Erne, and it was in his lifetime that the castle was burnt.

CROM CASTLE

A letter from Lord Shannon, dated September 1, 1764, is still in the family's possession, in which he condoles with his kinsman for the destruction of his castle. "Unhappy indeed to be consumed by a few accidental sparks of fire when it had so bravely withstood the firing of 6,000 men so many years ago."

To the south of the fortress along the side of the lake lay the castle gardens, in the centre of which still grows a magnificent yew-tree, under which tradition records an O'Neill and his lady-love parted in the reign of Queen Elizabeth upon the former being attainted for high treason.

Henry, however, writing in 1739, says it was only planted about seventy years previously. It is 25 feet in height, while the trunk is 12 feet in girth. The circumference of the branches is 120 feet.

It was the custom for many years for sportsmen on the lake to fire a salute when passing the ruined fortress, which produced a most wonderful echo, as if the shot had been answered by a volley.

Authorities Consulted.

The Earl of Erne, "Crom Castle" in *Ulster Journal of Archæology*.
King, "Henry's Upper Lough Erne in 1739."
Latimer, "Actions of the Enniskillen Men."
Joyce, "Irish Names of Places."
State Papers.
Proceedings of Royal Society of Antiquaries.

DOE CASTLE

THIS fortress is situated at the extremity of a small Donegal bay called Sheephaven, in the Barony of Kilmacrenan, about a mile east of Creeslough. It was the chief stronghold of the MacSweenys, and derives its name from MacSweeny Doe or MacSweeny " of the districts."

The castle is built on a projecting rock, surrounded by the waters of the inlet upon the north, east, and south, while on the west its entrance was guarded by drawbridge and portcullis, as well as a fosse filled with sea-water.

A modern house is attached to the old fortress, which has a rectangular tower, and a circular donjon used as a dairy in modern times.

M'Parland, writing in 1802, in his statistical survey, records that the castle was fortified with a strong tower by the grandfather of the then MacSweeny of Dunfanaghy.

There seems to be no record of the erection of the fortress, and different authorities ascribe its building to various persons. Manus Oge says Doe was erected by Nachton O'Donnell for one of his seven sons at the same time that the castles of Burt, Inch, and Ramelton were built, while M'Parland accredits a lady named Quinn with its erection, who married a M'Swine, shortly before Elizabeth came to the throne.

Dr. Allman believes it dates from about the beginning of Henry VIII.'s reign, and tradition states that Doe passed to the MacSweenys in the fifteenth century, when a peace was concluded between O'Neill and O'Donnell in 1440.

DOE CASTLE

Red Hugh O'Donnell lived at Doe Castle with his foster father, Owen Oge MacSweeny, and it was while in his care that he was kidnapped at Rathmullen by Sir John Perrott in 1588.

Sir Hugh MacSwine na Oge, surnamed the Red, was one of Queen Elizabeth's chief favourites, and a polished courtier. Very different, however, was the last of the MacSwines who occupied Doe Castle. This was Sir Miles MacSweeny of the Club, who was knighted by Queen Elizabeth, and about whom tales of great brutality are recorded.

He was called "of the club" from his bludgeoning the better classes of his clan to death with his own hand if they offended him, while the poorer ones he consigned to a retainer called Furey and his satellites to hang from the castle walls.

A legend is told of how his beautiful daughter, Eileen, fell in love with Turlogh Oge, son of The O'Boyle, against her father's wish. The lovers used to meet on the beach and in the woods near the castle. Her father discovered their trysts and confined her to the fortress under the care of a worthy matron. The young people were thus reduced to signalling to each other—the maiden from the battlements, and her lover from his canoe in the bay. This became known to The MacSweeny, and with two boats of armed men he waylaid the young man and a few retainers on their way back from Lackagh, and brought them prisoners to the castle.

Here he starved them to death, and as the bodies were being carried to the graveyard the fair Eileen saw and recognised her lover. She never recovered the shock and grief, and not long afterwards she was found dead on the top of one of the castle towers.

Fishermen say that the spirits of the ill-fated pair haunt the bay, and by moonlight a phantom skiff may sometimes be seen skimming the waters containing the two ghostly lovers.

The castle was included in a grant of lands made by James I. to the Earl of Tyrconnell.

In 1607 it was seized by Caffer O'Donnell and Neale M'Swine with some followers. These young discontents alleged as their reason an old grievance against the Earl, who was given authority by the Lord Deputy and Council to march against them.

Accordingly Sir Richard Handson, the Earl, and Sir Neale O'Donnell arrived before the stronghold, when some of the offenders submitted, and some were taken and hanged. Sir Neale O'Donnell was badly hurt in the fray.

In the State Papers Sir Arthur Chichester advises that the troublesome youths should be given grants of lands as the best way of making them peaceful subjects. It is also recommended that the castle should be garrisoned by the King's men.

The latter was evidently done, as shortly afterwards the Earl of Tyrconnell lodged a complaint against Captain Brook and his men being quartered in the castle with privileges, after he (the Earl) had in person expelled the discontents.

The following year (1608) Doe was again lost to the English in the rebellion of Sir Cahir O'Doherty. It was in charge of a man named Vaughan and six warders, when a cowherd and a friar arriving with the tale that a body of wolves had set upon the cattle, they easily managed to draw six of them from the stronghold, who were at once killed, and the castle seized and garrisoned for the enemy.

A party was organised to retake it, and in the encounter with the rebels Sir Cahir was killed.

The castle was captured by Sir Oliver Lambert, and it was said to be "the strongest hold in all the province, which endured a hundred blows of the demi-cannon before it yielded."

DOE CASTLE

Captain Elling was then appointed constable, and £76 13s. 4d. was granted him towards repairing the damage done by the cannon in the siege.

At this time it had a garrison of fifty men.

Sir Richard Bingley was appointed constable in 1610, and at the same time received a grant of land in the county. After this there seems to have been a succession of constables until it was captured by the Irish in 1641. Owen Roe O'Neill landed here the following year from Dunkirk, and, being met by Sir Phelim O'Neill with other chiefs and one thousand five hundred men, proceeded to Ballyshannon.

In 1646 Quartermaster Harrison asked for the possession of the castle, which the enemy had deserted, and offered to garrison and maintain it with thirty warders.

Sir Charles Coot captured it in 1650, and Colonel Miles M'Sweeny tried to retake it the same year.

The Harrisons sold it to the Harte family during the eighteenth century.

General Harte was present at the battle of Seringapatam, and the capture of Tippoo Sahib, whose servant was also taken prisoner at the same time, and afterwards came to Ireland with General Harte.

He lived at Doe Castle, and was devotedly attached to his new master. He always wore his native dress, and is reported to have slept fully armed on a mat at the General's door.

He did not long survive his master, the General meeting with a sad death by falling down the stairway leading to the tower.

Cannon captured at Seringapatam were mounted on the lawn of the castle.

The Hartes subsequently let Doe to a Mr. Maddison, but it remained in the possession of the family until 1866, when it was purchased by Mr. Ards.

The history of Doe Castle is not altogether as clear on

many points as could be wished, for the authorities seem to be greatly confused over many important points.

AUTHORITIES CONSULTED.

State Papers.
Harkin, "Scenery and Antiquities of North-West Donegal."
Joyce, "Irish Names of Places."
M'Devitt, "Donegal Highlands."
Parliamentary Gazetteer.

Drimnagh Castle.

DRIMNAGH CASTLE

ABOUT three miles from Dublin, between Crumlin and Clondalkin, is situated the old fortress of Drimnagh or Druimneach, which signifies the "ridged lands," so called from the proximity of the sand ridges called the Green Hills.

The castle is an oblong building with pointed battlements at the corners. A passage with an arched entrance high enough for a loaded cart to enter is visible from the road, above which rises three storeys, with a modern window in each.

A turret stairway also projects on this side and rises above the battlements. An ancient chimney flue is to be seen crowned by a modern addition.

A small turret rises above the battlements on the north side as well, at which side a strong, modern house has been added.

The castle is covered by a modern slated roof. Some outhouses bear marks of antiquity, and a little distance from the main building is a small, square tower, which, no doubt, formed an outpost for the garrison. The fortress was surrounded by a moat at the beginning of the nineteenth century, and its position can still be traced.

In 1215 the lands of Drimnagh were granted by King John to Hugh de Bernivall, and he is supposed to have built the castle early in this reign.

The lands were confirmed to his brother in 1221, and they remained in his descendants' possession for four hundred years.

In 1435 Wolfran Barnewall had licence to entail his estates, and in 1613 the family leased the castle to Sir Adam Loftus, a nephew of the Archbishop, with the reservation that no timber was to be cut.

Some time later a Peter Barnewall succeeded to the property, and he was unwilling to renew Sir Adam's lease, whereupon that gentleman endeavoured with some members of the Barnewall family to prevent his inheriting the estate, and proceeded at the same time to cut down the great trees which surrounded the fortress. After much litigation the King at length intervened on behalf of Barnewall, and Sir Adam was restrained from doing any more damage.

In 1649, after the battle of Rathmines, the Duke of Ormond seriously contemplated fortifying Drimnagh and making it his headquarters, but he was dissuaded by General Purcell.

Colonel Nicholas Walker, a Cromwellian officer, lived in the castle after the Restoration. It was said that he was present on the scaffold at the execution of Charles I. with his face covered by a vizor. The Hearth Money Returns of 1664 state that Drimnagh was occupied by "Lt.-Col. ———," and had three "smooks" or chimneys.

In 1841 the fortress was the property of the Marquis of Lansdowne. It was one of the castles of the Pale, and the scene of Mr. R. D. Joyce's romance entitled "The Rose of Drimnagh" is laid there.

Until lately it was inhabited by Mrs. Mylott, but it is now empty.

AUTHORITIES CONSULTED.

D'Alton, "History of County Dublin."
P., "Drimnagh Castle," in *Irish Penny Journal*.
E. Ball, "Descriptive Sketch of Clondalkin, Tallaght," &c., in *Journal of Royal Society of Antiquaries*, Ireland.
Dix, "Lesser Castles in the County Dublin," in *Irish Builder*.
Joyce, "Rambles Round Dublin," in *Evening Telegraph* Reprints.

DUBLIN CASTLE

DUBLIN CASTLE

THE situation chosen by the Norsemen for the first fortress of "Duibhlinn" (A.D. 840) was naturally strong, being on a hill at the junction of the Liffey and the Poddle. After this date we read of several raids upon the dun, or castle of Dublin, including the treacherous entry into the city of Milun DeCogan and Meyler Fitz-Henri during a truce, when all the defenders of the stronghold were put to the sword. This was shortly after the landing of Strongbow. The present area covered by Government buildings includes the ancient site.

When Henry II. came to Dublin a large wooden hall, covered with wattles, was erected in Dame Street, that he might entertain the Irish chiefs who came to pay homage. Upon his return to England he committed "Dublin with its castle and donjon to Hugh de Laci, Fitz-Stephen, and Morice Fitz-Gerald." Hugh de Lacy became the first Viceroy. It was while he was in England that Meyler Fitz-Henry, who had been appointed Lord Justice in his absence, wrote to King John complaining that he had no safe place to store the King's treasure, and asking for leave to erect a proper fortress. This he received in the form of a patent dated 1204, which says:—

"But you are first to finish one tower, unless afterwards a castle and palace, and other works that may require greater leisure, may be more conveniently raised, and that we should command you so to do."

The grant consisted of 300 marks, which was owed to

the King by G. Fitz-Robert, and there are no records to show whether FitzHenry ever collected the debt, or even began the castle in the three years afterwards for which he held office. It seems to be a very general opinion that the castle was built about 1220 by Henry Loundres, Archbishop of Dublin, either at his own expense, or that he advanced the money as a loan. A State paper, however, dated 1217, grants the Archbishop two cantreds without Dublin for damage done to his churches in fortifying the castle, and later there are many entries regarding compensation to be paid in money to Henry Loundres in lieu of land which had been encroached upon when extending the fortifications.

In 1242 an entry records that the windows of St. Edward's Chapel belonging to the castle were to be glazed, and divine service held. This building seems to have been outside the fortress walls, on the site of the present Chapel Royal which was erected in 1814. In 1243 a hall was to be built 120 feet long and 80 feet wide. It was to have glazed windows, with a round one at the gable end 30 feet in diameter.

The entrance to the castle was by a drawbridge on the north side, the site now being occupied by the gate to the Upper Castle Yard. This bridge was flanked by two towers, and defended by a portcullis, and later by ordnance as well. From the gate towers, often used as State prisons, a high curtain or wall extended east and west. In the westward direction it joined what in later years was known as Cork Tower, because it was rebuilt by the great Earl of Cork in 1629, it having fallen in 1624, and been only partly restored. He spent £408 on it.

From this the wall was continued south to the Birmingham Tower, which is said to have derived its name from its having been erected either by John Birmingham, Earl of Louth, Lord Justice 1321, or Walter Birmingham, who held office in 1348. It is more likely, however, that this tower is identical with that known as the high tower, and that it received the name Birmingham after William Birmingham and his son Walter had been imprisoned there in 1331, otherwise the fortress would have been incomplete prior to 1321, and the side with least natural defence unprotected. From Birmingham Tower the curtain extended eastward (intersected by two smaller towers) to Wardrobe Tower. From this the wall was continued northward to the Store Tower near Dame's Gate, which was in its turn connected with the eastern gate tower. There were two sallyports in the wall.

Of the eight towers which once protected the fortress only the Wardrobe Tower now remains, often erroneously called Birmingham Tower. This, as its name implies, is where the royal robe, cap of maintenance, and other furniture of state were kept. The sword of state is still preserved there, and also the records which were removed from Birmingham Tower. The lower portion is the original masonry, but an upper storey was added when the Chapel Royal was built. The Birmingham Tower was rendered unsafe by an explosion of gunpowder in Ship Street and had to be taken down. A lighter structure was erected on the site, which contains the present kitchen and viceregal supper-room. The other towers were gradually removed to make room for new buildings.

The Anglo-Irish used to decorate the gate and walls of the castle with the heads of the slain, and in 1316 some four hundred heads were sent from Wicklow for this purpose.

The castle did not become a permanent residence of the Viceroy until 1560 by order of Elizabeth, and in 1565 Henry Sydney took up his abode in it. He also enlarged and beautified it, and placed the State papers there in safe keeping.

The castle has stood several successful sieges. In 1478 Gerald, 8th Earl of Kildare, was superseded as Lord Deputy by Lord Grey of Codnor. He refused to resign, and Keating, Prior of Kilmainham, and Constable of the Castle, sided with him, and fortified the stronghold against the new Deputy. He destroyed the drawbridge, and Lord Grey, finding his numbers too small to force an entrance, returned to England, and Kildare was shortly afterwards reinstated.

Again, in 1534, young Lord Offaly, known as "Silken Thomas" from the splendour of his horses' trappings, hearing a false report that his father had been treacherously executed in England, returned the Sword of State to the Council, which he held as Deputy in the Earl of Kildare's absence, and commenced hostilities against the castle.

It is said the citizens readily admitted him within the walls of Dublin. His chief attack was from Ship Street, but the Constable of the castle getting the thatched houses there set on fire, the besiegers fell back into Thomas Street.

Lord Offaly having been obliged to commence hostilities against Ossary, the siege was not carried on with much heart. Many of the arrows sent into the castle were headless, and others bore letters saying some of the besiegers were really in sympathy with the King's party.

Upon the rumour of help from England, the citizens closed the gates and made prisoners of the attackers.

Lord Thomas hurried back, and at once laid siege to the city itself, but his force was too small to have any effect.

As he had seized the Dublin children who had been sent to outlying villages on account of the plague, the citizens agreed to liberate his party if the little ones were restored. This was done, and shortly afterwards aid from England quelled the rebellion.

Several exciting escapes have been made by prisoners from the castle. In 1587 Hugh O'Donnell was confined in one of the gate towers for three years, when he and a companion managed to escape on to the drawbridge by a rope. He was, however, treacherously sent back to Dublin by O'Toole of Castlekevin, upon whose hospitality he had thrown himself. At this time a partly dry and partly wet moat surrounded Dublin Castle, and O'Donnell was now imprisoned in the Wardrobe Tower round which the Poddle flowed. He, however, escaped again the next year through the water, and, arriving after much hardship at Glenmalure, eventually reached the North in safety.

In 1697 Lord Delvin was imprisoned in one of the gate towers for taking part in a conspiracy against the King. The Lord Deputy hearing that he meditated escape, desired Tristram Ecclesten, Constable of the Castle, to remove his prisoner from the upper to a lower storey. Not only did Ecclesten neglect to do this, but he allowed Lord Delvin to have visitors, who managed to convey him a rope, by which he escaped. Next year he surrendered himself and was pardoned.

Law Courts and Parliaments have at different times been held in the castle.

In 1689 King James made a State entry, and stayed one night there after the battle of the Boyne.

In 1783 St. Patrick's Hall was built. In 1784 the Viceregal Lodge was bought, and since then the State apartments of the castle have only been used during the Dublin season.

Authorities Consulted.

O'Donovan, "Annals of the Four Masters."
Calendar of Irish State Papers in England.
Wright, "Historical Guide to Dublin.
Harris, "History of Dublin."
Marquis of Kildare, "Earls of Kildare."
Brewer, "Beauties of Ireland."
M'Gee, "History of Ireland."
Joyce, "History of Ireland."
Gilbert, "Castle of Dublin" (*University Magazine*).
Haverty, "Ireland."
Collins, "Sydney State Letters,"

DUNDANIEL CASTLE

THIS castle is situated on the western margin of the Barony of Kinnelea, in the townland of Skevanish, County Cork. It stands on the left bank of the Bandon River, in the angle formed by the influx of the Brinny. It is half a mile above Innishannon, and three miles below Bandon.

The present name seems, from ancient documents, to be a corruption of Dundanier, or a word of the same phonetic sound. Different suggestions have been put forward as to the probable meaning of the original name, including "Dane's Fort," or "the fort of the foreigner," and "the fort of the two rivers." This latter would be a very appropriate appellation, its south and west sides being protected by the converging streams.

Nothing now remains of the castle save the keep, which measures 32 feet east and west, and 44 feet north and south.

The entrance is in a ruined state on the east side, and between it and the river on the south the masonry has almost wholly disappeared. The walls on the north and west are 6 feet thick, while on the south and east they measure 8 feet, although these sides have otherwise apparently less provision for defence.

Mr. Herbert Gillman gives a most interesting suggestion regarding this fact. He says that in all probability a winding stair was situated in the thickness of the walls at the south-east angle, the building of which has now disappeared, and that this stairway terminated at the hall or chief apartment of the castle usually occupied by the castellan. Upon the north-east angle of the tower is now the remains of a ruined turret, and Mr. Gillman thinks this is most likely to have been the protection for the egress to the *allur* or battlemented walk, which was reached from the main chamber by a second stairway in this part of the wall. By such an arrangement no watchman could leave his post of duty without passing through the room in question, and thus a greater protection would be secured.

We learn from the Lismore papers that the top of the fortress was reached by a very narrow "pair of stairs."

The tower is about 55 or 60 feet high. The stone arch which is usual in such buildings covering the internal space, is in this instance situated singularly high up, being immediately beneath the top storey, and there is no mark on the lower walls to show that a second ever existed. The ground floor was used for defence as well as for the usual store, and above it beams, on stone corbels, supported two oak floors between the basement and the arch. Light and air were chiefly admitted by long openings splayed for archery. It is interesting to note also the later apertures introduced after musketry superseded the bow and arrow.

Of the former outworks of the fortress little trace remains. On the east of the tower, at about a hundred yards distant, is what an old inhabitant stated to be a disused channel of the River Manghane or Brinny. This fact is borne out, and contradicted, respectively by several maps. The fact that the field lying west of the river is still called "Castle Garden" seems to point out that the channel of the Brinny has been changed. Also the north and west walls of the fortress have the greater number of crenellated openings, which show that they were considered the most vulnerable sides.

The Down Survey map of 1656 shows a dwelling-house to the east of the castle.

In the mortar on the inside surface of the arch, the marks of the twigs are still visible which formed part of the temporary support used when building. The mortar has much less lime than is usual in such work, no doubt from the distance it would have had to be brought.

These markings, as well as the general architecture, indicate that the date 1476, which is usually stated as the time of its erection, is likely to be accurate.

It is supposed to have been built by Barry Oge, or Barry the Younger, whose family displaced the O'Mahons in this district, being a descendant of Philip de Barry, the Anglo-Norman invader.

The lands of Innishannon were granted to the Barry Oge family either in Henry III.'s or Henry IV.'s reign.

In 1449 Barry Oge forfeited the confidence of the Crown, and his lands were seized for the King. But a letter of the time states that he was there "upon the King's portion, paying his Grace never a penny of rent." At this time wars at home and abroad had weakened the English power in Ireland, and it is most likely that Barry Oge built Dundaniel Castle to protect the lands he was holding in spite of the forfeiture.

In 1548 mention is made of a pirate called Colle coming to Kinsale in a pinnace and marrying Barry Oge's aunt, living in his castle, and not allowing any one to enter Kinsale. Probably this castle was Dundaniel, where the honeymoon was being spent, but the Barry Oge himself does not seem to have shared the odium in which his uncle-in-law was held.

Pirates were a very grave trouble to the south coast for many years following.

After the Desmond rebellion Barry Oge's land was again forfeited in 1588, and bestowed upon MacCarthy

DUNDANIEL CASTLE

Reagh, and in 1599 "Downdandier" is referred to as eing in his possession.

After the siege of Dunboy Castle, in 1602, Sir George Carew relates having sent some companies of foot soldiers to Macarthy's Castle of Dundaniel, to remain there until the army was leaving Munster.

Eight years later the estate was purchased by the East India Company for the sum of £7,000. They constructed a dock, where they built two ships, and colonised three villages with some three hundred English settlers.

They garrisoned the castle with "four light horse, six corslets, and ten muskets, trained at the Company's charge."

But this form of industrious innovation was not at all to the liking of the native inhabitants, and they so harassed the company's workers that they were obliged to appeal to the Government for protection in 1613. This does not appear to have been accorded, as a second petition in the same year asks for leave to place three or four pieces of ordnance in the castle for defence against the "wylde Irish."

The Company, still receiving no Government aid, relinquished their enterprise. In the "Castle Garden" slag, like the refuse of ironworks is still found, which is most likely the remains of the East India Company's industry.

After this the MacCarthys seem to have again taken possession of the castle, and a scion of the old house, named Teige O'Connor, occupied Dundaniel upon the breaking out of hostilities in 1642.

This O'Connor seems to have been a man of unqualified barbarity. A MS. in Trinity College records a most unwarrantable attack by him on five peaceful fishermen who were whipping the rivers near the stronghold. By his orders they were seized by some of the garrison and carried within the castle. Four of them were hanged at once, and the fifth offered £10 for his life. This was accepted, and some of them accompanied him to his house to receive it. Upon finding where he kept his money, they seized the whole of it, amounting to £35, and then hanged the unfortunate owner.

John Langton, writing to the Earl of Cork, gives a most graphic description of the assault upon Dundaniel Castle on the 20th of April, 1642, when the English forces marched from Bandon under the command of Lord Kinalmeaky and Captain Aderly of Innishannon.

It appears a party of rebels had seized some cattle and brutally killed four children and wounded a fifth, who were minding them near the town. The distracted parents traced the crime to the garrison of Dundaniel Castle, "neere the ould iron worke." So horse and foot marched out, recovered the cattle save one animal, and attacked the castle.

Three of the besiegers were killed and six wounded by shot and stone from the fortress, but the musketeers posted themselves round the castle and on the neighbouring hill, and kept up a fire of small shot so that each of the defenders who looked out was killed.

They next tried to drive in the door with sledges, and these failing they set it on fire, but they had to undermine the wall in the neighbourhood before the fire became sufficient to make the door yield.

They rushed into the lower room, and the enemy fled to the top of the castle above the vault.

The attacking party then loaded themselves with corn and oatmeal which was stored in the lower chambers, and having provided themselves with plunder they set fire to the wooden floors of the lower rooms. Night came on, and they returned to Bandon with their booty.

Next morning they came back to view the scene, and found that the rebels (who had escaped the fire which did not penetrate the vault), had let themselves down from the battlements in the night time by means of ropes

DUNDANIEL CASTLE

and other contrivances. Many lay dead on the top of the castle, and round about it.

The victors found four or five muskets and fowling pieces, some brass and iron pots and pans, and some money hidden in the oatmeal bins.

About forty of the enemy escaped and joined the Roches. They were pursued, and an encounter took place where over a hundred were killed, but the chiefs escaped.

After this the MacCarthy property was confiscated, and Dundaniel Castle was granted to Richard Earl of Cork, by whom it was leased to various tenants, and through whom it descended to the present Duke of Devonshire.

AUTHORITIES CONSULTED.

H. Gillman, "The Castle of Dundanier, miscalled Dundaniel" (*Cork Archæological Society's Journal*).
Parliamentary Gazetteer.
Calendar of State Papers.
G. Bennett, "History of Bandon."
Grosart, "Lismore Papers."

DUNDRUM CASTLE, COUNTY DOWN

SITUATED three and a half miles north by east of Newcastle, County Down, this donjon fortress commands an extensive view of Dundrum Bay and the surrounding district of Lecale. The castle was built on the site of an older fortification known as *Dun Rudhraidhe*, or Rury's Fort, which is said to have been the scene of the great feast given by Bricrin of the Poisoned Tongue, to King Connor MacNessa and the Red Branch Knights at which he induced them to make war on one another, as is chronicled in " The Book of the Dun Cow." The present village of Dundrum (Dundroma, signifying the fort on the ridge) lies between the castle and the shore, while to the east of the fortress are the ruins of an Elizabethan mansion erected by a former owner of the castle.

The circular keep or donjon is built upon a rock, and has an external diameter of some 45 feet, the walls of which are 8 feet thick above the projecting base. The tower at present stands about 50 feet in height. The cellar below is hewn out of the rock on which the building was erected, and is said at one time to have contained 200 tuns of Spanish wine belonging to O'Neill.

To the east of the entrance is a circular newel stair 3 feet 3 inches in diameter, constructed in the thickness of the wall and leading to the parapet. From this there are openings at each storey, and it is most likely from the position of the offsets in the wall that the floors were of

DUNDRUM CASTLE, COUNTY DOWN 149

wood supported on beams, the holes for the latter being still visible at different levels.

Round this tower was the courtyard or bawn, encircled by a high wall 4 and 5 feet thick, which was again protected by a fosse or moat, still to be seen on the north and west sides. The bawn was occupied by the buildings for the retainers, and perhaps the family in times of peace, and is of a roughly circular form about 150 feet across.

South-east of the donjon, in the line of wall, are the two

DUNDRUM CASTLE, CO. DOWN.

ruined towers which protected the barbican gate, the corbel blocks of which still remain over the archway, and originally supported the defences of the gateway. From these, numerous rebels were hanged in the rebellion of 1798.

The castle was built of stone quarried to form the fosse, mixed with land stones of the district. Little has been done to alter the twelfth or thirteenth century architecture, except the opening out of windows. On the side of the ruined manor the outer fortifications would seem to have been levelled to make terraced gardens to the later dwelling.

It is generally supposed that Dundrum Castle was built by John de Courcy at the end of the twelfth century for the Knights Templars, after his daring conquest of Ulster in 1177 with only a force of about a thousand men. The stronghold remained in the possession of the order (which was bound by vows of chastity, poverty, and obedience) until the suppression of the Knights Templars in 1313. It then passed into the hands of the Prior of Down, and is mentioned by Archdall in his "Monasticon Hibernicum" as a religious house. Upon the abolition of the monasteries the reversion of the castle and manor, with a yearly rent of £6 13s. 4d. reserved out of it, was granted to Gerald, Earl of Kildare.

In 1516, however, it appears to have been in the possession of O'Neill, who fortified it, with a boast he would hold it against the Earl of Kildare, at the same time sending to the King of France to come and help him to drive the English out.

The following year Gerald, 9th Earl of Kildare, and Lord Deputy, marched into Lecale and took Dundrum by storm, but it seems almost immediately to have reverted to the Magennises, who repaired it. In 1538 it was retaken along with seven other castles by the English, commanded by Lord Deputy Grey, who says: "I took another castell, being in M'Geeon's countrie called Dundrome, which, I assure your lordship, as it standeth is one of the strongest holds that ever I saw in Ireland, and most commodious for defence of the whole countrey of Lecayll, both by sea and land, for the said Lecayll is invironed round about with sea, and no way to go by land into the said countrey but only bye the said Castle of Dundrome."

After this the castle appears to have remained in the hands of the Crown for a few years. In 1551, we learn from the records of the Privy Council that Prior Magennis

DUNDRUM CASTLE, COUNTY DOWN

was seized and imprisoned in Dundrum Castle by Roger Broke without order of law. Six years later Lord Deputy Sussex asked that Lecale with the Castle of Dundrum might be granted to him in fee-farm for ever.

But again in 1565 it was occupied by the great Shane O'Neill, who placed his own ward in it for defence, and the Magennises (with whom O'Neill was intimately connected) were in possession of the stronghold in 1601, when Phelim Magennis surrendered it to Lord Mountjoy.

O'Neill is said to have been a constant visitor at the castle while it was possessed by the Magennises, Lords of Iveagh, and after a night of revelry would indulge in a strange kind of bath, by being buried to his neck in the sands on the shore of the bay.

Four years subsequently to the stronghold passing into the hands of the Crown, Lord Cromwell was commissioned to be governor and commander of Lecale and the tower and castle of Dundrum.

In 1636, Lord Cromwell's grandson, Thomas, Lord Lecale and 1st Earl of Ardglass, sold it to Sir Francis Blundell, from whom it descended by marriage to its present owner, the Marquis of Downshire.

Sir James Montgomery fought the Irish on the shore at the foot of the castle hill 1642, and placed a garrison in the fortress to protect the district. At this time Dundrum belonged to the Blundells, who afterwards built the now ruined mansion adjoining, and the ancient stronghold was finally dismantled in 1652 by the order of Oliver Cromwell.

AUTHORITIES CONSULTED.

Phillips, " Dundrum Castle."
Praeger, " Guide to County Down."
Joyce, " Irish Names of Places."
Grose, " Antiquities of Ireland."
Harris, " History of County Down."
Calendar of State Papers.
" Notes to Sir Henry Sidney's Memoir," and " Facsimiles of Signatures of Irish Chieftains" in *Ulster Journal of Archæology*.

DUNDRUM CASTLE, COUNTY DUBLIN

This fortress was one of the long chain of the Pale castles which defended the metropolis, but having been inhabited until the beginning of the nineteenth century it is in a much better state of preservation than most of these old buildings.

It is situated about three miles south of Dublin on a rise of ground above the Dundrum River, a tributary of the Dodder, at the junction of the Ballinteer and Enniskerry roads.

It is probable that the castle was built on the site of a more ancient stronghold, as Dundrum signifies "the fort on the ridge."

The principal ruin of the present castle is a keep which is battlemented in a slightly projecting form on the south-east, while the south-west wall rises in rather a high gable. The building is oblong in shape, and the entrance, which is on the south side, is evidently of more modern construction. A gate now gives egress to the interior, which is occupied by a flower bed.

Two large windows on the ground floor also point to later alterations, especially as they occur simultaneously with the remains of earlier openings.

The stairs are likely to have been situated in the south-west side. There are numerous small chambers and passages in the thickness of the walls.

Of the three fireplaces in the north-west wall that on the ground floor is the largest, measuring 9 feet long by 5 feet

DUNDRUM CASTLE, COUNTY DUBLIN

high, and as the flagstones of the hearth are covered by some inches of gravel its height was once greater. At the back of the fireplace and slightly to one side is an aperture about two feet square, which is framed in cut stone, and was probably used as an oven.

On the south-west end of the keep are the ruins of a smaller building several storeys high, which is connected with the main building by a square topped doorway. The dividing wall is nearly 6 feet in thickness.

Both buildings are largely covered with plaster, and on the south-east the keep has been partly rough cast.

The situation of a third building can be seen adjoining the tower on the north-east side, where the pitch of its roof may be traced about three-fourths of the way up, but very little of the walls remain.

The castle is partly covered with ivy.

The fortress seems to have been built soon after the Norman invasion, and as the lands of Dundrum were held by Hugh de Clahull, it was probably erected for their defence. It subsequently passed to the Fitzwilliams of Merrion, from whom it descended to the Earls of Pembroke, and it forms at present part of the Pembroke estate.

Robert le Bagod, ancestor of the Fitzwilliams, had license to convey the manor of Dundrum to his son William, and in 1332 Thomas Fitzwilliam was found seized of the lands round.

From this time on it is likely the fortress was occupied by cadets of the Fitzwilliam family.

In 1542 Sir Thomas Fitzwilliam was in possession of the manor, and in 1616 his grandson Thomas, afterwards first Viscount Fitzwilliam, recovered the lands of Dundrum and Ballinteer, with the castle and water mill.

His brother William, who had married Archbishop Ussher's widow, lived at Dundrum Castle about this time.

The building was slated and in good repair during the Commonwealth. It is stated to have had three hearths and a barn, with a garden.

It was tenanted by a Mr. Isaac Dobson during the reign of Charles II. He was a Nonconformist, and probably a trader in Dublin. When James II. came to the throne he left the country, and was attainted by Parliament in 1689.

His son, who was a bookseller, succeeded him at the castle. He greatly improved the grounds, and when he died in 1720 he left the use of the castle to his wife for her life, after which it went to his sons.

The last Dobson who lived in it died in 1762, and when Mr. Cooper visited it in 1780 it was most likely inhabited by a farmer, who was then cutting down the grove of ash which grew between it and the river.

He speaks of the inhabited part as a modern addition to which older remains were adjoining. He states that the principal entrance was from the courtyard by stone steps.

It soon afterwards fell into ruin, and at the beginning of the nineteenth century the present modern dwelling-house was erected. This was at first inhabited by the Walsh family, and later Dr. Reichel, Bishop of Meath, lived in it. Miss Hume is the present occupier.

AUTHORITIES CONSULTED.

E. Dix, "Dundrum Castle," in "The Lesser Castles in the County Dublin"; F. Ball, "Dundrum Castle," both *Irish Builder*.
Ball and Hamilton, "The Parish of Taney."

DUNLUCE CASTLE

DUNLUCE CASTLE

THE ruins of this stronghold are picturesquely situated upon a rocky promontory about three miles east of Portrush, in the County Antrim, which is divided from the mainland by a chasm 20 feet wide and 100 feet deep.

The name Dunluce, or *lis*, signifies "strong fort," and in all probability the castle is built on the site of an ancient *lis*.

The walls of the fortress are constructed of local basalt, and as the columnar structure has been taken advantage of in the dressings of windows and doors, it makes it a difficult matter to compare the date of its erection with other castles by the style of architecture.

It seems likely that the fortress was built in the sixteenth century by the M'Quillans (formerly M'Willies), who derived their title from De Burgo, one of De Courcy's followers. Experts think that no part of the building is of fifteenth-century workmanship.

The castle was originally confined to the isolated rock, which was connected with the mainland by a drawbridge. Now this part is reached by a footway about 18 inches wide and 20 feet long, supported by an arch.

The strongest walls are on the south and east sides. The drawbridge formerly led into a small enclosed courtyard, at the lower end of which stands the barbican, containing the main entrance, and with an embrasure at one side commanding the bridge. This has corbelled bartizans at the angles of the south gable, which are a Scotch type of architecture.

A strong wall, following the cliff, connects the barbican with a circular tower at the south-east angle called M'Quillan's Tower. The walls of this building are 8 feet thick, and a small staircase in them leads to the top of both tower and wall.

Formerly another curtain extended from M'Quillan's Tower along the edge of the rock northward to Queen Maud's Tower, which is also circular but of smaller dimensions.

On the west and north the castle walls are not so thick as elsewhere, and here the principal domestic offices are situated.

On the north side, over the mouth of the cave which penetrates below, are the remains of the kitchen, where a terrible accident happened during a storm. The date is placed at 1639. The young Duchess of Buckingham, who had married the 2nd Earl of Antrim, was giving a great entertainment, when suddenly the kitchen gave way, and eight servants, including the cook, sank into the waters of the cave below, and were drowned. It is said a tinker, who was sitting in a window mending pots and pans, was the only survivor of those present, and "the tinker's window" is still pointed out.

The state rooms of the castle are situated behind the towers at the eastern side. The great hall measures 70 feet by 23 feet, and has a large fireplace and three bay windows, which were probably later improvements made by Sorley Boy M'Donnell for his son Sir James, when he took up his abode at Dunluce.

The castle yard is situated between the hall and the parapet wall, and measures 120 feet by 25 feet.

A small vaulted room at the east side of the castle called the Banshee Tower, is pointed out as a haunted chamber.

The oak roof of the chapel, which had been restored in the Duchess of Buckingham's time (1637–40), was afterwards used to cover a barn in the district.

DUNLUCE CASTLE

The buildings on the mainland are of much later date than those on the rock. It is probable that they are later than 1640, though whether they were built, as tradition states, because the domestics refused to inhabit the older castle after the subsidence of the kitchen, or whether the increase of the family's importance required more accommodation, it is hard to say.

In 1513 a dispute arose between the descendants of Garrett MacQuillin and those of Walter MacQuillin for Dunluce, then in the former's hands. O'Donnell seems to have placed the Walter MacQuillins in possession.

Sir Thomas Cusake mentions the castle in his account of the expedition against the MacDonnels in 1551, and four years later a fierce dispute arose between the MacQuillins and MacDonnels for the chieftainship of the Route district.

These MacDonnels were of Scotch descent, and in 1565 the famous Shane O'Neill set out to expel the Scots from Antrim.

A great fight ensued, in which James and Sorley Boy (yellow or swarthy Charles) MacDonnel were taken prisoners.

Dunluce held out for three days longer, but Shane kept Sorley Boy without food until the garrison should surrender, which they accordingly did for his sake as well as their own.

O'Neill then put his men in the castle, and is reported to have "kylled and banyshed all the Skottes out of the north."

James MacDonnel died in Tyrone Castle in 1567—probably from poison. Two years later his death was avenged by one of the clan, who assassinated Shane, and after this Sorley Boy was set at liberty.

At this time an English garrison was in possession of Dunluce, and Sorley Boy crossed to Scotland, and returned with eight hundred picked Redshanks to demand his castles and lands returned by a grant from the Crown.

This request not being at once acceded to, he commenced hostilities, and in a year had re-possessed himself of all his strongholds and lands, except Dunluce. He then renounced all allegiance to the Queen, raised some more Scotch troops, and took the surrounding country without opposition.

In 1573 he made a partial submission to the Crown, and asked to have the part of the Glynns, which he claimed through the Bysetts, confirmed to him by letters patent, but when the title deeds arrived he cut them up and threw them in the fire, saying—

"By my sword I got these lands, and by the sword I will hold them."

The next year Mr. Francis Killaway was granted Dunluce under Essex's scheme of plantation, but in those days possession was more than "nine points of the law," and when the Lord Deputy, Sir John Perrott, set out with a great army against the Scots of Ulster, in 1584, Sorley Boy's warder occupied Dunluce.

In the official despatches it is styled the "impregnable" fortress.

The MacDonnels were unprepared for the attack. Cannon was landed at the Skerries and drawn up by men, but when the castle was summoned to surrender, the Scotch captain replied he would hold the fortress to the last man for the King of Scotland.

The siege lasted nine months; the ward of forty men, mostly Scotch, surrendering in September, 1585.

St. Columkill's Cross was found amongst the treasure by Perrott, who forwarded it, with a jeering letter, to Burghly. It has since been lost sight of.

The Lord Deputy appointed a pensioner called Peter Carey as constable, and a ward of English soldiers.

Perrott reports that Carey dismissed them, and re-filled

DUNLUCE CASTLE

their places with Northerns, some of whom were in league with MacDonnel, and that one night fifty men were drawn up the rock by ropes made of wythies. He also says they offered Carey his life, but he refused, and retired to a tower with a few men, where he was eventually slain.

This seems a rather unlikely story, and another account states a good many of the garrison were slain, and that Carey being hanged over one of the walls of the stronghold, the English soldiers fled. Carey's widow was granted a pension.

Having recovered his castle, Sorley Boy made overtures of peace to the Government, which were eagerly accepted, and he travelled to Dublin and prostrated himself before Elizabeth's portrait. The Indenture, dated 1586, amongst other things, states he was appointed Constable or Keyholder of Dunluce Castle.

His son, Sir James MacDonnel, occupied the stronghold in 1597, and the Governor of Carrickfergus lodged numerous complaints against him, amongst which were his refusal to give up the ordnance he had taken from Don Alonzo's ship of the Spanish Armada, and his having fortified himself in Dunluce.

The following year Tyrone's two sons and their tutor were lodged in the castle, and Sir Geffrey Fenton had suspicions that they were placed there as hostages to the Scotch King.

Shortly afterwards open hostilities began between MacDonnel and the Government until Sir James died suddenly at Dunluce in 1601.

The castle was granted to his son, Randel, by letters patent in 1614, to be surrendered if required for a garrison, and he was created Earl of Antrim in 1620.

His son, who succeeded in 1636, married the widowed Duchess of Buckingham. The castle was summoned by the Irish in 1641, and they also burned the town.

The Earl did not join the Rebellion, though many of his

relations were in arms. In 1642 Munro came to Dunluce on pretence that some of the Earl's tenantry were implicated. After having been well entertained, he treacherously seized Lord Antrim and sent him prisoner to Carrickfergus, at the same time plundering Dunluce.

The Earl escaped to England, and his lands, which had been confiscated during Cromwell's time, were restored to him in 1663; but in the meantime Dunluce had fallen to decay, and does not seem to have been inhabited since.

The Antrim family at present reside at Glenarm Castle.

AUTHORITIES CONSULTED.

G. Hill, "Macdonnells of Antrim."
Calendar of State Papers.
Parliamentary Gazetteer.
Proceedings of Archæological Association of Ireland, Papers by R. Young and J. O'Laverty.
Joyce, "Irish Place Names."
"The Description and Present State of Ulster," in *Ulster Journal of Archæology*.

DUNSOGHLY CASTLE

DUNSOGHLY CASTLE

This castle is situated eight miles north-by-west of Dublin, near the village of St. Margaret's, off the Ashbourne road.

It consists of a splendidly preserved keep about 80 feet high, flanked by four square towers which rise above the roof at each corner. One of these contains a winding stair leading to the battlements, at the top of which a flight of ten steps gives egress to the summit of the watch tower.

The other three towers have little rooms opening off the different storeys.

The ground floor, which was most likely a kitchen, is a large vaulted apartment into which a door has been quarried in later years.

The first floor was once a fine wainscotted room, the walls of which were yet hung with family pictures when D'Alton visited it in 1838.

A flight of wooden stairs connects this apartment with the ground.

The two upper storeys had wooden floors, and the building is still covered by a good slated roof, which is evidently a modern addition. So too are the large square windows, some of which are glazed and others protected by wire netting. The doorways are Gothic.

In the south-west tower is the prison with no entrance except through a hole in the roof by which captives and their food were let down.

Tradition states an underground passage connects the castle with St. Margaret's Church, as well as having many hidden vaults.

Beside the keep is the ruined chapel with an arched doorway, which has been used as a cowshed. At the side towards the castle is a low built-up archway over which is a slab carved with the symbols of the crucifixion, and having under it the inscription:—"J.P.M.D.S., 1573," which is supposed to mean Johannes Plunket Miles de Dun-Soghly, 1573.

There seems to be no record of the building of the castle.

In 1288–89 it is noted that the rent paid for Dunsoghly by Geoffrey Brun was 74s. and fivepence. Nearly two hundred years later (1422) the King granted to Henry Stanyhurst the custody of all the messuages which had belonged to John Finglas to hold rent free during the minority of the heir. Two years later Roger Finglas is forgiven his arrears of Crown rent out of the lands and tenants of Dunsoghly and Oughtermay.

Soon after this the land seems to have passed to Sir Roland Plunkett, the younger son of Sir Christopher Plunkett, Baron of Killem, and Lord Deputy of Ireland, 1432, this family being a branch of the Fingall family.

In 1446 Sir Rowland Plunkett, of Dunsoghly Castle, was appointed Chief Justice of the King's Bench, and later his son, Sir Thomas Plunkett, became Chief Justice of Common Pleas.

The Crown leased, in 1547, to John Plunkett, of Dunsoghly, gent., all the tithes in Dunsoghly and Oughtermay, in the Parish of St. Margaret of Dowanor, part of the possessions of the Chancellor of the late Cathedral of St. Patrick, at a rent of five marks. He was also to provide a chaplain for the church of Dowanor.

This John Plunkett was grandson to Sir Thomas, and also received knighthood. He was made Chief Justice of

DUNSOGHLY CASTLE

the Queen's Bench in 1559. He died twenty-three years later, seized of the manors of Dunsoghly and Oughtermay.

Sir John built the private chapel belonging to the castle, and also the chantry of St. Margaret's.

In 1590 Christopher Plunkett, of Dunsoghly, is included in the list of the English Pale ; and twenty years later he surrendered Dunsoghly to the King, who re-granted it to him with additional lands on account of his own and his family's service to the Crown.

Colonel Richard Plunkett, of Dunsoghly, was an active supporter of the Lords of the Pale in 1641, and a reward of £400 was offered for his head by the Lords Justices and Council.

In 1657 the Down Survey says that the "chiefest places in the Barony of Coolock are Malahide and Dunsoghly." "There is in Dunsoghly a good castle, and a house adjoining it (James Plunkett)."

The House of Commons granted Sir Henry Tichbourne £2,000 in lieu of his wardship of Nicholas Plunkett, of Dunsoghly, in 1666. This Nicholas was succeeded by his son, at whose death the property was divided between his three daughters, and the castle is still in possession of their descendants.

The fortress is said to have been bombarded in Cromwell's time from a mound near, which is now occupied by a dwelling-house, and a long crack made in the south wall by the cannon is still visible.

The castle was inhabited up to the middle of the eighteenth century.

AUTHORITIES CONSULTED.

J. D'Alton, "History of County Dublin."
Proceedings of Royal Archæological Association of Ireland.
W. Wakeman, "Rambles near Dublin," in Dublin *Evening Telegraph* Reprints.
Carew MSS.
State Documents.

ENNISCORTHY CASTLE

SITUATED on the Slaney, about twelve miles north-by-west of Wexford, in the Barony of Ballaghkeen, is the town of Enniscorthy. The origin of the name does not seem to admit of a satisfactory explanation. Some writers say that it was originally Corthœ, and the capital of Ptolemy's Coriandi. Hence the prophesy, " Enniscorthy was, Dublin is, and Drogheda will be." Again Enis-scorteach, signifying "the stud-house pastorage," has been mentioned as a possible explanation.

The castle is a massive square structure, flanked by three round towers. It is in good preservation. Two of the towers can still be ascended.

It is built of hard blue slate, dug on the spot, and the cases of the doors and windows are of grey grit stone.

It is believed that the manor of Enniscorthy was granted by Strongbow to Maurice de Prendergast, and that he commenced to erect the castle in 1199, it being finished by his son Philip in 1205 or 1206.

Again, it is stated to have passed to the De Prendergasts through the De Quincey family, and that it was originally erected by Raymond le Gros.

Between 1225 and 1228 it was walled in and entrenched by Gerald Prendergast, who died in 1251.

The Rochfords held it from 1252 to 1327 through Maurice Rochford marrying Matilda Prendergast.

The land had formerly been part of the MacMurroughs'

ENNISCORTHY CASTLE

territory, and they regained it in 1328, although their claim was fiercely disputed by the Rochfords.

Donogh MacMorrough, King of Leinster, resided in the castle from 1368 to 1375, in which year he was slain near Carlow by Geoffrey Wall. Two years later Art Mac-Murrough, King of Leinster, recovered the castle, and held it until his death in 1418.

Donald Kavanagh, King of Leinster, lived in state in the castle from 1428 to 1476, and he it was who founded the Franciscan monastery close to the stronghold in 1460.

Murrough, King of Leinster, died in the castle in 1518.

In 1550 it passed to the Crown after Cahir MacArt Kavanagh relinquished the title " MacMurrough."

Richard Kettyng complained in 1551 that the Council would not confirm the King's letters, which granted him the castles of Ferns and Enniscorthy. He requested that they might be granted by patent.

The following year Enniscorthy was leased to Gabriel Blake.

In 1566 a ruined castle and the manor of " Innescortye " was leased to Nicholas Hearon, Esq., for twenty-one years, and the following year it was surrendered by his assignee, Thomas Stucley, Esq., who then received a lease of it.

It was sacked by Sir Edmund Butler in 1569, and remained uninhabited for thirteen years, though it was leased to Richard Synnot for twenty-one years in 1575, and in 1581 the great poet Edmund Spenser received it upon like condition.

" Lease (under commission, 15 July, XXII.) to Edmund Spenser, gent., of the site of the house of friars of Enes-cortie, with apputences ; the manor of Enescortie, a ruinous castle, land, and a weir there, lands of Garrane, Killkenane, Loughwertie, Barrickcrowe, and Ballineparke, and the customs of boards, timber, laths, boats bearing victuals, lodgings during the fair, and things sold there, and fishings belonging to the manor, and all other appurtenances as well within the Morroes country as without. To hold for 21 years. Rent, £13-6-4. Maintaining one English horseman. Fine, 20s."

It is stated that fear of the Kavanaghs prevented his coming into residence, for the year afterwards his lease was transferred to Sir Richard Sinnot, of Ballybrennan, and ratified by the Crown for a term of forty years.

In 1595 Queen Elizabeth granted the estate to Sir Henry Wallop, Treasurer of War, by letters patent.

He restored the castle, but his son preferred to reside in the more modern dwelling of the Franciscan monks, which was close to the fortress. He died here in 1624, and was succeeded by his son Robert.

Sir Henry's grandson was one of the judges at the trial of Charles I., and after the Restoration he was imprisoned in the Tower of London, where he died in 1667. His great grandson was created Earl of Portsmouth in 1743.

The castle was in the hands of the Confederates in 1642.

In 1649 (whilst in the possession of Mr. Robert Wallop) the army of the Commonwealth laid siege to the stronghold. It was well manned and provisioned.

Close to its walls was the "fair house," formerly the largest Franciscan monastery in Ireland, and then the residence of the Wallop family, who deserted it upon the approach of the army.

When the castle was summoned the garrison refused to surrender, but they shortly afterwards reconsidered their decision and left their great guns, arms, ammunition, and provisions in the hands of the victors.

Shortly afterwards the castle was, however, re-taken by a trick. Some Royalist supporters feasted the men of the garrison and sent women to them to sell whiskey. When they were helplessly drunk the Irish overpowered them and took possession of the castle.

The Governor, Captain Todd, and his wife, as well as

ENNISCORTHY CASTLE

the officers under him, were all put to death. Only four of the soldiers were spared, they having betrayed the fortress for the sum of £7.

As soon as Colonel Cooke, the Governor of Wexford, heard of the outrage he marched to Enniscorthy and took the castle by storm, killing every one of the Irish garrison.

The first Earl of Portsmouth repaired the building and leased it to Adam Colclough in 1745.

During the rebellion of 1798 it was used as a prison by the insurgents during the period that Enniscorthy remained in their hands.

They greatly defaced the place, but the Earl of Portsmouth restored it between 1806 and 1812, altering it to the requirements of a modern residence for his agent. After this period it had many tenants.

From 1852 to 1863 it was used as an estate office, and a printing press was also erected within the walls. It was from here that the *Enniscorthy News* was first issued.

It fell into a state of dilapidation about 1863, though in 1867 it was used as a temporary barracks for the extra police required in the town during the Fenian rising.

In 1898 it was sold to Mr. P. J. Roche of New Ross.

AUTHORITIES CONSULTED.

Flood, " History of Enniscorthy."
D. Murphy, "Cromwell in Ireland."
Brewer, " Beauties of Ireland."
Proceedings of Royal Society of Antiquaries of Ireland.
Parliamentary Gazetteer.
State Papers.
Calendar of Patent and Close Rolls, Ireland.
Fiants of Elizabeth.

ENNISKILLEN CASTLE

THE chief part of the town of Enniskillen is situated on an island in Lough Erne, seventy-five miles west-by-south of Belfast, in the County Fermanagh.

The name is supposed to be derived from a small islet near to the eastern bridge where the heroic wife of a great chief is buried, and which was called Enis-Cethlenn or "the Island of Cethlenn."

The castle stands at the western side of the town, where it commanded the lake.

It is now incorporated with the Castle Barrack, but the original quadrangular keep (a storey lower than in former times) is still to be seen, while the curtain wall and towers, which were erected in 1611, and figure in the arms of the town, are in a good state of preservation. The ditch which once surrounded it has now been filled up. The castle was the chief fortress of the Maguires, lords of Fermanagh. In 1439 it was surrendered to Donall Ballach Maguire, and three years later Thomas Oge Maguire gave it to Philip Maguire.

In 1593 Maguire had the houses round the castle burnt for fear of attack. Nevertheless, early the following year, during his absence, Captain Dowdall laid siege to the fortress.

On the ninth day he attacked the castle "by boats, by engines, by sap, by scaling." He placed 100 men in a great boat covered with hurdles and hide, which, with

ENNISKILLEN CASTLE

Connor O'Cassidy as guide, drew up close to the wall of the barbican.

Here a fierce onslaught was made, and the garrison retreated to the keep. This, Captain Dowdall threatened to blow up unless they surrendered, which they accordingly did.

The steersman of the boat gives the number as thirty-six fighting men, and nearly the same of women and children; whereas Captain Dowdall states he put a hundred and fifty to death, which is most likely an exaggeration.

He says it came into her Majesty's hands with small loss, though it was very strong, with walls seven feet thick and "soundrie secret fights within it of great annoyance uppon the barbican."

He remained ten days mending the breaches, gates, and doors, and laid in three months' provisions. He elected a constable, and, garrisoning it with thirty soldiers, took his departure.

Marshall Bagnall was on his way to ward the castle, but Dowdall reported that he was too ill to await his coming.

The same year Maguire laid siege to the fortress, it is said, at the instigation of the Earl of Tyrone. The relieving party was defeated, and the Lord Deputy himself set out to the rescue of the garrison.

They had been reduced to eating horseflesh, and had only one more animal when they were relieved. The ward was then reduced from forty to thirty, and the castle victualled for six months, which supply was to be augmented by fishing for eels under the walls.

Shortly after this the bawn was seized and seven warders killed; and in 1595 the whole fortress surrendered. In the State Papers the Lord Deputy declares he cannot understand why this should have been, as the castle was well provisioned. He says that he hears the constable and fifteen warders were promised life and goods, but that when they came out they were all put to death. It does not seem that this report was confirmed.

In 1596–97 the Lord Deputy asks for three falcons with their carriages and ladles, to replace those which Maguire had taken with the castle, and which had belonged to Dublin.

Maguire's brother held the fortress in 1598.

It was again in English possession in 1607, and Captain William Cole was constable in 1610, when he asked for some land to be allotted to his office. That immediately round the castle was in the hands of Scottish settlers, and there was no demesne land attached to the building.

In 1611 he built "a fair house" on the old site, adding numerous outhouses.

A moat surrounded the bawn, and the river was crossed by a drawbridge. He also erected a wall 26 feet high with flankers and parapet, which still remains.

The castle was granted to Sir William Cole in 1620 on a lease for twenty-one years, and he was responsible for its repair. The Earl of Enniskillen at present represents the family.

Four hundred pounds was granted for State repairs in 1646, some of which had been expended on the castle of Enniskillen.

During the famous siege of the town in 1689 the Governor, Gustavus Hamilton, took up his residence in the castle, which belonged to Sir Michael Cole, who was absent in England.

In 1749 the fortress was in ruins.

Authorities Consulted.

State Papers.
MS. Ordnance Survey.
Parliamentary Gazetteer.
Proceedings of Royal Society of Antiquaries, Ireland.
King, "Henry's Upper Lough Erne."
Witherrow, "Derry and Enniskillen."
Earl of Belmore, "Governor Hamilton and Captain Corry," and Ancient Maps of Enniskillen, both in *Ulster Journal of Archæology*.

FERNS CASTLE

THIS ancient seat of royalty is situated five miles and three-quarters north-by-east of Enniscorthy, on the River Bann, in the County of Wexford. The name comes from Fearna, meaning alders, or "a place abounding in alders."

The erection of the first stone castle is ascribed to Strongbow, and it is supposed to have been built upon the site of the fortress or dun of his father-in-law, Dermot MacMurrough, King of Leinster.

The present ruins are the remains of four round towers, which were joined by high curtain walls enclosing a courtyard. The building is one of great strength, and occupies an imposing situation above the town.

The most perfect of the towers contains a chapel, with a beautifully groined roof springing from consoles. Richard Donovan, who inherited the property in 1773, is said to have converted the sanctuary into an Orange Lodge, where high revel was held, and a visitor in 1864 states that an equestrian statue of William III. occupied the site of the altar beneath the east window.

Mr. Baranger, however, writing in 1780, says that the chapel was without a floor, and made one with the under apartment. He describes the room above it as arched, and also remarks that the edges of the stones of the long loophole windows had been cut underneath as if for cannon to be pointed through. A brass fieldpiece found in the castle was used for the defence of Wexford, 1641.

Three kinds of masonry are visible in the construction

of the tower, each occupying about a third of its height. The bottom layer consists of small stones, the middle part of larger ones, while those at the top are hewn.

At one time part of the wall connecting the towers was used as a ball-alley (the ground being flagged for this purpose), until the owner of the castle enclosed the ruins with a wall for their preservation.

In 1865 part of the fortress on the north side fell in a thunderstorm, and the tenant of that date procured leave to blast the rest of this wall for fear of accident. The ground is littered with broken masonry.

After Strongbow's death in 1177, Henry II. bestowed the manor and castle of Ferns upon William FitzAdelm de Burgo. The same year FitzAdelm seized the Black Castle of Wicklow from the three sons of Maurice Fitzgerald, giving them Ferns by way of compensation.

The brothers at once began to rebuild and strongly fortify their new possession, but it was hardly completed before Walter Allemand, a nephew of FitzAdelm, attacked the castle and left it in a ruined condition.

William Marshall, Earl of Pembroke, who married the grand-daughter of Dermot MacMurrough, began to erect a much larger fortress on the same site in 1192. He was succeeded by his son, who had married the daughter of King John, and he completed the stronghold in 1224. He then presented it to the Bishop of Ferns as restitution for Church land which his father had seized.

It remained in the possession of the Church from 1224 to 1364, during which time it was used as an Episcopal Palace.

In 1243 Geoffrey St. John, Vicar-General of Ferns, and Escheator of Ireland, came into residence, and was succeeded by Bishop Lambert in 1282, who died in the castle.

He was followed by Richard of Northampton, who had been Canon of Kildare, while in 1304 Robert Waldrond was consecrated, and took up his abode at Ferns. During this time the neighbourhood was much disturbed, and the next Bishop was arraigned for high treason in 1317, but was pardoned the following year.

In 1331 the clan of O'Toole seized the castle, pillaged, and burned it. Next year the Crown took possession again, and three years later they thought it expedient to appoint Lord Gerald Rochford constable of Ferns Castle. He held office for ten years, and was summoned to Parliament as a Baron.

In 1347 Bishop Esmond came into possession of the stronghold, and was succeeded by Bishops Charnels and Denn. The latter prelate was the last Bishop to reside in the castle, for from 1402 to 1530 the stronghold was in possession of the MacMurroughs.

At the end of this period it was captured by Lord Deputy Grey. He was on his way from Kilkenny to Dublin, when he sent word from Leghlyn to Stephen FitzHenry at Kilkea, to meet him at Ferns Castle with his guns and men.

Lord Grey marched by night, and arrived in the morning before the fortress. He demanded its surrender, which was refused by the garrison, "using very spiteful language." The day was spent in preparing for the attack. He posted his men round the building in the ditches and other cover, so that none of the besieged should escape, and the troops broke down the gate leading to the drawbridge. A Mr. Thomas Allen, who was with the attacking party, noticed that one of the garrison kept watch every now and then from one particular place, and he sent a gunner to hide himself where he could cover the spot with his weapon. This was successful, and the man was shot as soon as he returned. He was the governor and chief gunner of the castle.

The rest of the garrison then asked for a parley, which was granted.

Lord Grey told them that unless they surrendered before

the arrival of the ordnance, which was within a mile of the stronghold, he would not accept a surrender, but kill them all. They then agreed to give the castle up, and two of the English were stationed in it during the night.

The next day the Lord Deputy appointed a garrison of the MacMurroughs to guard the stronghold, taking their chief with him to Dublin as a hostage.

A writer of this time describes the castle as the old inheritance of the Earl of Shrewsbury or the Duke of Norfolk, and "oon of the auncientis and strongest castells within this lande."

In 1536 Cahir MacInnycross Kavanagh, the Mac-Murrough, was appointed constable by the Crown, but two years later he was superseded by Sir Richard Butler.

At the time great anxiety was felt for fear of an attack from the Kavanaghs; and in 1550, we learn from the State Papers that Cahir M'Arte Kavanagh had managed to get possession of the castle by treatment.

The next year Richard Kettyng asked the Privy Council to confirm the King's letter granting him the stronghold, but they refused.

It was considered necessary to have English captains in the castles of the districts to hold the Kavanaghs in subjection, so that a list of constables to Ferns Castle is recorded, the most remarkable being the Mastersons, father and son, the former being accused of conspiring against the Queen in 1569.

Thrilling traditions are related regarding his wife, Catherien de Clare, who was said to decoy the neighbouring chiefs and Irish gentlemen within the fortress under the guise of hospitality and murder them by pushing them down a trapdoor.

In 1588 Masterson entered a petition for land, as recompense for thirty-four years' service.

His son spent large sums on rebuilding the castle; nevertheless it was granted to Lord Andley in 1608.

FERNS CASTLE

Sir Charles Coote occupied the stronghold in 1641, but finding he was unable to hold it against the insurgents, he dismantled the outworks, blew up part of the building, and left the neighbourhood.

It must, however, have been partly repaired, for eight years later, when Cromwell's commander, Colonel Reynolds, appeared before it, the garrison fled, leaving their arms, ammunition, and provisions behind them.

In 1669 Charles II. granted the castle to Arthur Parsons; while in 1689 it seems to have been in the possession of Alderman Thomas Keiran, who gave it to his brother-in-law, Richard Donovan, in 1694, from whom it descended to its present owner, Richard Donovan, Esq., D.L., of Ballymore House, Camolin.

AUTHORITIES CONSULTED.

Calendar of State Papers.
Calendar of Carew MSS.
Parliamentary Gazetteer.
W. G. Flood, "History of Enniscorthy."
G. Bassett, "Wexford."
G. Stokes, "Ireland and Anglo-Norman Church."
G. Griffiths, "Chronicles of County Wexford."
Savage, "Picturesque Ireland."
Proceedings of Royal Society of Antiquaries of Ireland.

FERRYCARRIG AND SHANA COURT CASTLES

THE chief interest attaching to the castles of Ferrycarrig and Shana Court is the fact that one or other of them was the first Anglo-Norman fortress erected in Ireland.

The sites of the two strongholds occupy positions one on each side of the Slaney, a little more than two miles west of Wexford. The parish of Carrig lies on the right bank of the river in the Barony of West Shelmalier, and here on an isolated rock commanding the ferry is situated Ferrycarrig Castle—Carrig signifying a rock.

It is a square tower of great age and occupies the whole summit of the rocky point on which it stands, and does not seem, therefore, to have ever been of larger dimensions than at present. The masonry is rough and massive and the loopholes unusually small, while the door is so low and narrow that it is necessary to stoop when entering.

An opening in the wall is usually called the "murdering hole," but as there is another aperture to correspond with it in the exterior at the base they are likely to have had some other use.

The close resemblance which this tower bears to Trajan's Tower at Paboquaipass on the Danube, even to a similar entrance, has been the subject of remark.

On the south bank of the river, where the Crimean monument now stands, were traceable some years ago the fosse and outworks of Shana Court. They occupied about half an acre, but the walls of the fortress had been

FERRYCARRIG AND SHANA COURT

demolished to supply stones for the building of the old mansion of Belmont.

Tradition asserts that Ferrycarrig was erected by FitzStephen, who landed in Ireland in 1169, and that Shana Court was built by King John, it deriving its name from his having held court there as Viceroy.

We know FitzStephen de Marisco erected a castle at Carrig from the following passage in Giraldus Cambrensis:

"MacMorogh marched to besiege Dublin, but left FitzStephen behind, who was then building a hold or castle upon a certain rocky hill called the Carricke, about two miles from Wexford, which place, although it was very strong of itself, yet by industry and labour it was made much stronger."

From the same source we also learn that it was environed on two sides by the river, but this might apply equally to either fortress.

A further description says: "It was at first made but of rods and wiffes, according to the manner in those daies, but since builded with stone, and was the strongest fort then in those parts of the land; but being a place not altogether sufficient for a prince, and yet it was thought too good and strong for a subject, it was pulled down, defaced, and razed, and so dooth still remane."

The most likely assumption, on the whole, seems to be that King John erected on the ruined site of FitzStephen's stronghold the castle known as Shana Court, the stones of which were used in building Belmont, and that Ferrycarrig was an outwork of the larger fortress or else was erected by the Roches of Artramont as a watch-tower to protect the ferry.

FitzStephen suffered a memorable siege in his castle in 1170. He had weakened his garrison by sending a detachment to serve with Strongbow, when the men of Wexford and Kinsellagh rose and laid siege to Carrig Castle with a force of about three thousand.

Several desperate assaults were successfully repulsed before the attackers asked for a parley. This was granted, and they informed FitzStephen that Strongbow and his followers had been utterly routed, and that King Roderic was marching with a great army to annihilate his garrison, but that out of respect to his person they wished him to escape.

FitzStephen could not be induced to believe the tale until three bishops took a false oath as to its truth, whereupon he capitulated upon honourable terms. These were at once violated, and, against the conditions, he was made prisoner and sent to Beggery Island, while many of those with him were killed.

Donald Kavanagh, with great difficulty, arrived in Dublin to inform Strongbow that FitzStephen could not hold out more than three days. It was on this occasion that Maurice FitzGerald made his famous speech, in which he said: "FitzStephen, also, whose courage and noble daring opened to us the way into this island, is now with his small force besieged by a hostile nation. What should we, therefore, wait for?"

Stirred by his eloquence, the English forces, though of small numbers, set out and carried victory before them, but in the meantime Carrig had surrendered.

Strongbow was warned that if his forces marched on Wexford all the prisoners would be at once slain, so that FitzStephen was not liberated until King Henry arrived in Ireland in 1172.

Ferrycarrig is situated on the Earl of Donoghmore's estate.

AUTHORITIES CONSULTED.

J. Ryan, "History and Antiquities of Carlow."
Brewer, "Beauties of Ireland."
Giraldus Cambrensis.
Parliamentary Gazetteer.
Proceedings of Royal Society of Antiquaries.
Marquis of Kildare, "Earls of Kildare."
Joyce, "Irish Place Names."
"Ferrycarrig," in *The People*.

GEASHILL CASTLE

> "Oh, sweetly rural is the scene
> Where Geashill Castle stands;
> Beneath the line of green old hills
> This lovely vale expands."
>
> E. EGAN.

THE village of Geashill is situated in the barony of the same name, about eight miles south-east of Tullamore, in the King's County. On a long ridge near are the ruins of the castle, adjoining a modern lodge usually occupied by the agent of the Digby estate. The ancient fortress is three storeys high, and a spiral stairway still leads to the summit, where there is an iron chair. An underground passage is said to run to the ruined Abbey close by.

The date of the castle's erection by the Fitzgeralds is ascribed to the twelfth century, and in 1203 or 1204 the King commanded it to be delivered to William Marshall, Earl of Pembroke, as the guardian of Maurice, second Baron of Offaly, who was heir to Gerald FitzMaurice.

In 1305 the sept of the O'Dempseys slaughtered a great number of the O'Connors near the castle, and the following year the stronghold was destroyed by these native Irish. The Book of Howth says: "The Lord of Offalye builded the castle of Geschell" in 1307, so it was, no doubt, rebuilt this year by Thomas FitzMaurice, "the crooked heir," who died in 1298, and who is supposed to have been prevented from inheriting as head of the family on account of some deformity. Juliana FitzGerald granted the castle to his son, who was her cousin, and afterwards 1st Earl of Kildare.

An inquisition was held at Kildare in 1282 upon the estate of the late John FitzThomas, when his heir, Thomas FitzMaurice, came of age. It was shown that the former had held lands from Maurice FitzGerald "for a moiety of the service of one knight whenever royal service should be summoned, rendering suit nevertheless at the court of the said Maurice FitzGerald at Geashill."

Lord Leonard Gray and the chieftain O'Mulmoy seized the castle, and abbey of Killeigh in 1538. In both they found great stores of corn, part of which they burnt and part carried off.

On an ancient map of Leix, dated about 1563, both the castles of Lea and Geashill are marked as ruins, but in Sir Henry Sydney's account of Ireland shortly afterwards he writes: "Geshell, in the King's County, is very necessary to be had of the Earl of Kildare; it is a matter of consequence for her Majesty's service in that county."

James I. granted the barony of Geashill in 1619 and 1629 to Lady Lettice Digby, widow of Sir Robert Digby, of Warwickshire, as compensation for not inheriting as heir-general of the house of Kildare, she being the only child of the eldest son of the 11th Earl of Kildare. At the same time he created her Baroness of Offaly, and she lived quietly at Geashill from that date until 1642, when the great rebellion broke out and the Confederate Catholics laid siege to her stronghold.

A kinsman of hers named Henry Dempsy, brother of Lord Clanmalier, was in command, and despatched a letter "To the Honourable and thrice virtuous Lady, the Lady Digby," demanding that she should surrender the castle to his Majesty and offering her and her household a free pass to wherever they wished, threatening at the same time if she did not comply to murder every Protestant in the town.

GEASHILL CASTLE

To this demand the Baroness sent the following answer: "I received your letter, wherein you threaten to sack this my castle, by his Majesty's authority. I have ever been a loyal subject and good neighbour among you, and, therefore, cannot but wonder at such an assault. I thank you for your offer of a convoy, wherein I hold little safety; and, therefore, my resolution is, that being free of offending his Majesty, or doing wrong to any of you, I will live and die innocently, and will do the best to defend my own, leaving the issue to God. And though I have been, and still am desirous to avoid the shedding of Christian blood, yet, being provoked, your threats shall no wit dismay me.—LETTICE OFFALY."

The castle was surrounded by bog and wood, and was, in consequence, somewhat difficult of access, so that upon receiving her letter the enemy retired to make more elaborate preparations for attack.

They collected a number of pots and pans, with which a man from Athboy constructed a cannon. It had to be cast three times before it was successful.

After two months the attackers returned to the castle with Lord Clanmalier in command. He despatched another letter demanding surrender to the brave lady, which received a spirited reply, reiterating her determination to endeavour to hold her own against all comers.

Upon its receipt they discharged the gun, which burst at the first shot, but a fusilade of muskets was kept up until the evening.

As the Baroness was looking out of one of the windows a ball struck the wall near her, and taking out her handkerchief, she contemptuously dusted the spot.

It is said that one of her sons, having fallen into the enemy's hands, was brought before the castle in chains, with a threat that they would kill him unless she surrendered. She, however, replied that if they touched a hair of his head she would at once put to death a Roman Catholic priest who was within the walls.

At dark the enemy retired, again sending her a letter offering her terms, which received the same refusal as the others had done, and the messenger she sent was kept a prisoner.

Lady Offaly managed to let Sir Charles Coote, then at Naas, know that she needed assistance, and Philip Sydney, Viscount Lisle, at once set out from Dublin to her relief, accompanied by Sir Charles Coote, Sir George Wentworth, Lord Digby, the Baroness's eldest son, and a considerable force of horse and foot.

Lady Offaly had also despatched an appeal for help to the FitzGeralds, but the letter fell into the enemy's hands instead, who at once renewed the siege when they learnt of her straits.

As the English forces advanced the besiegers skirmished and retreated. The relieving party supplied the fortress with food and ammunition, but at Lady Offaly's request she remained in the castle.

The following October she was again attacked by Charles Dempsie, but this time was shortly relieved by Sir Richard Grenville, and after this she retired to Cole's Hill, in Warwickshire, where she died in 1658.

Her eldest son, Lord Digby, inherited the castle, and it is still in the family's possession.

AUTHORITIES CONSULTED.

Marquis of Kildare, "Earls of Kildare."
J. Wright, "King's County Directory."
State Documents.
Carew MSS., including Book of Howth.
Parliamentary Gazetteer.
Hore, "Rental Book of Gerald, 9th Earl of Kildare," and "Notes on a Fac-Simile of an Ancient Map of Leix," both in *Journal of Royal Society of Antiquaries, Ireland*.

GLENARM CASTLE

GLENARM CASTLE

THIS castle is situated in the Barony of Lower Glenarm, a little more than twenty-five miles north of Belfast, in the County Antrim, where the Glenarm rivulet enters the bay.

The original stronghold was erected by the Byset family about the middle of the thirteenth century, and came into the MacDonnell family through the marriage of Margery Bisset.

The castle stood on the southern side of the river at the head of the street which leads from the barbican, and on the opposite bank from the present building.

In 1278 an inquisition was held after the death of two John Bysets to determine if the Earl of Ulster was right in making the fortress over to the Bishop of Connor as ecclesiastical property, and it was decided that the Bysets had not held the castle from the church.

Captain Pers and Malbie placed Randal Oge in possession of the stronghold in 1568, but the same year his ward surrendered it.

In 1597 it is reported James and Randal M'Donnell "broke" the castle, and it does not appear to have been afterwards rebuilt, although the ruins were standing for many years.

Sir Randal MacDonnell was granted the estate in 1603, and began to erect the present castle.

Sir Awla M'Awla petitioned against his possession of Glenarm in 1610, but apparently without effect.

Sir Randal greatly enlarged the dwelling in 1636, and the following inscription was placed over the entrance:—

"With the leave of God this castle was built by Sir

Randal McDonnel, Knight, Erle of Antrim, having to wife Dame Aellis O'Neill, in the year of our Lord God, 1636. Deus est adjutor meus."

Shortly after this the family made Glenarm their chief place of residence instead of Dunluce Castle.

The fortress is approached by a barbican standing on the northern side of the bridge, while an avenue of limes leads to the hall door. The building is flanked by towers crowned with cupolas and vanes, and the gables are decorated with heraldic devices.

An embattled wall guards the terrace on the river side.

The hall, which is also used as a billiard-room, is especially handsome, while the dining-room and drawing-room are also fine apartments.

Some treasure chests said to have belonged to the Spanish Armada are preserved in the castle, but a doubt has been thrown upon their being of such a date.

During the rebellion of 1798, the castle was used as the headquarters of the Yeomanry. The rebels had decided to attack it on the 8th of June, and the wives of the Yeomen, whom they had captured, were to be placed in front of the insurgents in their advance.

This diabolical plan was frustrated on the very morning of the intended attack by news of the defeat at Antrim, whereupon the camp was broken up.

Glenarm is the seat of the Earl of Antrim, the present representative being the sixth peer.

Authorities Consulted.

Hill, "MacDonnells of Antrim."
State Documents.
State Papers.
Thomson, "Highways and Byeways in Donegal and Antrim."
Parliamentary Gazetteer.
"Guide to the Giant's Causeway," in *Dublin Penny Journal*.
Drew, "Old Iron Treasure Chests"; Smith, "Memories of '98," in *Ulster Journal of Archæology*.

GLIN CASTLE

THE origin of the title Knight of Glin, or Knight of the Valley, seems not to be accurately known, but the designation has been recorded as in use during the reign of Henry III. The Knights of Glin, also called the Black Knights, belong to the great Geraldine family, and owed a certain allegiance to the Earls of Desmond, which is described as follows: "Divers customs of meat and drink, together with rising of men at the Earl's calling to the number of 60 kearne."

The housing and feeding of some of the Earl's men were also included.

Glin is a small market town and seaport in the Barony of Shanid, in the County Limerick, at the junction of a rivulet with the Shannon, twenty-six miles west by south of Limerick City.

Of the ancient fortress situated in the town, nothing now remains but the keep. It measures 38 feet by 35 externally, and the walls are 8 feet in thickness. It is at present about 40 feet in height, but was at one time crowned by a turret in the eastern corner. The courtyard walls were 102 feet in length and 92 in breadth. The chief entrance, to the north, was defended by a semicircular outwork. The great hall was situated on the western side of the courtyard, while the keep was in the south-west corner. The two eastern angles were defended by small towers. A moat surrounded the castle filled with water from the Shannon tributary.

The Knight of Glin was a very important chieftain in Limerick, maintaining an ordinary force of ten horsemen and a hundred and forty foot soldiers. During the Desmond wars he shared the fortunes of the Earl, and in 1569 both the Knight and the son were attainted, the latter being executed.

The estates were, however, very shortly afterwards restored, and in the rebellion of the Northern Earls and the "Sugan Earl" of Desmond, the Knight of Glin was again amongst the disaffected.

In the summer of 1600 Sir George Carew started on an expedition to the west to restore peace in that quarter. He had with him a force of one thousand five hundred men, and was accompanied by the Earl of Thomond.

The army marched through Kerry to Askeaton, where there was a halt for four days awaiting provisions, which had been sent by water from Limerick. On the 4th of July they marched twelve miles to Ballintare, the enemy moving in front within view. The next morning's march brought them before Glin Castle, the rebels still offering no opposition.

The Four Masters describe the route taken as having been from Limerick along the northern bank of the Shannon through Clare, the troops ferrying themselves across the river at Glin, but it is most likely that Sir George Carew's biographer gives the correct line of march.

Captain Gawin Harvey's ship, with the ordnance on board, had been anchored in the Shannon for fourteen days awaiting their arrival, and the guns were at once unshipped upon the arrival of the troops.

That night the forces entrenched themselves between the castle and the river, and the next day, under the guise of a parley, they managed to plant the cannon without opposition.

The next day the Knight of Glin, who was not within

GLIN CASTLE

the castle, asked for a safe conduct to the English camp, which was granted. Upon arrival he demanded to see the President, but was refused unless upon an unconditional surrender. This he would not consent to, and was, therefore, ordered to depart. Seeing his son in the camp, whom he had delivered as a hostage some time previously, he seemed to hesitate, but as he still held out for terms the Earl of Thomond broke off the negotiations, and the Knight and his attendants retired to a neighbouring hill to watch the attack.

Later the Constable of the fortress sent a message to the Earl of Thomond begging an interview, which was granted. He began by stating that the love he bore the Earl, being a Thomond man himself, had induced him to warn the English to depart, as the Earl of Desmond with three thousand Connaught men were only two miles off, and would most likely attack the camp and drive them all into the river. The Earl laughed at his forebodings, and told him to deliver the castle and so save himself and the warders from death. This offer he refused, and the President, hearing he had done so, sent a message to say that he hoped to place his head on a stake in two days' time.

One of the cannon becoming clogged, Sir George Carew ordered it to be filled with a charge in inverted order and the fire put to the mouth, so as to clear the touch-hole by the explosion. This was carried out with great success, much to the relief of the besiegers.

A fire of small shot was kept up from the castle at the ordnance, and the President, placing the Knight's son on one of the cannon, sent a message to the garrison to say he had given them a mark to aim at. The Constable replied that the Knight of Glin might have more sons, and that the child should not deter him from firing.

Sir George Carew, however, removed the child, and commenced the battery. A breach was made into the cellar under the great hall, one gunner only being killed.

Captain Flower then led the attack and entered the hall through the breach, forcing the ward to retire. The flag of the besiegers was hoisted from the turrets of the hall, and night coming on Captain Slingsby was ordered to hold the position until the morning.

A dropping fire was kept up all night. The Constable, seeing that to successfully hold the castle was impossible, tried to escape with some of the warders, but he and others were killed in the attempt, one only getting away. His head was placed upon a stake in the camp as the President had said.

The rest of the garrison retired to the keep. In the morning the attackers burned the heavy wooden door which guarded the stairway, but they had to wait two hours for the smoke to clear away. As soon as it had done so, one of the garrison appeared to ask for the lives of his comrades if they surrendered, but it appears he gave himself up before an answer was returned.

The officers and men then ascended the stairs in single file as the width of the passage necessitated, but met with no opposition, the garrison having retired to the battlements, which were protected only by one door.

Here a terrible hand to hand encounter took place. Some of the warders were killed, while the rest jumped from the parapet into the water below, and were either drowned or killed by the guards stationed beneath the tower.

The English lost ten soldiers and one ensign, while about twenty-one men were wounded. Of the defenders of the castle about eighty men were killed, while the Four Masters state that some women and children also lost their lives. They remark that the place would not have been so easily won had not the "Earl of Desmond's people dispersed from him."

The rebels had burned the town of Glin upon the approach of the Royal troops.

GLIN CASTLE

During the rising the castle had been used as a storehouse for the "Sugan Earl's" forces, and a Limerick merchant called Anthony Arthurs seems to have dispensed his goods from it.

Sir George Carew placed a guard of twenty-one soldiers in it under the command of Captain Nicholas Mordant.

Edmund FitzGerald, Knight of the Valley, was restored to most of his estates in 1603, and six years later he appealed to the Lords of the Council against Patrick Crosby obtaining Glin Castle by the King's letter, on the pretext that it was kept from the Knight to prevent his rebelling. Crosby had undertaken to repair and fortify the fortress at his own cost. The Knight stated he had been pardoned by Lord Mountjoy, that his lands had been restored, and shortly afterwards the castle as well.

The next year Sir Arthur Chichester explains that the building was occupied only by Anthony Arthur, who sold wines in it, and that he had therefore given it to Crosby. He also stated that the Knight's eldest son was abroad.

In 1681 the castle was in the possession of Major FitzGerald.

The present Glin Castle, seat of Desmond FitzJohn Lloyd FitzGerald, Knight of Glin, is situated about a mile west of the town. Over the yard gate is an engraved stone bearing the following inscription: "Edmond Gerrald, Knight of the Vally. Onnor Cartie, his wife. Fear God always and remember the Poor. I.H.S. Anno Domoni, 1615."

Authorities Consulted.

Pacata Hibernia (Dublin reprint, 1810).
J. Dowd, " County of Limerick."
Calendar of State Papers.
Parliamentary Gazetteer.
Carew MSS.
Donovan, " Annals of the Four Masters."
Journal of Thomas Dineley (*Kilkenny Archæological Society's Journal*).

GREENCASTLE, COUNTY DONEGAL

THIS castle is situated on the west side of the entrance to Lough Foyle, two and a half miles north-east of Moville, in the Barony of Innishowen.

It was erected upon a rock and defended by two towers which contained the chief apartments, while a third tower defended the northern end.

It is built of green fire stone, from which its present name may have been derived.

In Macator's map, which was published in 1629, it is marked as "New Castle," and it is still known in Irish by that name.

Hanmer's "Chronicle" and Grace's "Annals" state that Arx Viridis in Ultonia was thrown down in 1260, so that it is likely that the present building, which was erected by Richard de Burgo, the Red Earl of Ulster, in 1305, replaced a former fortress.

In 1332 William de Burgo, or the "Dun Earl," owned the fortress, which he had inherited from his father, and having taken prisoner Walter, son of Sir Walter de Burgo, he starved him to death in the castle. Sir Arthur Chichester excavated one of the pillars of the dungeon in which it is supposed he was confined, and a mark was discovered that most likely had held a ring to which the prisoner was chained. The "dreary and dismal" prisons are still to be seen.

The Dun Earl was stabbed to death the next year in revenge for the murder.

The following legend is told regarding Walter de Burgo's death. The Earl had a beautiful daughter who one day, in

GREENCASTLE, COUNTY DONEGAL

GREENCASTLE, COUNTY DONEGAL

crossing the sands on the shore under Benevenagh, became engulfed in quicksands, and was nearly losing her life when Sir Walter Burk's son, who was serving in the army of O'Neill and O'Donnell, seeing her danger from the heights above rushed down and saved her from the peril.

The same year this young man was taken prisoner by the girl's father in his war with the O'Donnells and starved to death at Greencastle. The Earl one day, during his unfortunate victim's captivity, discovered his daughter carrying food to the prisoner, and seizing her by the hair, dragged her to the battlements and hurled her over on to the rocks below.

The fortress was for many years in possession of the O'Dohertys.

In 1555 Calvagh O'Donnell went to Scotland to raise forces with the help of Mac Calin (Gillaspick Don), and returning with them and a cannon called *gonna cam*, or "crooked gun," he set to work and demolished the New Castle.

It was, however, reported as wardable in 1586. The last of the O'Dohertys to hold the fortress was knighted by Queen Elizabeth, but shortly afterwards he went into rebellion, and his estate was forfeited.

In 1610 it was granted with other property to Sir Arthur Chichester with an allowance to maintain the garrison. Two years later he asked to be allowed for horsemen at Greencastle instead of the ten warders, and in 1615 Lord Chichester was granted Greencastle for three lives by letters patent.

In 1752 it was on the Earl of Donegal's estate.

Authorities Consulted.

O'Donovan, "Annals of the Four Masters."
MS. Ordnance Survey.
Stokes, "Pococke's Tour in Ireland in 1752."
State Papers.
Carew MSS.
Parliamentary Gazetteer.
Blackley, "A Tour through Innishowen."

GREENCASTLE, COUNTY DOWN

UPON the northern shore of Carlingford Lough, in the Barony of Mourne, four and a half miles south-west of Kilteel, County Down, are situated the ruins of this castle. It is a very fine specimen of Norman architecture, and was erected soon after the landing of the first English settlers so as to secure communication between the Pale and the outlying district of Lecale, as well as to command the entrance to Carlingford Lough.

At present the remains chiefly consist of the keep, which was a high rectangular building, with square towers at the angles. A winding stair in the south-west turret leads to the top. The stone floor of the great hall, measuring 70 feet by 40, is supported by arches which form vaults in the basement. The upper floors have disappeared, and were probably of wood.

The traces of extensive outworks can be seen round the building. On the west side stands a house which is at present inhabited by a farmer, but which for many years formed the chief residence of the Bagnall family during the seventeenth and eighteenth centuries.

The castle belonged to the Du Burgos or Burkes, Earls of Ulster, and in 1312 Sir Maurice, the son of Thomas, married Catherine, daughter of the "Red Earl" of Ulster, and the next day, being the 16th of August, Thomas, the 2nd Earl of Kildare, "a prudent and wise man," married her sister, Lady Joan de Burgh, also in the castle. The Lady Joan had two other married sisters, one being the

GREENCASTLE, COUNTY DOWN

GREENCASTLE, COUNTY DOWN

wife of King Robert Bruce, and the other Countess of Desmond.

In 1335 there was an order to send six "balistas" to furnish "Viride Castrum," or the Greencastle. The same year William de Logan was ordered to pay Henry de Maunderville 20 marks out of the rents of the late Earl of Ulster, which were in the King's hands, on account of the minority of the heir. This reward was for De Maunderville having twice relieved the castle of Greencastle with men-at-arms when it was besieged by the "felons" of Ulster.

It was again attacked by the Irish in 1343, and this time it was carried by storm and dilapidated, but was shortly afterwards restored.

The late Constable, William de Doun, received pardon in 1356 for having seized and imprisoned Rosea, daughter of Richard Foy.

During Henry IV.'s reign there was only one constable between the castles of Carlingford and Greencastle. It is reported that Stephen Geron received £20 a year for the guardianship of Greencastle and £5 for Carlingford.

In 1403 John Moore, who was then constable, petitioned for a rise of salary, and he was granted £40 a year on condition he spent 10 marks of it on repairs. The amount was to be paid out of the rents of Carlingford, Cooley, and "le Mourne."

None but Englishmen were permitted to hold the appointment in 1495.

Notwithstanding this, when M'Donell made his submission in 1542 he requested to be granted Greencastle, and the lands lying waste around it, for which favour he promised military service.

The Government did not evidently see their way to accede to his request, and seven years later it is reported that the fortress was in a "wretched condition."

In 1552 it was granted to Sir Nicholas Bagnall, in whose family's possession it remained for many years.

Sir Arthur Chichester was granted means to provide ten warders for Greencastle in 1612, but this does not seem to have interfered with the Bagnall possession, as in 1620 Arthur Bagnall held the manors and lordships of Greencastle and Mourne.

Three years later it is recommended that the ward be moved from Culmore to Greencastle, and the stronghold was garrisoned during the rebellion of 1641.

Authorities Consulted.

J. O'Laverty, "Diocese of Down and Connor."
W. Harris, "County of Down."
R. Praeger, "Official Guide to County Down."
State Papers.
Marquis of Kildare, "Earls of Kildare."
Carew MSS.
Parliamentary Gazetteer.

HOWTH CASTLE

HOWTH CASTLE

About seven miles east-north-east of Dublin, in the Barony of Coolock, is situated the village of Howth, on the promontory of the same name.

A short way from the town, nestling under the lee of the hill is the castle, the seat of the Earls of Howth.

It is a long battlemented building, with square towers at each end.

A large flight of steps gives admission to the hall, which extends along the whole length of the building. Here is preserved the two-handed sword of Sir Amoricus Tristram (the founder of the St. Laurence family in Ireland) with which he is said to have fought his first Irish battle. Also three inscribed bells, which were removed from the Abbey, are preserved in the castle.

The fortress seems to have undergone much alteration since its first erection, and the great gateway tower, which now flanks the main building on one side, appears to be of sixteenth-century architecture and is no doubt part of the original building.

The stronghold was erected in 1564 by Christopher, the twentieth baron, but whether it was built on the site of an older castle or whether Corr Castle, also situated on the peninsular, was the ancient fortress of the St. Laurence family, does not seem to be known.

The mortar of the early building, like the Tower of London, is reported to have been mixed with blood.

Until far into the nineteenth century the castle was surrounded by a fosse.

There are several inscribed and figured stones over the entrance to the stable-yard, and also one built into the wall near the garden gate.

Sir John de Courcy and his sister's husband, Sir Amoricus Tristram, arrived at Howth in 1177. Their companionship in arms is said to have been the outcome of a compact to share each other's fortunes made in the Church of St. Mary at Rouen.

Upon the arrival of the ship at Howth, De Courcy, being ill, remained on board, while Sir Amoricus took command of their forces in the first engagement with the Danes, who fiercely opposed their landing.

After a great battle, in which Sir Amoricus lost seven blood relations, the enemy were completely defeated at the bridge of the Evora, and the lands of Howth were granted to the victor as a reward of prowess.

He then accompanied Sir John de Courcy to Down, where he also gained possessions and did great deeds of valour. A story is told that after the first battle in the north Sir Amoricus was found leaning on his shield under a hedge, bleeding from three large wounds, and having sustained himself by eating the wild roses and honeysuckle which grew within his reach. His life was despaired of for nine days, but he eventually recovered, and lived to die heroically among a group of outnumbered infantry, having slain his horse so that he could not save himself by flight.

The St. Laurence coat of arms is a shield with cross swords and roses in a bloody field, which may have originated from the wild flowers Sir Amoricus gathered.

An early chronicler says of him that he might " be chosen from amongst a thousand knights for beauty and heroic courage, as well as for humility and courtesy to his inferiors, yielding to none but in the way of gentleness."

After his death his sons gradually lost his northern

possessions, and King John confirmed the grant of the lands of Howth to the third baron by charter. It may have been at this time that the family name was changed from Tristram to St. Laurence. There seems to be no historical evidence for the tradition that the name was altered to commemorate a victory gained upon St. Laurence's Day.

In 1575, as Grace O'Mailley was returning from her famous visit to Queen Elizabeth she landed at Howth, but found the castle gates closed, the reason assigned being that it was the dinner hour. Shocked at such want of Irish hospitality she seized the young heir, who was playing on the strand, and carried him off to her castle in Mayo. She refused to restore him until she received a promise that the gates of Howth Castle should never again be closed at dinner hour. This child was Nicholas, afterwards twenty-first baron. A picture at the castle is supposed to represent the incident.

Lord Mountjoy, as Lord Deputy, and Sir George Carew, as Lord President of Munster, landed at Howth in 1599, and spent a night at the castle before proceeding to Dublin.

In 1607 the State Papers report that the old Countess of Kildare and Lady Dowager of Delvin and her children were at Howth in Sir Christopher St. Laurence's house, and the following year it is mentioned that Sir John Talbot's house is near the castle of Howth.

King William slept a night in the castle in 1690, and his room was kept unaltered from the time he had used it.

Dean Swift was a constant visitor at Howth, and an original portrait of him, painted by Bindon in 1735, hangs in the castle.

Near the garden stands the old elm known as " The Tristram Tree," which has been carefully propped and preserved in every way on account of the tradition attaching to it. It is said that as long as this tree lives there will be an heir to the noble house which was founded by Sir Amoricus Tristram.

To "follow as closely as Lord Howth's Rat" was at one time a common simile for any faithful or attached animal, and the legend which gave rise to the saying is the following:—

One of the former Lords of Howth had retired to his castle to retrench a somewhat diminished heritage, and one night while living thus in solitary state there was a fearful storm.

Word was brought to the fortress that a ship was being wrecked under the cliffs near the Abbey, and every one rushed off to the spot to render what assistance was possible, and amongst them Lord Howth.

Every effort was, however, unavailing, and the ship went down apparently with all hands. But as morning broke the eager watchers espied a frail, roughly-put-together raft floating towards them, and on this was a beautiful woman, with a wooden chest beside her.

As soon as she landed Lord Howth courteously offered her the hospitality of the castle, and ordered his servants to carry the heavy coffer thither.

She continued to live at Howth Castle, and her host became passionately enamoured of her, and wished to marry her, but she persistently refused his offers, and urged him daily to seek another bride.

At last he gave way to her entreaties, and became affianced to the daughter of a neighbouring nobleman.

As the time for the marriage drew near the fair stranger presented Lord Howth with a ribbon wrought with strange characters, which she told him to wear on his wrist and guard as his luck. Then she left the castle and was heard of no more.

In due course Lord Howth brought home his bride, and with true womanly curiosity she wanted to know why he never removed the ribbon from his arm.

One night, while he was asleep, she untied it, and took

HOWTH CASTLE

it over to the fire to decipher the inscription, but it accidentally ignited, and was burnt to ashes.

Lord Howth was terribly distressed at its loss, declaring that his good fortune would now forsake him.

Shortly after this there was a great feast in the castle. In the midst of the festivities the dogs in the courtyard began to give tongue, as if in pursuit of game, and in a minute a terrified rat had jumped on the banqueting table, and, pausing before Lord Howth, looked up piteously in his face for protection.

He ordered the dogs to be called off, and from that hour the rat never left him.

His wife and family did not approve of his faithful attendant, and his brother persuaded him to go to the Continent, and by thus crossing the sea rid himself of the animal. However, the morning after his arrival in France the rat was found sleeping on his bed. He then pushed on to Marseilles, but not long after his arrival the rat entered his room wet and draggled from its long journey.

The animal approached the fire to dry itself, when the nobleman's brother took up the poker in a rage and killed it with one blow.

"You have murdered me," cried the Earl, and, falling back, he died.

The rat is sometimes said to have been white, and to reappear when evil is about to befall the house of St. Laurence.

The present Lord Howth is the fourth earl.

Authorities Consulted.

D'Alton, "History of Co. Dublin."
Proceedings of the Royal Society of Antiquaries of Ireland.
Brewer, "Beauties of Ireland."
Parliamentary Gazetteer.
Calendar of State Papers.
R. A., "The Abbey of Howth," in *Dublin Penny Journal*.

KILBARRON CASTLE

"Broad, blue, and deep the Bay of Donegal
　　Spreads north and south, and far a-west before
The beetling cliffs, sublime and shattered wall,
　　Where the O'Cleary's name is heard no more."

　　　　　　　　　　　　　　T. D. McGee.

THIS castle is situated on the shores of Donegal Bay about three miles from the town of Ballyshannon, in the Barony of Kilbarron, County Donegal.

The name Cill-Barrainn signifies "the Church of St. Barrfhionn."

The fortress was built on a high and nearly insulated cliff, and from its romantic and wild situation a tradition falsely sprang up that it had been the stronghold of freebooters. The promontory is nearly circular in form and rises a hundred feet above the sea, along the edge of which a wall was built, while on the landward side a thick wall, the whole width of the neck protected this direction from attack.

To the north of the small open courtyard thus enclosed was the keep, and here are traces of a subterranean passage, now filled up, which was used for "distillery purposes" in the eighteenth century.

The remains of two chambers at the cliff side seem older than the other buildings. The sea wall is pierced by an oblong passage with a small square mouth popularly known as "the murdering-hole."

The castle was probably erected in the thirteenth or

KILBARRON CASTLE

fourteenth century by the O'Sgingins, who were ollaves or historians to the great O'Donnells.

In 1391 the Four Masters tell us it was demolished by Donnell, the son of Murtough (O'Conor of Sligo).

The last of the O'Sgingins to be chief historian to O'Donnell in the fourteenth century had no son, and only one beautiful daughter, with whom Cormac O'Cleary, who was on a visit to the Abbey of Assaroe, from Galway, fell in love.

O'Sgingin gave his consent to the marriage, and instead

KILBARRON CASTLE.

of the wedding gift which it was usual for the bridegroom to present to his wife's father, O'Sgingin asked that if a son were born of the marriage he should be brought up with a knowledge of literature and history.

Hence Kilbarron passed into the O'Cleary family, and this great race of historians occupied it for several centuries.

It is likely Cormac O'Cleary re-edified it, but the "stone houses," of which the building is recorded, were erected by Diarmaid, one of the celebrated sons of Tadhg Cam (or The Stooped) O'Cleary.

The fortunes of the Ollaves of Tirconnell began to wane with that of their patrons, the O'Donnells, although the last O'Cleary to hold lands was not dispossessed until 1632, yet many of their possessions were lost to them at the flight of the Northern Earls in 1607. Most of the estate passed to Lord Folliott and the Bishop of Raphoe.

AUTHORITIES CONSULTED.

Donovan, "Annals of the Four Masters."
Allingham, "History of Ballyshannon."
P., "Kilbarron Castle," in *Irish Penny Journal*.
Donovan, "Genealogies, Tribes and Customs of Hy-Fiachrach."
Parliamentary Gazetteer.
Proceedings of Royal Society of Antiquaries, Ireland.

KILBRITTAIN CASTLE

THE castle is situated about five miles south of Bandon, at the Kilbrittain inlet from Courtmacsherry Bay, in the County of Cork.

Smith says the castle before being rebuilt " was a stately building environed with a large bawn, fortified with six turrets on the walls." Mr. Jones Stawell erected the present mansion, with which a portion of the ancient castle is incorporated. The kitchen, servants' hall, and housekeeper's room have vaulted roofs, and date from the twelfth century or earlier. There is also a tower and adjoining wall which belonged to the former fortress, as well as the steps leading from the old courtyard. There are supposed to be vaults underneath the building, which are not now accessible, as well as an underground passage leading to the sea.

The castle is pleasantly situated on rising ground between hills. It is usually supposed to have been erected by the Lords Courcey, who received a grant of the lands shortly after the Anglo-Norman landing, but in 1743 Robert Clayton, Bishop of Cork, sent copies of two inscribed stones, found at Kilbrittain, to John, Earl of Egmont. These stones bore the date 1035 in the Arabian characters, which seems to indicate an earlier date of erection. He says: " The stone from which the inscription was taken was found by Mr. Stawell in an old castle, which he has since pulled down, called Kilbrittain, which signifies in Irish the ' church or cell,' or rather the ' burial place of the Britains.' Mr. Stawell says there was likewise the figure of a woman carved in *bas-relief* on another stone, the workmanship of which being most curious. He neglected it, and it has since been lost."

The manor of Kilbrittain passed into the King's hands in 1295 upon the death of John de Courcey, who was slain on the Island of Inchydonny by M'Carthy. Walter de la Haye, the King's escheator, delivered the lands to James Keating in keeping for De Courcey's heir.

Lord Courcey, it is said, borrowed a white weasel or ferret from M'Carthy, and pledged his castle as surety for its safe return, but the animal dying M'Carthy claimed Kilbrittain, and it thus passed out of De Courcey's hands.

In 1430 M'Carthy Reagh and James, Earl of Desmond, "The Usurper," began hostilities, and the castle was stormed by the Earl and given to his brother Donough, who had assisted at its capture, but it subsequently returned to the M'Carthys.

In 1537 Lady Eleanor M'Carthy resided in the castle after her husband's death. She was sister to Gerald, 9th Earl of Kildare, and, therefore, aunt to Thomas, the "Silken Lord," and his half brothers. After Lord Offaly's rebellion, and execution, and the attainting of the house of Kildare, the young heir Gerald escaped from the Government by the aid of his tutor Thomas Leverous, afterwards Bishop of Kildare, who wrapped him in a blanket, and fled with him although the lad was sick with smallpox. After a hot pursuit they reached Kilbrittain where the Lady Eleanor took charge of her nephew. She subsequently married O'Donnell of Ulster to gain protection for the boy, but finding her husband was treating with the Government to betray him, she sent the future Earl to France and returned to her son's territory in the County Cork.

In 1572 Kilbrittain is spoken of as M'Carthy Reagh's chief dwelling-place, and it is mentioned that he paid a yearly rent of 67 beefs for it to the Earl of Desmond,

KILBRITTAIN CASTLE

besides rendering him military service at times. Eighteen plough lands are mentioned as attached to it in 1599.

During the great rebellion of 1641 it was the scene of much bloodshed, a gallows having been erected before the castle windows "for hanging the English." One morning a Richard Mewdon was hanged after two days' imprisonment, having been bound to a Mrs. Stringer with great cruelty. The rope was then put round her neck, but M'Carthy's mother looking out of the window, and thinking to save her, sent a priest to know what religion she was. She, however, boldly declared she was a Protestant.

The castle was shortly afterwards taken by the Bandonians.

Some ancient fir-trees are still to be seen called "M'Carthy's Bagpipes," where the executions took place, and the ground beneath having been cursed by one of his victims no grass will grow on it, although there is plenty of light and air.

After the confiscation of the M'Carthy estates the castle passed to Colonel Thomas Long, who was left at the head of affairs when Henry Cromwell retired. At the Restoration it reverted to the Crown and James II. bestowed it on Donough M'Carthy, Lord Cloncarty, a relative of its former owner.

It was sold in Queen Anne's reign to the Hollow Sword Blades Company, and it is now in the possession of Colonel W. St. Leger Alcock-Stawell.

To the castle belonged privileges of fairs and markets.

Authorities Consulted.

Smith, "State of the County and City of Cork"; also Copenger, "Historical Notes in New Edition" of same.
Gibson, "History of the County and City of Cork."
Bennett, "History of Bandon."
Marquis of Kildare, "Earls of Kildare."
Carew MSS.
Parliamentary Gazetteer.

KILKEA CASTLE

"And, oh! through many a dark campaign
  They proved their prowess stern,
In Leinster's plains and Munster's vales,
  On king, and chief, and kern.
But noble was the cheer within
  The halls so rudely won,
And generous was the steel-gloved hand
  That had such slaughter done.
How gay their laugh, how proud their mien,
  You'd ask no herald's sign—
Amid a thousand you had known,
  The princely Geraldine."

THIS castle was built by Hugh de Lacy, Chief Governor of Ireland, for Walter de Riddlesford, Baron of Bray, who had been granted the surrounding district of Omurethi by Strongbow. De Riddlesford's granddaughter, Emelina inherited the manors of Kilkea and Castledermot through her mother, and she, marrying Maurice FitzGerald, 3rd Baron of Offaly, the property passed to the Geraldines who still possess Kilkea Castle, which is one of the seats of the Duke of Leinster, where some of the family at present reside.

Kilkea signifies the Church of St. Kay, or Caoide, and the barony derives its name from the churchyard situated a few perches north-west of the castle.

The fortress is built on the banks of the River Greese, a tributary of the Barrow, about five miles south-east of Athy. Its position was a particularly exposed one, being

KILKEA CASTLE

situated in the Marshes which lay between the English pale and the territories of the native Irish. During the centuries since its erection it has undergone many alterations and enlargements down to its final restoration in 1849.

In 1356 Maurice, 4th Earl of Kildare, was commanded by the king to "strengthen and maintain his castles of Kilkea, Rathmore, and Ballymore, under pain of forfeiting the same." In 1426 the castle was enlarged by John FitzGerald, 6th Earl of Kildare. Again, about the year 1573, Gerald, the 11th Earl, repaired Kilkea after he was restored to the title and estates of which his half-brother, the "Silken Thomas," had been dispossessed. Three sculptured stones are still in existence belonging to a chimney-piece placed in the dining-hall by this Earl, and have, after various vicissitudes, been replaced in somewhat their original positions.

This Earl was called the "Wizard Earl," and the haunted room of the castle (which also contains a carved stone) is said to have been the place where he practised the Black Art. A legend regarding him runs thus:—His wife, not liking that he should have any secrets from her, begged him to let her be witness to some of his transformations and sorcery. At length he consented to give her three trials, but warned her that any sign of fear on her part would be fatal to him. First, the river Greese rose and flowed through the castle; secondly, an animal, half fish, half serpent, crept out of the water and twined round the lady's feet; and thirdly, a ghost flitted to and fro, but all these failed to frighten the Countess. Then the Earl was transformed into a little black bird, which lit on her shoulder; but the devil, in the form of a cat, springing at it, she stretched forth her hand with a cry to protect her lord. Hence he and all his knights were spirited away to the Rath of Mullaghmast, where they sleep by their horses' sides, fully clad in armour, and from thence they ride to

Kilkea Castle every seven years. The Earl's steed is shod with silver shoes, and as soon as they are worn out the spell will be broken, and he will return again to Kilkea, when, after about half a century, he will drive the ancient enemies of Ireland out of the country.

A lady writing of the castle in 1817, mentions the grand staircase being of massy oak, and amongst other things speaks of the ancient kitchen containing seven ovens. The building seems to have been somewhat dilapidated when the 3rd Duke of Leinster began to restore it (1849). Nearly all the battlements were thrown down, and its last tenant had made matters worse in searching for treasure. This same man, writing to the Duke in 1839, speaks of a carved oak ceiling in what had once been the castle chapel. This is said to have been on the north side.

During restoration a few quaint-shaped bottles containing liquid were found in a recess, and previously it is stated that an old gentleman sitting at a table, had been discovered built up in some part of the walls, but that he fell to dust at once when air was admitted.

Two underground passages are believed to connect the castle with the churchyard on the one hand, and a pagan tumulus or burial moat on the other.

The grooves of the portcullis by which the main entrance was protected are to be seen at the hall-door, and also the square holes for fixing beams of timber, which added to the security. The hall had a stone vaulted ceiling at the time of restoration, which was removed to give greater height. A new storey was also added to the building at this time.

The "Evil Eye Stone" is carved with a group of grotesque figures, and is situated 17 feet above the ground, in the quoin of the "Guard Room," near the entrance-gate of the ancient bawn of the castle.

Maurice FitzGerald, 3rd Baron of Offaly, seems to have parted temporarily with his interest in Kilkea to Christiana

KILKEA CASTLE

de Marisco, a niece of his wife's, through whom a royal claim on the manor was established. In 1317 it appears to have been in possession of the Wogan family. Sir Thomas de Rokeby, Lord Justice of Ireland, died in the castle in 1356.

In 1414, the O'Mores and O'Dempseys, having invaded the pale, Thomas Cranly, Archbishop of Dublin, and Lord Deputy, accompanied the Royal troops as far as Castledermot, where he and his clergy remained praying for the success of the arms. The opposing forces met at Kilkea, where a battle was fought, in which the Irish were defeated. A great many human bones having been found in a field south of the castle, it is likely to have been the scene of this conflict.

John FitzGerald, 6th Earl of Kildare, nicknamed "Shaun Cam," or Hump-back John, again defeated the native Irish at Kilkea in 1421.

It was here, too, that the "Great Earl," Gerald FitzGerald, 8th Earl of Kildare and Lord Deputy of Ireland, got his death wound. In August, 1513, he started on an expedition against a castle belonging to the O'Carrolls, and now known as Leap Castle, in the King's County. While the Earl was watering his horse at the River Greese, near Kilkea, attended by the Mayor of Dublin and a splendid retinue, he received a wound from one of the O'Mores of Leix, which in a few days proved fatal. He was moved by gentle stages to Kildare, where he died. He was thirty-three years Chief Governor of Ireland.

During the rebellion of the "Silken Thomas," 10th Earl of Kildare, in 1535, Kilkea seems at first to have formed one of the headquarters of his native sympathisers. The surrounding country having, however, been laid waste by the Earl of Ossory, we read that he made an appointment with Sir William Skeffington, the Lord Deputy, to meet him at Kilkea. He waited with his army for three days, but the Lord Deputy being ill, he did not arrive.

In 1537 the King appointed Lord (James) Butler to be Constable of the Castles of Catherlagh (Carlow) and Kilkea. Some years later a Walter Peppard, one of the gentlemen ushers of the King's chamber, seems to have been in possession of the castle.

The 11th Earl lived largely at Kilkea after the restoration of his title and lands. In 1575, when apprehended on suspicion of treason, one of the charges was that he had interviewed and entertained rebels at Kilkea.

Elizabeth, widow of the 14th Earl of Kildare, was granted the Manors of Kilkea and Graney by the King, as she had no jointure. She was a daughter of Lord Delvin, and had married the Earl by dispensation of the Pope, she being a Roman Catholic. In 1618 she wrote a most touching letter from Kilkea to the Privy Council, beseeching them to allow her the guardianship of her little son Gerald, the 15th Earl—then just over six years old—until he should be older and stronger, urging that he was "the only son of his father." The infant Earl died some two years later at Maynooth, being succeeded by his cousin George, known as the "Fairy Earl."

In 1634 the Countess gave Kilkea to the Jesuits, who retained possession of the castle until 1646, in which year the Superior of the Order entertained the Pope's Nuncio sumptuously at the castle.

During the civil war, which began in 1641, Kilkea was taken and re-taken several times; but on the restoration of peace, both the 16th and 17th Earls seem chiefly to have resided there.

In 1668 it was leased to Lord Brabazon, and afterwards, for nearly two centuries, the castle was inhabited by strangers, to whom it was let at different times.

In 1797 it passed into the hands of Thomas Reynolds, the '98 informer through the influence of Lord Edward FitzGerald. He somewhat repaired and furnished the castle. His son gives a graphic description of the wanton

KILKEA CASTLE

destruction of property by the soldiers sent from Dublin to arrest his father. It appears they tore up floors and down wainscotting, in a search for Lord Edward, who it was thought was hidden in the castle.

Shortly after this it became a regular garrison and a refuge for the Loyalists. It was attacked by the insurgents without success.

The castle was leased once more, in 1799, before the family again took possession of their ancient home.

Authorities Consulted.

Lord Walter FitzGerald, "Kilkea Castle" (*Kildare Archæological Society's Journal*).
Marquis of Kildare, "The Earls of Kildare."
State Papers.

KILKENNY CASTLE

THERE seems to be a difference of opinion regarding the derivation of this name. The most popular belief is that it signifies the Church of St. Canice or Kenny. Again it is put forward that a settlement of the Gaels having been along the banks of the Nore, the high ground towards the present castle was wooded, and so called Coil or Kyle-ken-uï, " the wooded head " or "hill near the river," and so it became Cillcannegh or Kilkenny.

The city is situated seventy-two miles south-west of Dublin, in the county of the same designation.

The fortress is said to occupy the site of the ancient Irish castellum of the kings of Ossory. It is built on high ground above the town, and the present entrance is through a handsome gate-house of Caen stone which was brought up the River Nore in boats. The 2nd Duke of Ormond, who succeeded in 1688, spent £1,500 on its erection, but the carving has only been completed in later years. A massive wooden door gives admittance from the Parade.

The castle seems formerly to have been a quadrangular building flanked by towers, having its entrance on the south side opposite the present gate-house. The building now forms three sides of a square, but in 1861 the foundations of the south curtain and the two bastions which protected the entrance were uncovered during alterations.

Thus up to the beginning of the eighteenth century the castle practically had its back to the town, and it is there-

KILKENNY CASTLE

KILKENNY CASTLE

fore likely that the architects of the Norman stronghold followed the ground plan of the old Irish fort, where King Donnchadh held his court during the greater part of the tenth century, and which existed long before the English town was built.

In the northern side of the building is situated the hall, billiard room, ante-room, library, and drawing-room. The west wing is occupied by the private rooms of the family, while the picture gallery forms the eastern block. This wing was added by the 2nd Duke of Ormond. It is 120 feet long by 30 broad, and contains some valuable portraits by Vandyck, Holbein, Lely, Kneller, &c.

The dining-room is part of the original building, and its walls measure some 15 feet in thickness.

The tapestry in the castle is very handsome. Some of it is supposed to have been manufactured in Kilkenny, where Piers, Earl of Ormond, and his wife, Margaret FitzGerald, started a tapestry industry, some of the records of which are still preserved. A set of panels representing the "History of Deceus" is the most valuable tapestry in the castle.

Of the three towers, that on the south being the largest is called "The Tower." The small turret in the north-west angle is part of the oldest masonry in the castle, and is supposed to belong to the twelfth-century fortress.

The Evidence Chamber contains an immense number of valuable historic documents and family records, among which are some deeds executed by Strongbow.

The first Norman fortress is supposed to have been erected by Richard, Earl of Pembroke, better known as Strongbow, shortly after his arrival in Ireland. In 1173 Donald O'Brien, King of Thomond, descended and seized the castle, its garrison of Flemings retreating to Waterford. They returned when the Irish had withdrawn and occupied what remained of the stronghold until William, Earl Marshal, arrived with Isabel, his bride, in 1191. She was the daughter and heiress of Eva and Strongbow, and had been brought up at the English Court. They were married in 1189, and he began to rebuild the Castle of Kilkenny in 1192. Thomas, 10th Earl of Ormond and favourite of Queen Elizabeth, repaired the castle. James, the 1st Duke of Ormond, remodelled the whole building after his return from exile with Charles II., in a style of architecture then common in France and Holland. Dr. Molyneux, writing in 1709, says: "There is not one handsome or noble apartment. The Rooms are Darke, and the stairs mighty ugly."

It is at present in castellated Tudor style. In 1826 the change of architecture was entrusted to Mr. William Robertson, and during the minority of the present Marquess his mother carried out many improvements.

A passage is reported to exist from the castle to Dunmore cave.

In Earl Mareschal's charter he granted the tenth part of the provisions in the castle to the Brotherhood of St. John. They were also to officiate in the castle chapel while the Earl was absent, but when at home his chaplain took their place.

The stronghold was inherited in succession by the Earl's five sons, who all died without heirs, and Kilkenny passed to his third daughter Isabel, who married Gilbert de Clare, 6th Earl of Clare, Hertford and Gloucester, and in 1290 we find him surrendering Kilkenny Castle to the King to hold at his pleasure.

In 1334 the 9th Earl of Clare died without issue, and was succeeded by his sister Eleanor de Clare, whose husband became Earl of Gloucester through her right. His grandson Spencer, Lord of Glamorgan and Kilkenny, sold the castle in 1391 to James Butler, 3rd Earl of Ormond.

Theobald Walter had been made Chief Butler of Ireland by Henry II., which appointment granted him a tun of

KILKENNY CASTLE

wine out of every nine brought to Ireland, and this privilege remained in the family until 1810, when the Government purchased it from Walter, the 1st Marquess of Ormond.

The gilt key which was worn at the girdle when the Butlers attended the King is still preserved at the castle.

A few years after the fortress had changed hands, King Richard II. spent a fortnight at Kilkenny as the guest of the Earl of Ormond.

The Carew MSS. inform us that the Earl of Ormond made Kilkenny Castle his chief residence in 1596.

The 1st Duke of Ormond was born in 1610, and is generally known as the "Great Duke." He was for many years Lord Lieutenant of Ireland.

In 1642 the castle was taken by the "Council of Confederate Catholics," and was held by them for some years.

Oliver Cromwell besieged both town and castle in March, 1650. On the 23rd he opened fire on the castle, and two days following a breach was made at noon, but the garrison twice beat off the besiegers and quickly repaired the damage.

Cromwell's time being short for the work before him, he was about to retire when the mayor and the townspeople offered to give up the town, and he was shortly reinforced by Ireton.

Sir Walter Butler had received instructions from Lord Castlehaven to surrender, in case no help arrived before a given time, so considering the weakness of his garrison he made terms with the Parliamentarians which were of an honourable nature. As the garrison marched out Cromwell complimented them on their gallantry, saying he had lost more men in the storming of Kilkenny than in the taking of Drogheda.

The estate was restored to the Duke upon the Restoration. The Count de Lauzun had been commander for

James II. at Kilkenny, and the castle had been carefully preserved by him.

The Duke died in 1688, and was succeeded by his son, who also was Lord Lieutenant of Ireland. William III. dined in the castle in August, 1690, as the Duke's guest.

In 1715 he was accused falsely of conspiring against the Crown, and in anger at the charge he crossed to France, and joined the Stuarts.

His estates, valued at £80,000 a year, were forfeited and he died at Avignon, supported by a pension from the Court of Spain.

The Irish House of Lords restored part of the estates and the Irish Earldom to another branch of the Ormonds, and John Butler became 17th Earl of Ormond.

Walter, the 18th Earl, was created Marquess in 1816, and from him the present representative is descended, who in 1904 entertained King Edward VII. and Queen Alexandra at the castle.

Authorities Consulted.

J. Hogan, "Kilkenny."
Brewer, "Beauties of Ireland."
J. Robertson, "Antiquities and Scenery of Kilkenny."
P. Egan, "Kilkenny Guide."
E. Ledwidge, "History of Irishtown and Kilkenny" in "Collectanea de Rebus Hibernices."
J. Graves, "Journey to Kilkenny, 1799" (*Journal of Kilkenny Archæological Society*).
MacMahon, "Kilkenny Castle" in "Historic Houses."
Calendar of State Documents.
Calendar of Carew MSS.

KILLIANE CASTLE

THIS fortress is situated in a parish of the same name in the Barony of Forth, about three miles south-east of Wexford. The name, which is written Killyan in the *Liber Regalis* visitations, signifies "The Church of St. Liedania."

The building consists of a castellated rectangular keep, to which a modern house has been attached. There is also an enclosed bawn with most excellently preserved walls. Near the castle stand the ruins of its chapel.

In the notes attached to the Down Survey Maps, dating from about 1657, it is stated that at Great Killiane is "a Castle with a slate house adjoining, a decayed windmill, and seven cabbins."

The castle is supposed to have been erected by the family of Hay, whose first representative in Ireland was Richard de Hay, Lord of Hay in Wales, who crossed with the Normans in 1196. From this family Killiane passed to a younger branch of the house of Chevers, of Ballyhally, early in the sixteenth century. Hamond Chevers, of Killiane, was one of the jurators to hold an inquisition on Tintern Abbey in 1543. He held his castle and lands from the Mayor of Wexford.

In 1627 Killiane was still in possession of a Hamond Chevers, and his son George held it with 237 acres when the rebellion broke out in 1641. He was present at the siege of Duncannon Fort in 1645, when it was defended against the Confederate Catholics by Laurence, Lord

Esmond, and in consequence of the part he took in the insurrection Killiane was confiscated. In 1666 it was granted to Francis Hervey, Esq., with 220 acres, and it has remained in this family's possession ever since.

One of the daughters of the house, who married the Very Rev. Samuel Adams, D.D., Dean of Cashel, in 1809, was so famous for her beauty that she was called "The Rose of Killiane." The family has not lived in the castle for some years, and it is let by the present owner, Arthur Hervey, Esq.

AUTHORITIES CONSULTED.

MSS. Ordnance Survey.
Down Survey Maps.
Inquisitions of Leinster.
Hore, "History of Wexford."
Lewis, "Typographical Dictionary of Ireland."
B. Adams and M. Adams, "History of the Adams Family
Proceedings Royal Society of Antiquaries, Ireland.
Chancery Patent Rolls, Act of Settlement.

KILLYLEAGH CASTLE

KILLYLEAGH CASTLE

> "Downpatrick too may boast
> Of the great fort by its side,
> Where a monarch may have lived,
> And have rul'd in savage pride ;
> But what is Patrick's grave,
> Or cathedral old and grey,
> To the proud baronial castle
> That adorns Killileagh ?"

THIS castle stands on rising ground above the town of Killyleagh, five miles north-east of Downpatrick, in the County of Down. It was the principal fortress of seven which formerly guarded the shores of Strangford Lough.

About a mile distant is *Loch Cleath*, or "The Lake of the Hurdles," so it is probable that Killyleagh signifies "the Church of the Hurdles."

The gate tower of the castle is entered under a Gothic arch of Glasgow stone from the main street of the town. It is 59 feet in height, and crowned with turrets. Curtain walls on each side connect it with flanking towers, which are again joined by other castellated walls to the castle itself, thus enclosing a rectangular courtyard, which is laid out in grass and flower-beds.

The mansion has an imposing frontage, flanked at both sides by circular towers. One of these dates from the castle's erection, and the other, which is a copy, from the year 1666. The centre block of masonry was entirely restored in the middle of the nineteenth century. Some of the walls, which were removed at that time, were

15 feet thick, being composed of rubble and excellent mortar.

The old carved stone over the door was copied in Caen stone. The Royal Arms are surmounted by a figure of Charles I., while below are the family arms. The original stone, which was much weather worn, has been placed over a small door at the side.

Most of the stone used at the restoration was quarried on the estate, but the facing stones were brought from Scotland.

One of the special attractions of this charming residence is the beautiful terraced gardens lying to the south. They consist of three tiers of cultivation beginning with the "Box Garden" of trim flower-beds, from which you descend by a flight of rustic steps to "the Rockery Garden" abounding in Alpine plants. Here some beautiful and extremely ancient yew-trees are to be seen, their branches being 120 feet in circumference, while below a small lake in the centre of rose-beds leaves nothing to be desired in its delightful effect.

The castle was erected by Sir John de Courcy shortly after his conquest of Ulster, and in 1356 Edward III. appointed John de Mandeville warden.

After this it fell into the hands of the O'Neills, who retained it up to 1561, when Queen Elizabeth granted the territory to Hugo White. He rebuilt the castle and removed the ward from Dufferin Castle near, to garrison it. After this it was known as "White's Castle" for many years.

In 1567 the fortress was gallantly defended against a fierce attack made by the great Shane O'Neill, and he was successfully repulsed. The strength of the White family gradually decreased, and in 1590 they could only muster a hundred and twenty foot soldiers and twenty horsemen to defend their lands, while eight years later twenty footmen was the total of their fighting strength.

KILLYLEAGH CASTLE

The M'Artans and O'Neills joined together and dispossessed them, the former family taking possession of Killyleagh. Their estates were, however, forfeited at the close of the sixteenth century for the part they took in the rebellion of the Northern Earls, and some time after this the lands were granted to the Hamiltons.

General Monk partly demolished the castle in 1649, and the Hamiltons began to rebuild it in 1666.

James I. had created the head of the family Earl of Clanbrassil and Viscount Clandeboye, but the last to hold the title died in 1676. It is said he was poisoned by his wife, Lady Alice of Clanbrassil, a daughter of the Earl of Drogheda, who was a beautiful and vicious woman, and after plunging the estate into debt desired to contract a wealthy marriage.

At this time the Earl's mother, Lady Anne, resided at Killyleagh Castle in accordance with the wishes of her husband's will.

As Earl Henry left no children the estate was divided amongst his cousins, Killyleagh falling to the lot of James Hamilton. When James died in 1683 his lands were divided between his brother Gawin, ancestor of the present Colonel Rowan-Hamilton, D.L., of Killyleagh Castle, and his daughter Anne, whose granddaughter, Dorcas, married Sir John Blackwood, and was created Baroness Dufferin and Clandeboye.

The division of the estate was accurately made and decided by lot, which had the effect of putting one branch of the family in possession of the half of the courtyard of the castle which lay nearest the town, while the other part was attached to the castle.

This division caused a family feud of some two hundred years in duration. A house was built on the disputed land between the town and castle, and it was only upon the coming of age of the late Marquis of Dufferin, who said it should never be said of him that he kept any man out of his own hall-door, that the contention ended.

The young nobleman presented the land to his kinsman of the castle, to be held by the tenure of the annual tribute of a red rose to the lady of Clandeboye, or should there be no such person, a pair of gilt spurs to the Lord Dufferin of the time. He added to his gift a castellated gate-house, which was erected from designs by Mr. Ferrers.

The last stone was laid by Lord Dufferin upon the morning of his marriage with Miss Rowan Hamilton on the 23rd of October, 1862.

It bears an inscription to that effect, as well as the name of its sculptor, Mr. Samuel Hastings, of Downpatrick.

In 1688-89 Sir Robert Maxwell resided in the castle, having married the widow of the Earl of Clanbrissal. Captain Savage asked to be allowed to garrison the gate-tower so as to be some check upon the disturbances the Protestant party were making in the North. Sir Robert took two days to consider the matter, but in the meantime the soldiers were attacked by Hunter, and the captain and lieutenant taken prisoners.

Soon after the castle was reduced by the Royalists, and in the investigation which followed much credit was taken from the fact that no plundering was allowed. It was stated that such forbearance was wonderful in the face of great provocation, inasmuch as the very day the castle was taken part of Colonel Mark Talbot's wig was shot off by a bullet from the fortress.

The celebrated United Irishman, Archibald Hamilton Rowan, owned and lived in the castle. He was secretary of the Dublin Society of United Irishmen in 1791, and in 1794 he was sentenced to two years' imprisonment for seditious libel.

The embroidered lavender dress coat, which he wore at his presentation to Marie Antoinette in 1781 or 1782, when

KILLYLEAGH CASTLE

in attendance on the Duchess of Manchester, is still preserved as an heirloom in the castle. A pair of pistols presented to Captain Hamilton, R.N., C.B., after the battle of Navarino, by the French Admiral De Rigny, for his gallant services to the French squadron, are also to be seen at Killyleagh.

In 1842 Captain Archibald Rowan Hamilton married Miss Caldwell, of Cheltenham, and seven years later they began to restore the castle.

In 1862 the marriage of the late Lord Dufferin and Clandeboye, with Hariot Georgina, eldest daughter of the late Captain Archibald Rowan Hamilton, 5th Dragoon Guards, was celebrated in the evening of October 23rd, in the drawing-room of the castle.

When the present owner of the castle, Colonel Gawen Rowan Hamilton, came of age in 1864, Lord Dufferin handed him the keys of the gate-tower, to which reference has already been made, saying, " The time is now come for me to hand over to you this gate-house, a gift which I had originally destined for your father, but which, with equal pleasure, I now make to you. I trust that you and your descendants may long continue to enjoy it."

AUTHORITIES CONSULTED.

Lowry, "The Hamilton Manuscripts."
Knox, "History of County of Down."
Praeger, "Official Guide to County Down."
S. M. S., "Killyleagh Castle, County of Down," in *Dublin Penny Journal*.
Hanna, "The Break of Killyleagh," in *Ulster Journal of Archæology*.
Newspaper Cuttings lent by Mrs. Rowan Hamilton.

KING JOHN'S CASTLE, CARLINGFORD

THIS is one of the few names in Ireland which clearly show a Danish influence. The Irish designation was Cairlinn, and the present name simply means the "*fiord* of Cairlinn," or Carlingford.

It is situated in the County of Louth, on the southern shore of the bay at the foot of the Mourne Mountains, about eleven miles east-north-east of Dundalk.

It was a most important town of the Pale, and at one time nearly every building of any size was of a fortified type. There are still to be seen the remains of three strongholds called at the present time King John's Castle, Taffe's Castle, and Lee's Castle.

King John's Castle is traditionally supposed to have been erected by that monarch's orders in 1210 to protect the mountain pass of Goulin. We know that King John was at "Kerlingford," but Grose considers that it is more likely the fortress was built by De Lacy or De Courcy.

It is situated on a rocky promontory which projects into the sea, and having been built in accordance with the natural formation of the rock is triangular in shape. It is divided in the centre by a "cross wall" nearly 12 feet thick. On the southern side the divisions of apartments are still to be seen, and there are also the remains of galleries with recesses for archers. The walls are about 11 feet in thickness, and on the sea side there is a small underground passage some 20 feet in length.

The chief entrance from the water was protected by a

KING JOHN'S CASTLE, CARLINGFORD

KING JOHN'S CASTLE, CARLINGFORD

platform or battery, which also commanded the harbour. It is said the promontory once extended further into the sea, and being covered with soft grass was called the "Green Quay."

In 1215 the King commanded Roger Pipard to deliver up the castle to any one the Archbishop of Dublin appointed to receive it. Richard de Burgh was ordered to give up the fortress to Geoffrey de Mariscis in 1216 or 1217, but this order was immediately followed by a similar one to William de Lacy, who had evidently taken the King's Castle at Carlingford.

In 1388 Stephen Gernon, the constable of the time, was licensed by the King to take corn tithes in the lordship of Cooley to supply the castles of Carlingford and Greencastle. Five years later Esmond de Loundres was appointed Warden of Carlingford, Greencastle, and Coly, with the profits due to the office. The O'Neill of that day so pillaged the country round that De Loundres was unable even to meet his expenses, and he petitioned that, the seignory being laid waste, he might be either relieved of office or properly supplied with means to meet the charges attached to it. Whereupon an order to provision the castles under his command was issued.

Fishing rights seem to have been attached to the castle in 1425, and more than a hundred years later they still formed a Government revenue. In 1535 the Treasurer went to Carlingford to inspect the King's castle. He reported that it and Greencastle with the country round had been almost destroyed, and that if the war was to continue English workmen would have to be sent over to put the castle in repair. He suggested that the expenses should be defrayed by the fishing dues.

This does not seem to have been done, for in 1549 both castles were in a dilapidated condition. Three years later Sir Nicholas Bagenall was granted "the Manor of Carlingford and an old castle there, and the whole demesne and manor of Mourne and Greencastle, the castle and demesne of the Black Friars in Carlingford." Ten years later it was still in his hands.

In 1596 the Earl of Tyrone, after having pretended to submit to the Government, made an incursion into the Pale. It seems that his foremost troops were commanded by his son-in-law, Henry Oge, who endeavoured to surprise the castle at Carlingford. This he was unable to accomplish, but, " missing of his principal purpose, there were carried away as prisoners, in lamentable manner, two gentlewomen, daughters of Captain Henshaw, the one married and the other a maid."

The Earl, who was following, had intended to reinforce the troops after the seizing of the town and fortress, but the failure of the enterprise prevented his doing so. He acknowledged having carried off the ladies from the castle " in time of peace," and refused to return them until O'Hanlon's son was liberated in exchange.

Marmaduke Whitechurch was constable of Carlingford in 1610, and had six warders under his command.

In 1641 " Sir Con Maginse tooke the forte and castle of the Neurie and Carlingfoorde."

The next year it was captured by a ruse graphically described as follows : " 5th of May. Newes came from Dundalk to the Lords Justices by Captaine Cadogan (who came thence through Maday with ten horse-men only) that the Newry was not only retaken by the Lord Conway and Munroe, the Scots commander, from the rebels, but also that the towne and castle of Carlingford were taken by a ship that came from Knockfergus. Their policy was to put up the Spanish colours, which the rebels discerning, sent a fisher-boat, with ten or twelve of their commanders, to goe aboard the ship, supposing that some ammunition was come unto them ; but the captaine of the ships, instead of shewing them any such commodities, clapt them up under decks, and so landing his musketiers,

KING JOHN'S CASTLE, CARLINGFORD 249

they took the towne, which they of the castle soone perceiving, fled away, and left both unto our forces."

In 1648 Lord Inchiquin marched on Carlingford after capturing Dundalk, and seems to have had little difficulty in getting possession of the town and fortress. The following year Colonel Venables appeared before the walls with Parliamentary forces. Upon his making preparation for the landing of cannon the town and castles were surrendered. In a letter to Oliver Cromwell he speaks with great praise of Captain Ferns, who "came to the harbour's mouth with his fregot, and upon a signal agreed between us, came gallantly in under fire," although his mainmast was split by a shot from the castle. He captured a small Wexford vessel then in the bay.

Carlingford was no mean prize, as it formed the chief storehouse of their opponents' arms in Ulster.

The three castles and the sea-fort contained in all seven pieces of ordnance, nearly 40 barrels of powder and the same of small shot, over a thousand muskets, and 480 pikes.

They did not find much provision in the town. The next day Newry surrendered.

The fortress must have been subjected to bombardment at some time, as cannon-balls have been found among the ruins.

AUTHORITIES CONSULTED.

Murphy, "Cromwell in Ireland."
Grose, "The Antiquities of Ireland."
Gilbert, "Affairs in Ireland, 1641–1652."
Graves, "King's Council in Ireland."
Joyce, "Irish Names of Places."
Parliamentary Gazetteer.
Calendar of Carew MSS.
State Documents.
State Papers.
Reeves, "Ecclesiastical Antiquities of Down, &c."
D., "Carlingford," in *Dublin Penny Journal*.

KING JOHN'S CASTLE, LIMERICK

LIMERICK CITY is situated on the Shannon, ninety-four miles south-west by west of Dublin. The name is a corruption of Luimneach, signifying "barren spot of land."

King John's Castle is one of the finest examples of Norman military architecture in the country. It was erected to guard Thomond Bridge, and was the citadel of the English town of Limerick.

The curtain wall by the river is about 200 feet long, and is flanked at both ends by round towers, each having a diameter of 50 feet, and with walls 10 feet thick. A third tower protects the north-east angle, while the corner towards the town had a square platform raised to the level of the battlements and capable of mounting five or six cannon. In the lower part of this structure was the sally port of the fortress.

The modern entrance is in Nicholas Street, but the former gate led into Castle Street, and was protected by a drawbridge. It was exceedingly narrow, and flanked by two massive towers, one circular and the other semi-circular. The arms of the city surmount the gate. A wet ditch surrounded the castle, and was supplied with water from the Shannon.

The oldest part of the structure is the tower nearest the bridge, which shows marks of bombardment.

The dilapidations caused by the guns have been

King John's Castle, Limerick

renovated with red brick, which was a happy idea of the contractor so as to preserve the old war marks.

The ancient battlements were not removed until the close of the eighteenth century, up to which time they were a favourite city promenade.

The castle, as its name indicates, was constructed at the command of King John, and the builders were ruthlessly encroaching on church land until the bishop remonstrated with the King, who issued a proclamation in 1207, ordering that the work should cease until his return, which was in 1210. He furnished the stronghold with every requisite of defence, and appointed a constable and chaplain.

There was a long uninterrupted line of constables from 1216, when Godfrey de Rupe, or Roche, was appointed, until the office was prospectively abolished by Act of Parliament in 1809 to cease with the life of the constable of that date, the Right Hon. Colonel Vereker, afterwards Viscount Gort, who died in 1842.

The chaplaincy was also an office of importance.

In 1217 Reginal de Breouse received the custody of the castle and city for a stated period of years, and in 1226 it was the only castle in Ireland which was not fortified against the King, Richard de Burgh holding it for him.

Twenty pounds were granted to Thomas de Winchester in 1326 to repair the walls, which were much decayed; and six years later the followers of the Desmonds, who were prisoners in the fortress, took possession of it, after killing the constable. The citizens soon recovered possession and put all the occupiers to death.

The Earl of Desmond was made constable for life in 1423, with leave to discharge the duty by deputy. He was granted £10 and some fishing dues to repair the building as "the greater part of it had fallen to the ground."

We learn from the State Papers that, Mr. Zouche having liberated O'Sullivan Beare, who had been captive at

Limerick in 1582, the castle no longer required a ward. But the following year it is stated that John Sheriff having let Patrick Fitzmaurice and his brother out of the castle cost the Queen £20,000.

Three years later the fortress was occupied only by a constable and porter, and was in much need of repair and a garrison.

Sir George Carew received an order to repair the building and provide a ward in 1600, so that it would be a fit residence for the President. He reported that unless part of the town were removed it was impossible to make the fortress really strong, and so he was merely able to add some storehouses, which he regretted, " for that this insolent town has need of a straight curb."

The death of the President prevented the intended repairs being carried out, and two or three hundred pounds were needed shortly after to roof the towers and the Great Hall, which had been begun, so that the assizes might be held in it. The arms were being much injured through the stronghold not being weather-proof.

In 1602 Father Archer informed the Spaniards of a way they could surprise the castle, he having learned it in Limerick during the previous rebellion.

The plan consisted of two or three Irish galleys coming up the river at night with the tide, and carrying about three hundred men, who would at once force the northern gate by breaking the wooden door with a "pittarr," as no watch was kept there. The castle once in their hands, attacks could be made from all the other sides of the town.

King James I. granted a charter to the city of Limerick in 1609, from which the castle is exempted.

In 1608 it was stated that a cellar existed under the stronghold, which could be entered from the town without observation. The following year great dilapidations are reported by Sir Josias Bodley. He said that the round towers near the river were so undermined by the water that

KING JOHN'S CASTLE, LIMERICK

a cart might pass below their foundations. He repaired the walls and towers, and built the square platform for cannon on the town side. He surrounded the whole with a moat and erected the drawbridge. A constable's house was still needed.

Repairs were again required in 1618 and 1624.

Captain George Courtenay with two hundred men maintained a most gallant siege in 1642. Though short of provisions, and with a garrison who were not all regulars, he managed to keep the Irish forces at bay for a considerable time.

The besiegers threw a great boom across the Shannon, formed of aspen trees fastened together with iron links, so as to prevent Sir Henry Stradling provisioning the castle by the water gate.

A steady fire from the fortress delayed the work for some days, but the boom was eventually fixed and the remains of it could be seen at low water so late as 1787.

The castle was next bombarded from the cathedral, but still the brave defenders held out. Then mines were begun in three places, the roofs being propped with dry timber smeared with tar. When completed this was ignited and the cavern falling made a large breach in the wall of the castle.

Seeing defence was no longer possible Captain Courtenay capitulated on the 21st of June, obtaining honourable terms for himself and the garrison. Lord Muskerry took possession the next day.

The captured cannon were used to reduce the neighbouring castles. It is said that the great gun which was mounted on the platform next the town took 35 yoke of oxen to draw it.

Ireton arrived at Limerick in 1651, and began to bombard the castle from the foot of Thomond Bridge. As soon as a breach was effected twenty dragoons, in complete armour, led by Captain Hackett, rushed in, followed by infantry. The Irish fled across the bridge into the further town, breaking two of the arches to prevent pursuit. Barrels of gunpowder were found in the vaults of the castle with lighted matches ready to ignite them.

It seems from the following inscription which was inserted in the south-west tower near the platform that repairs were carried out after these sieges : " Contrived by Lef. Vanderstam, General of their Majesties' Ordnance, Anno 1691–2."

In 1787 infantry barracks for about four hundred men were erected within the old walls.

The castle is now used as a Government ordnance store.

Authorities Consulted.

M. Lenihan, " Limerick : Its History and Antiquities."
J. Ferrar, " History of Limerick."
J. Dowd, " Limerick and its Sieges."
FitzGerald and M'Gregor, " History of Limerick."
Proceedings of Kilkenny Archæological Society.
Joyce, " Irish Place Names."
Parliamentary Gazetteer.
State Papers.
Carew MSS., with Book of Howth.
State Documents.

LEA CASTLE

This castle is situated on the banks of the Barrow in the north-east corner of the Barony of Pornahinch, in the Queen's County.

The name is sometimes spelt Ley or Leagh, and is said to signify "grey" or "grey land," though a legend traces its origin to the name of a great chieftainess who lived, and was treacherously slain, on the plain of Lea.

The fortress consisted of a three-storeyed rectangular building 60 feet by 46 feet, flanked by round towers and having walls varying in thickness from 8 to 10 feet. The west side of the structure has been blown up, but the remaining tower contains five rooms, one of them having thicker walls than the rest, *i.e.*, 13 feet instead of 12.

The centre of the castle was built on arches, and the projecting angles of the towers were connected by a curtain wall nearly 8 feet thick.

The approach was by a causeway 100 feet in length. It was surrounded by a ditch 25 feet wide, which could be filled by water from the Barrow. From this it was called Port-na-hinch, or the "Castle of the Island," from which the barony takes its name. Inside the moat was a low wall, which can still be traced. All the arches are round except one leading from the causeway to the bawn, which is pointed.

Two drawbridges and two bastions defended the gate into the inner ballium, which measured 140 feet by 130 feet. The remains of the barbican can still be seen.

The outer ballium includes the bawn, and the inner one contained a tennis court and tilt yard.

Some authorities state the castle was erected by Baron Offaly, while again it is said to owe its origin in about 1260 to William de Vesey, who had married the Earl of Derby's daughter, whose mother was heiress to William Mareschal, Lord Palatine of Lea. The daughter of O'More, Prince of Leix, is also said to have built Lea Castle on the Barrow in the marches of Inch, 1260.

LEA CASTLE (INTERIOR).

It appears, however, to have been in existence in 1203, as there is an order to the Justiciary of Ireland to have the castle delivered, as well as other possessions, which had belonged to Gerald FitzMaurice, and in 1257 William Marshall, Earl of Pembroke, received a grant of the wardship of Maurice, 2nd Baron of Offaly, and also his castles of Lea and Geashill.

In 1264 a meeting was held at Castledermot to settle some dispute about land in Connaught, but at it Maurice, Baron of Offaly, and his nephew, John FitzThomas, seized

LEA CASTLE

Richard de Burgh, heir to the Earl of Ulster, the Lord Justice Richard de Capella, Theobald Butler, and John Cogan, and imprisoned them in Lea.

Thomas de Clare sold the wardship of Maurice FitzGerald's heirs and the guardianship of Lea Castle to Sir William de Valence in 1270 for 3,500 marks. The wardship had been granted to De Clare by the King's eldest son. At this time, the Book of Howth states, it was the only fortress held by the English in Offaly. In 1274, however, an order was issued to restore the custody of FitzGerald's heirs to Roger and Matilda de Mortimer, who had, it seems, inherited the privilege, and De Valence only having paid 2,300 marks was not held liable for the rest of the money in consequence.

The castle was burnt by the O'Dempseys, O'Dunnes, and O'Carrols in 1284, and Theobald Verdon going to avenge the outrage was entirely routed. It was shortly afterwards restored by De Vesey, the Lord Justice of Ireland.

Here, with the assistance of Baron Offaly, he imprisoned the Red Earl of Ulster and his brother in 1294, but they were liberated the following year by order of the Parliament at Kilkenny, and the Earl's sons were surrendered as hostages instead. It is said De Vesey then quarrelled with John FitzThomas FitzGerald, Baron Offaly, and fled to France to avoid meeting him in single combat, and by this means Lea Castle lapsed again to the Geraldines.

John FitzThomas was ordered to repair to the King abroad in 1297, and £40 was granted to him to fortify his Castle of Ley.

The castle was besieged and the town burnt in 1307 by the "tories" of Offaly, but the former was relieved by John FitzThomas and Sir Edmund Butler, afterwards Earl of Carrick.

Baron Offaly restored the fortress and erected a church with steeple and bells, but in 1316 Robert Bruce burnt the castle and town, and carried off the bells.

Sir Walter Eustis is said to have been stabbed to death in the castle by his wife's sister, daughter of the O'More, who had formerly rejected his addresses, but upon the birth of her sister's child, she murdered Sir Walter in a fit of jealousy, and retired to the convent at Kildare, where she confessed her crime and died penitent.

The O'Dempseys' seized the fortress in 1329, but the next year it was surrendered to Sir John Darcy, Lord Justice, who restored it to the Earl of Kildare to keep for the King. The O'Dempseys again laid siege to the castle in 1339, but were driven off by the Earl.

O'More, Chief of Leix, burnt Lea in the spring of 1346, but in the following November he was defeated by the Earl of Kildare, who rebuilt the town, castle, and church, but not the steeple.

The fortress was again taken by O'More and O'Dempsey in 1414. Seven years later they were defeated near Kilkea Castle by the 6th Earl of Kildare, nicknamed "Shaun Cam," or Hump-backed John.

Lea Castle was restored to the Earl after the battle of the Red-bog of Athy.

The Four Masters mention the castle in 1452.

In 1533 the Earl of Kildare furnished the stronghold with guns and ammunition out of the King's store, and in direct opposition to his commands, which the Master of the Rolls pointed out to him in the presence of the Bishop of Meath.

The following year it is reported to have been one of the six best castles of the Geraldines, and it was the chief stronghold of Lord Offaly, the "Silken Thomas," during his rebellion, after the fall of Maynooth.

There is a letter from the former constable of this latter fortress, written in 1535, to Cromwell, saying that Lord Thomas had removed the Countess's apparel to Ley, as well as other valuables, and that he, Boyce, had resigned his office in consequence of the insurrection.

LEA CASTLE

The Carew MSS. record the Castle of Ley was of "no value" in 1537, and state it was granted to James Fitz-Gerald after the attainting of the Earl. In 1548 he required two gunners at the King's charge, and powder and shot.

Thomas Scotte petitioned to lease it in 1549.

In 1554 the Lord Deputy, Thomas Earl of Sussex, is said to have taken it from Patrick O'More, but it was regained by Anthony O'More in 1598, after which he defeated Essex at the Pass of Ballybrittas, called the "Pass of Plumes" from those worn by the gay English soldiers.

Lea was held by the Irish in 1641 upon the breaking out of the rebellion, but afterwards the loyalists took possession under the command of Lord Lisle. They planted an ash-tree to commemorate the event which lived 170 years, and had a girth of from 29 to 33 feet, while its shade had a diameter of 60 feet.

In 1642 Lord Castlehaven retook Lea, and at this time some of the brass money known as St. Patrick's halfpennies was struck here. These coins have the letter L on them and are very rare.

O'Neill is said to have lodged in the castle.

The Parliamentary Colonels, Hudson and Reynolds, took and dismantled the fortress in 1650.

It was repaired and held by lease under the Crown by an O'Dempsey until confiscated after the fall of the Stuarts. In 1695 it was granted to the Earl of Meath as part of Sir Patrick Trant's estate.

A horse stealer called O'Dempsey and nicknamed "Shamas a Coppuil," or "James the Horse," inhabited it at the beginning of the eighteenth century until the Government interfered.

Hampden Evans owned it in 1791, and it afterwards passed to Viscount Carlow.

The following legend was related by Widow Gorman

in 1818 to Miss French of Glenmolire, and noted by her:—

Redmond M'Comon O'Byrne, chief of Donamace and Leagh, had two gigantic sons named Roderick and Maurice. The latter was married to a daughter of The O'Neill and had one son called Connell.

Upon the death of the old chieftain O'Byrne, he divided his territory between his sons, leaving Donamace to the elder, Roderick, and Leagh to the younger, Maurice.

Roderick, believing he should have inherited all his father's possessions, determined to murder his brother.

LEA CASTLE (EXTERIOR).

One stormy night he set out alone from Donamace, and having tied his horse beneath a grove of ash-trees near the castle of Lea, he let himself in by the postern, with the key of which his unsuspecting brother had entrusted him.

Reaching Maurice's chamber he murdered him in cold blood, but not before his victim had cried out to his son to revenge his death by a brother's hand.

Roderick seized the body and, carrying it to where he had left his horse, put it into a leather bag that he had brought with him. Arriving at Dunamace he threw the body into a very deep well, thinking it would never be discovered.

Maurice's son, Connell, had heard his father's cry for

LEA CASTLE

vengeance in his dreams, but upon awaking and finding his father gone, with blood stains on the floor and stairs, he knew he had actually heard his voice.

The young chieftain, armed with two great sabres of equal size, proceeded to his uncle's stronghold, and presenting himself before him, demanded satisfaction. In the duel which followed both combatants were killed, and it is said no grass grows in their footsteps on the rock until this day.

The old well is still shown, and if two friends visit it together one is said to die within the year.

There seems to be no historical record of the fortress ever having been in possession of the O'Byrnes.

Authorities Consulted.

Grose, "Antiquities of Ireland."
O'Byrne, "History of the Queen's County."
MS. Ordnance Survey.
Comerford, "Kildare and Leighlin."
Marquis of Kildare, "Earls of Kildare."
Joyce, "Irish Names of Places."
State Documents.
State Papers.
Carew MSS.
Parliamentary Gazetteer.
"Lea Castle, Queen's Co.," in *Dublin Penny Journal*.
Lord Walter FitzGerald, "Kilkea Castle," in *Journal of Kildare Archæological Society*.
Miss French, MS.

LEAP CASTLE

THE ancient stronghold of the O'Carrolls, of Ely-O'Carrol, is situated in the parish of Aghancon, in the Barony of Ballybritt, King's County, about five miles south-east of Birr.

Its former name of Leim-Ui-Bhanain denoted "The Leap of O'Banan," and it is still known as "The Leap" in the district.

There are several legends to account for its designation. One is that two brothers came to the rock on which the castle is built, and they decided that whichever of them survived, after leaping to the ground below, should erect the stronghold. One of the two was killed by the jump.

Another story of a leap is told of a period long after the castle was built. Sometime during the sixteenth century the O'Carrolls' fortress was besieged by the English forces, and in a sortie the garrison took prisoner a young Captain Darby, who was with the attacking party. The room where he was imprisoned in the castle is still shown. The daughter of the chief was deputed to carry him his food, which was delivered through a hole in the wall. But the young Englishman made good use of his slender opportunities by winning the heart of the Irish maid, so that she connived at his escape by unbarring his prison. When running down the stone stairs which led to the cell in which he had been confined, he met her brother coming up, who raised the alarm regarding the escaping captive. Nothing daunted, young Darby turned and

LEAP CASTLE

ascended to the battlements, where, it is said, he leaped from the castle roof into a large yew-tree, the roots of which have only lately been removed. That the young couple were eventually married is a satisfactory ending to the romance, and certain it is that Leap Castle passed to the Darby family as the marriage portion of an O'Carroll's daughter who married a Darby, son of an English knight.

The castle is supposed to have been built by the Danes prior to the English invasion, during their conflicts in these parts with the more recently landed Norwegians. The structure resembles their form of defence, being of pyramidical shape, and built in the rubble masonry of that period, with pre-Norman arches and small loopholes for the discharge of arrows and javelins. The walls vary from 15 to 25 feet in width. There are several stone stairways in the thickness of the walls, and parts of them are brightly polished from constant use. The keep is the oldest construction, and it forms the hall of the present edifice. The wings, one at each side, were built at the end of the sixteenth or beginning of the seventeenth century. That on the north-west connects what is known as the "Priest's House" with the main building. This dwelling is of fourteenth-century masonry, and was used as the chief residence of the family in times of peace.

In the top of the keep is situated what is known as "The Bloody Chapel," having been desecrated by one Teige O'Carroll, who murdered his brother before the altar. It was formerly covered with a stone roof, but this gave way last century. A curious old stone-fastening remains that formerly received the bar of the door.

Off the chapel is the oubliette, formerly supplied with a spring death-trap. Not so very long ago three cart-loads of bones were removed from it and buried in consecrated ground. Bits of several old watches were found among the remains.

Large dungeons are situated below the keep, and there are many bricked-up passages and secret chambers. One of the former is said to lead to a neighbouring rath. The guard-room on the south-east side is hewn out of the rock. Numerous bones have been found in different parts of the building.

The site of the castle was evidently chosen to guard the river ford and the pass of the Slieve Bloom Mountains into Tipperary. Many bones have been found in a field near the river. A village once surrounded the castle, but only the ruins of the houses now remain.

The O'Carrolls, whose chief stronghold the castle was, are supposed to have wrested it from its original builders, the Danes.

In 1154 Henry II. granted Ely O'Carroll to Theobald de Walter, but he was entirely unable to take possession of any but the lower portion of the kingdom.

In 1489 John O'Carroll died of plague at Leap. The visitation was at this time so bad that hundreds of bodies lay unburied.

Gerald Fitz-Gerald, 8th Earl of Kildare and Lord Deputy of Ireland, set out for Leamyvannan in 1513 to put down a rising of the O'Carrolls. He failed to take the castle, "as was seldom the case with him," and retreated to collect fresh forces.

Returning with a splendid company he was shot by an O'More while watering his horse at the River Greese, near Kilkea, and he died a few days later at Kildare.

Three years afterwards his son attacked Leap, and took the stronghold, of which it is recorded, "there was scarcely any castle at that period better fortified and defended than this, until it was demolished upon its warders."

In 1522 the Earl of Kildare made it a charge against his rival, Sir Piers Butler, Lord Deputy, that he had lent O'Carroll cannon to defend Leap against him in 1516.

The charge was hardly denied, but the defence was put forward that the attack on O'Carroll was unwarranted.

Mulrony O'Carroll died at Leap in 1532. It is recorded that he was "a triumphant traverser of tribes; a jocund and majestic Munster champion, a precious stone, a carbuncle gem, the anvil of the solidity, and the golden pillar of the Elyans."

He was succeeded in the chieftainship by his son, Ferganainm, but the succession was disputed by a senior branch of the family who were in possession of Birr. Ferganainm enlisted the aid of his father-in-law, the Earl of Kildare, who received a wound during the dispute which hurried his end.

It was, no doubt, at this time that a terrible massacre took place at Leap Castle upon the rival branch of the sept, who had been invited to the stronghold under the guise of friendship. Lord Deputy Grey may have had this act of treachery in his mind when writing of O'Carroll, Baron of Ely, in Edward VI.'s reign, he speaks of him as "false." It is stated that this O'Carroll made submission to Lord Leonard Grey in 1537.

Twenty years later (1557) the Earl of Sussex, Lord Justice, made a hosting into Fircall, penetrating into Ely, where he took Leap Castle. But this expedition seems, mainly, to have been directed against the O'Connors, who had taken refuge there after their escape from Meelick Castle, and "the goodness of his steed" is said to have saved O'Connor from his pursuers, who took the Leap without opposition. O'Carroll became repossessed of the stronghold shortly afterwards.

There was a Jonathan Darby, Captain of Sussex Horse, in 1553, and perhaps it was during this expedition that the romance before related took place. A tomb in the neighbouring graveyard records the death of a Jonathan Darby in 1601.

It is said an inquisition was called at Lemyvanane

in 1568 for the preparation of a deed by which Ely O'Carroll was surrendered to the king by "Sir William O'Kerroll," to whom it was restored by letters patent, but there is some confusion about the dates and conditions of the several transfers.

In 1604 Ely O'Carroll was annexed to the King's County.

During the Parliamentary wars, Mr. Darby, of Leap, espoused the King's cause, and tradition avers that Cromwell appeared before the castle saying that if they did not surrender in twenty-four hours he would blow them out with a pump-stick. The fortress was not tenable in the event of cannon being used, as it is commanded from many points.

A weird story is told of the Jonathan Darby of the time, usually known as "the wild Captain." It is said before he surrendered the castle he collected all his money and treasure and with the aid of two servants hid it somewhere in the walls of the fortress. He then sent one of them for his sword and in the meantime threw the other over the battlements. Upon the messenger returning he slew him with the weapon he brought, evidently thinking "a secret is only safe with three when two are dead." Later he was arrested on a charge of high treason and imprisoned in Birr. He was several times reprieved, and at last liberated, his legs having mortified. Upon his return he was only capable of murmuring "My money, my money," but was quite unable to say where it was concealed.

In 1691 a Captain Darby, of the Leap, is alleged to have committed many deeds of daring against rapparees. It would appear that the estate was mortgaged for a nominal sum to one John Holland for fear of confiscation, for Charles II. re-granted the land to this Holland as mortgagee.

Admiral Darby, who commanded the *Bellerophon* at

the battle of the Nile, 1798, was one of the Darbys of Leap.

The present owner is Jonathan Charles Darby, Esq., D.L., who resides in the castle.

AUTHORITIES CONSULTED.

Donovan, "Annals of the Four Masters."
Cooke, "History of Birr."
Cooke, "Picture of Parsonstown."
G. Story, "Impartial History of Ireland."
R. Bagwell, "Ireland Under the Tudors."
J. Brewer, "Beauties of Ireland."
Parliamentary Gazetteer.
Lord Walter Fitzgerald, "Kilkea Castle" (*Kildare Archæological Society's Journal*).

LEIXLIP CASTLE

THE castle is situated in the portion of Leixlip which extends into North Salt Barony in the County Kildare. The fortress occupies a commanding position at the juncture of the Rivers Rye-water and Liffey, above the famous Salmon Leap from which the designation Leixlip is derived, being a Danish name from the old Norse word "Lax-hlaup," *i.e.*, Salmon Leap. From the word "Saltus," a leap, the baronies of Salt have also taken their name.

The castle is generally supposed to have been erected by the De Hereford family towards the close of the twelfth century. The present building consists of two blocks at right angles, facing east and south. The east wing probably incorporates part of the twelfth-century keep, and with the north-east circular tower represents the oldest portion of the structure, although it has been pierced by modern windows.

In this part a room is still shown in which tradition states that King John slept during his stay in Ireland.

The square south-east tower is not so old, and its erection is generally ascribed to the Geraldines.

The lands of Leixlip were granted to Adam de Hereford by Strongbow shortly after the Normans arrived in 1170. At the close of the thirteenth century the castle and lands had passed to the Pypards. In 1302 Ralph Pypard surrendered all his castles, &c., to the Crown, and in consequence Richard de Bakeputz, who was constable of Leixlip, was ordered to deliver it up to the King.

LEIXLIP CASTLE

Leixlip Castle was included in the list of those fortresses that were only to have Englishmen as constables by the statute passed in 1494.

Henry VII. granted the castle and lands to Gerald, 8th Earl of Kildare, upon his marriage with Dame Elizabeth Saint John, between the years 1485 and 1509, and they remained in the possession of the FitzGeralds until the rebellion of "The Silken Thomas" in 1534, in which the owner, Sir James "Meirgach" (*i.e.*, the winkled) FitzGerald was concerned. In 1536 an Act was passed by which the Crown became possessed of the castle and manor.

Two years after Mathew King, of Dublin, surrendered the castle, which appears to have been granted to him for twenty-one years. In 1568 William Vernon, gentleman, was leased the manor of Leixlip, containing castles, &c., by the Crown. Nine years later Sir Nicholas Whyte, Master of the Rolls, came into possession. He was a son of James Whyte, of the County Waterford.

In 1570 he was granted the manor of Leixlip, two castles, a water-mill, a salmon-weir, two fishing-places called the Salmon Leap, on the River Anna Liffey, Priortown Meade, and other demesne lands. Two years later he was made Master of the Rolls.

Sir Nicholas Whyte was succeeded by his son Andrew, whose son was again Sir Nicholas Whyte, Knt.

This Sir Nicholas held the manor of Leixlip upon the breaking out of hostilities in 1641. In company with Lord Dunsany, Patrick Barnwall, Sir Andrew Aylmer, and other chief men of the Pale, he surrendered himself to the Lords Justices Parsons and Borlace. This was done in obedience to the King's proclamation to show that they had no part in the rebellion, but they were imprisoned in Dublin Castle and most inhumanly treated.

In the diary of Captain William Tucker he records going from Dublin to Naas in 1641 with the Marquis of

Ormond, and sleeping a night in Leixlip Castle. He mentions that the owner, Sir Nicholas Whyte, was at the time a prisoner in Dublin.

In 1646 General Preston established his chief quarters in the fortress, and in November of that year the Confederate Catholics halted in their march on Dublin between Leixlip and Lucan. They were commanded by Generals Preston and Owen Roe O'Neill. The King's secretary and minister, Digby, was at Leixlip with Preston.

Plots and counter plots among the Confederate commanders made the once formidable army of no avail. Owen Roe, fearing some treachery, threw a wooden bridge across the Liffey, as a flood had destroyed the permanent one, and withdrew his forces into Meath.

Sir Nicholas Whyte recovered his lands of Leixlip by a Decree of Innocence. He died in 1654, and was buried at Leixlip.

Various historians have confused the fortress popularly called Leixlip Castle with a stronghold of less note designated the "Black Castle" of Leixlip, situated at the eastern end of the town. Although still known as the "Black Castle" this building has been so modernised that its original fortified structure is not noticeable.

That some discrepancies as to ownership existed in the written history of Leixlip Castle was first noted in 1901, but it was not until the following year that Lord Walter FitzGerald, in a note in the *Journal of the Kildare Archæological Society*, gave an extract from "The Civil Survey" of James Peisley and Henry Makepeace of 1654, in which the "Black Castle" of Leixlip is mentioned as belonging to the Earl of Kildare and "one ruined castle" to Sir Nycholas White, thus establishing the fact that there were two distinct castles at Leixlip owned by different persons.

The "Black Castle" is therefore no doubt the fortress alluded to in an inquisition held in September, 1612, which states that Gerald FitzGerald, son of Gerald, late Earl of Kildare, and uncle of Gerald, late Earl of Kildare, was seized of one castle, three messuages, one ruined water-mill, and forty acres of arable land at Leixlip. And again in 1621 the inquisition taken upon the death of Gerald, 15th Earl of Kildare, includes the Castle of Leixlip, &c. While the rental of the Earl of Kildare in 1657 mentions the black castle of Leixlip with sixty acres of land valued at £15 a year.

Leixlip Castle was purchased by the Right Hon. William Conolly, Speaker of the Irish House of Commons, at the beginning of the eighteenth century. He subsequently built the mansion of Castletown at Celbridge, but his nephew and heir occupied Leixlip Castle during the famine years of 1740 and 1741.

After this period the castle has been inhabited by many distinguished tenants.

It was a favourite residence of Primate Stone, and during Lord Townshend's period of office he usually passed the summer there.

Many stories are told of this Viceroy's fancy for mixing incognito with "all sorts and conditions of men."

One day Lord Townshend met a journeyman cutler named Edward Bentley in the demesne of Leixlip Castle and began to talk to him. Bentley was loud in his praises of the Lord Lieutenant's kindness in allowing the public into the grounds of his residence, but he was equally vehement in denouncing the political views he held.

Mistaking the proprietor for one of the retainers, he offered him half a crown upon leaving, and when it was refused the cutler commented on the difference between his action and that of the gate-keeper who had demanded that amount.

Lord Townshend then took him to the castle and provided him with a cold repast, but as he was escorting his departing and grateful visitor through the hall the unfortunate gate-keeper came in.

The Lord Lieutenant asked him why he had dared to disobey orders and receive money from visitors. Whereupon the man fell upon his knees and asked pardon. Bentley, at last realising who had been his entertainer, immediately followed suit. Lord Townshend sent for his sword, and the cutler was quite certain that his last hour had come. The Lord Lieutenant flourished the weapon over his head and brought it down smartly on the terror-stricken man's shoulder, saying, "Rise, Sir Edward Bentley." The new-made knight was appointed cutler to His Excellency, and lived long to enjoy his honour.

Viscount Townshend's wife died at Leixlip Castle.

The Hon. George Cavendish remodelled the building and brought it up to modern requirements during his tenancy before 1837.

John Michael, Baron de Robuck, subsequently lived there, and was drowned in the Liffey in 1856 during a flood.

In 1878, Captain the Honourable Cornwallis Maude, son of the Earl of Montalt, took the castle after his marriage. He was killed at Majuba Hill.

The present occupier is William Mooney, Esq., J.P.

This fortress is one of the oldest inhabited houses in Ireland. It has been said that the novelist Maturin founded one of his weird plots on a legend relating to Leixlip Castle, but the statement requires verification.

An underground passage runs from the castle, beneath the Byewater, to St. Mary's Church, where it terminates in a vault under the building, the end being now walled up.

AUTHORITIES CONSULTED.

Lord Frederick FitzGerald, "Leixlip Castle," and Lord Walter FitzGerald, Note, in *Journal of the Archæological Society of the County Kildare.*

LEIXLIP CASTLE

Proceedings of Royal Society of Antiquaries.
"History of St. Wolstan's," in *Irish Builder* for 1899.
P. (Petrie ?), "Town and Castle of Leixlip," in *The Irish Penny Journal*.
Parliamentary Gazetteer.
Book of Survey and Distribution.
Calendar of Patent Rolls, Ireland.
Book of Inquisitions of Province of Leinster.
Fiants of Elizabeth.
Transcripts of Inquisitions.
MS. Ordnance Survey of Ireland.

LISMORE CASTLE

THIS castle takes its name from a rath now known as Round Hill, *lis* meaning "fort," and *mor* "great." It is situated on the right bank of the River Blackwater, about four and a half miles north-by-east of Tallow, in the county of Waterford.

When Henry II. visited Lismore in 1171 he seems to have formed the plan of turning the ancient and famous Abbey of Mochuda into a fortified episcopal residence; hence in 1179 Milo de Cogan and Robert FitzStephen were sent by his directions to choose the site for this stronghold, which was to act as a protection against the "mere Irish."

In all probability the tapering tower, now known as "Sir Walter Raleigh's Tower," formed part of the ecclesiastical buildings. It is constructed of rude rubble, and has plain loops and cornices. The entrance is on the second floor, and this leads into buildings of later date, so that it has no external doorway. A somewhat similar tower was destroyed by fire prior to 1864, which may (with the one now standing) have protected a gate between the upper and lower courts.

The outer wall, with its beehive-roofed bastions at the corners, and the old gate, which has its archway decorated with chevrons, are likely to have been of twelfth-century construction.

The entrance to the castle is by "the Riding House," so called from its having formerly been guarded by two

LISMORE CASTLE

mounted sentries, the niches for the horses being still shown. This leads into a long shaded avenue, flanked by high walls which extends to the opening of the lower courtyard. Over the gate are the arms of the first Earl of Cork, and the motto "God's Providence is our inheritance." "King John's Tower" is situated to the right of the entrance, and the "Carlisle Tower" on the left. This latter is about 240 feet in height, and was erected to commemorate the Lord Lieutenancy of the Earl of Carlisle. It is constructed of coarse rubble. The stone for the dressing of its windows and for other parts of the castle was quarried at Chatsworth, and brought over in specially chartered vessels.

The "Flag Tower" flanks the north-east angle, and the oldest wing faces east towards the garden. The upper court is reached through a passage on the west of the entrance, and here Sir Walter Raleigh's tower is situated to the north.

The whole fortress is built upon a rock, which on one side descends precipitously to the Blackwater, the base being clothed with trees.

The Earl of Cork employed "a free Mazon of Bristol" during his alterations. The modern improvements were principally designed by Sir Joseph Paxton.

The main door has an Ionic porch executed in Bathstone, said to have been the work of Inigo Jones.

The hall is square, and is used as a billiard-room. A stone stairway ascends on the left side of the entrance. The present banqueting hall was originally a chapel, and has a Gothic roof of open woodwork. The drawing-room contains a large bay window overhanging the river, known as "King James's Window." During his stay in Ireland in 1689, he spent a night in the castle, and dining in this room, he approached the window, but started back when he saw the depth below.

The sword and mace of Youghal are exhibited in the

hall, where is also the Pastoral Staff of Lismore, which was discovered built up in a doorway of the castle with a valuable Irish manuscript book, since called the "Book of Lismore."

In 1181 Cullen O'Cullane, and O'Phelan, Prince of the Decies, attacked the fortress, which had been somewhat hastily constructed, and they killed fifty to eighty of the garrison and razed the stronghold.

LISMORE CASTLE.

Prince John, Earl of Morton, landing at Waterford in 1185, rebuilt the castle on a larger scale.

Nine years later the men of the Decies took the fortress by surprise and killed Robert Barry, brother of Giraldus Cambrensis. In the autumn of the same year (1189) the Irish, finding they could not hold the castle, decided to destroy it, but they afterwards surrendered it upon terms. From this time it appears to have been an episcopal residence for some four hundred years.

In 1218 the Bishop of Waterford wrote to Henry III.

complaining that the castle of Lismore had been taken from him by Thomas FitzAnthony and Griffin FitzGriffin. The King ordered that it should be restored to the bishop.

When Robert de Bedford was elected Bishop of Lismore the fortress was transferred to him, but not without the Bishop of Waterford declaring it belonged to his see. Bishop de Bedford appealed to Rome, and after a dispute of twelve years it was finally confirmed to the see of Lismore.

In 1271 Lord Justice Audley came on a visit to the castle, and Roger de Mortimer, after he landed at Youghal as Lord Justice, was the guest of Bishop Fleming at Lismore in 1317.

Some time before his resignation in 1589, Meler Magrath, Bishop of Lismore and Archbishop of Cashel, granted the castle to Sir Walter Raleigh at a rent of £13 6s. 8d., and three years later Sir Walter sold it to Sir Richard Boyle, afterwards the first Earl of Cork, who restored and enlarged it.

His great son, the philosopher, was born in the castle in 1626.

The stronghold was besieged three times during the civil wars of 1641. It was first attacked by five thousand Irish troops under the command of Sir Richard Beling, and was successfully defended by Lord Broghill, the Earl's third son.

The following year an unsuccessful attempt was made to burn it by the Irish.

In 1643 it was again besieged by Lieutenant-Colonel Purcell with seven thousand foot and nine hundred horse. This time Captain Hugh Croker commanded the garrison. The Earl records in his diary that the rebels demanded the surrender of the fortress, but "we retorned them defyance." None of the defenders were killed, but their enemies lost about three hundred in killed and wounded. The following month cannon was brought to bear on the stronghold, and a breach was effected in the brewhouse, but it was quickly repaired with earth, and the fire from the castle was so great that the enemy did not dare to storm the opening. The guns were then shifted to the south-west, and the orchard was attacked, but the shots from the turrets protected the curtain wall.

After a siege of eight days, the Earl's sons, Lords Dungarvan and Broghill, landed at Youghal and made a treaty with Lord Muskerry for a six days' truce. Of the besiegers twenty were killed, while the defenders escaped injury.

The great Earl died in 1644. The following year the castle was again besieged, this time by troops under Lord Castlehaven. Major Power, with a garrison of a hundred of the Earl's tenants, managed to kill five hundred of the besiegers and to make terms before they surrendered.

The 4th Earl of Cork died without male heirs in 1753, and Lismore Castle passed to his eldest daughter, Lady Charlotte Boyle, who had married the 4th Duke of Devonshire in 1748. It thus passed to its present owner, the 8th Duke of Devonshire, who entertained King Edward VII. and Queen Alexandra at the castle in 1904.

Authorities Consulted.

Boyle, "Lismore Papers."
C. Smith, "State of Waterford."
R. Ryland, "History of Waterford."
Egan, "Waterford Guide."
Proceedings of Royal Society of Antiquaries of Ireland.
Parliamentary Gazetteer.
W. Flood, "Lismore" (*Journal of Waterford Archæological Society*).
Windele Manuscript (*Cork Archæological Society's Journal*).
MacMahon, "Lismore Castle" (Historic Houses).

LOHORT CASTLE

THIS fortress is situated in the Barony of Duhallow, four miles and a half east-south-east of Kanturk, County Cork.

The name was sometimes spelt Loghort, and means literally "herb-plot" or "garden," from *luibh*, "herb," and *gort*, "an enclosed field."

The central tower is circular, and measures about 80 feet in height. It was strongly machicolated, and had only a few apertures for light and air. The walls are about 10 feet thick at the base, diminishing to 6 feet.

The castle was formerly surrounded by a moat, which was crossed by a drawbridge, but this has been removed.

Richard Sainthill, writing in 1831, describes the castle thus:—

"Six miles from Liscarroll is Loghort Castle, the residence of Lord Arden when he visits his Irish estates. It is a square keep about 90 feet in height. The ground floor is now the kitchen. The first floor was the armoury, and contained arms for 100 soldiers, which were removed and lost in the year 1798. This is now the dining-parlour; above this is the drawing-room. We then rise to the state bedroom, beside which there are six others. From the battlements an extensive prospect is commanded."

The castle also contained a good library. In the armoury was preserved the sword of Sir Alex. MacDonald, who commanded the Highlanders at the battle of Knockninoss in 1647, and was treacherously killed by a soldier after the encounter.

The fortress dates from the reign of King John, and was a former stronghold of the MacCarthys.

In 1641 Sir Philip Perceval garrisoned it with a hundred and fifty men during the rebellion. Nevertheless the Irish gained possession of the stronghold by treachery, and held it until May, 1650, when Sir Hardress Waller reduced it with a battery of cannon.

In his letter to the Parliament he writes of it as a place of great strength.

After this it seems to have remained in a state of dilapidation until the middle of the eighteenth century, when Sir Philip Perceval's descendant, the Earl of Egmont, put it into a state of repair.

The agents of the estate resided in the castle during many years of the last century, and it is now the residence of Sir Timothy O'Brien, Bart.

There are many legends relating to the old fortress.

AUTHORITIES CONSULTED.

C. Smith, "County of Cork," with "Historical Notes from Croker and Caulfield MSS."
Joyce, "Irish Names of Places."
Brewer, "Beauties of Ireland."
Gibson, "History of Cork."
Parliamentary Gazetteer.
Lewis, "Irish Topographical Dictionary."

LOUGH CUTRA CASTLE

In the Barony of Kitartan, County Galway, about three miles south-by-east of Gort, is situated Lough Cutra Castle, the beautiful mansion of Viscount Gough.

The demesne extends along the west and south shores of the lake, and the gardens slope to the water's edge in terraces.

Mr. Blake Foster, in "The Irish Chieftains," says that the name was derived from a leader of the Belgic tribe, called Cutra, who owned the district before the arrival of the Milesians.

The mansion is a castellated building of Tudor style. It has massive walls of finely-cut limestone, and was erected during the last century at a cost of over £50,000.

Mr. Paine was the architect, but he died before the building was finished, and the lodges, &c., were carried out in the same style by Mr. Nash, while the gardens and grounds were exquisitely laid out by Mr. Sutherland.

It is considered one of the show places of the west.

John Prendergast Smith was created Viscount Gort in 1816. He had inherited the O'Shaughnessy estate through his uncle, and he began to build the present mansion.

The story goes that being enchanted with East Cowes Castle, in the Isle of Wight, which belonged to, and had been designed by, Mr. Nash, Lord Gort decided to erect a similar building on the shores of his beautiful lake. It is strange that the present Lord Gort now lives in East

Cowes Castle, from which the design of his ancestor's castle in Ireland was borrowed.

The first Viscount Gort adopted his nephew, Colonel Vereker, as his heir.

This soldier so distinguished himself at the battle of Coloony that he and his heirs were granted supporters to the family arms and allowed to adopt "Coloony" as their motto.

When the 3rd Viscount Gort succeeded to the estates they were heavily encumbered, and the famine of 1848 completed the ruin of the family.

The castle was sold for £17,000 to Mrs. Ball, Superioress of the Religious Order of Loretto, Dublin. She turned it into a novitiate house and opened a school. After a few years the community was recalled, and the castle was again put up for sale. This time it was purchased for £24,000 by the first Lord Gough.

Two pieces of ordnance which he captured in India are mounted at the entrance.

The present Viscount Gough is Resident British Minister at Dresden.

AUTHORITIES CONSULTED.

Fahey, "History and Antiquities of Diocese of Kilmacduagh."
Blake Foster, "The Irish Chieftains."
Parliamentary Gazetteer.
Ward's Guide to Limerick, Clare Coast, and Lower Shannon.

MACROOM CASTLE

THIS fortress is situated in West Muskerry, County Cork, about twenty miles from Cork City, on the bank of the River Sullane, the ford of which it was evidently built to command.

Various derivations are given of the old name Macromp. Some authorities state that it signifies the "Plain of Crom," the supreme deity of the ancient inhabitants of Ireland. Smith says the name came from a crooked oak under which travellers used to pass, but it seems more probable that it simply meant "a crooked plain," and referred to the undulating country round.

In Smith's History of Cork he describes the building as consisting of two square towers about 60 feet high connected by a large modern building. Windele, however, says that the present residence is a huge square mass of masonry which formed the keep of the original castle.

It has a handsome gallery and other good apartments, and is now covered with ivy. At the beginning of the last century Gothic windows were introduced and part of it weather-slated, which, being entirely out of keeping with the style of architecture, has not added to its picturesqueness.

It occupies a slight rise on the east bank of the Sullane River, which flows through the demesne. The gardens lie to the south.

The castle appears to have been erected in the twelfth century, and its building has been variously attributed to the Carews and Daltons, while its Irish name of Caislean-i-Fhlionn, signifying "O'Flyn's Castle," seems to indicate that it owes its origin to this family, who formerly owned territory in Muskerry and Carberry. It afterwards came into the possession of the MacCarthys, and Tiege MacCarty, father of the famous Lord Muskerry, died in the castle in 1565, having restored and enlarged it.

In 1602 its owner, Cormac MacDermot Carthy, Lord Muskerry, was suspected of hostile intrigues and imprisoned in Cork, while Captain Flower and then Sir Charles Wilmot were sent to lay siege to the castle. Lord Muskerry, however, escaped, and the Lord President fearing he might cut off Sir Charles's retreat, ordered him to return to Cork.

The night before the intended march the garrison killed a pig, but water being too scarce to scald it they decided to singe it instead with fern and straw. This they did in the castle bawn, but some sparks lighting on the thatched roof of a cabin flamed up and set fire to some tallow through one of the windows of the castle.

The flames quickly spread through the building and the garrison was obliged to take speedy refuge in the bawn. From thence they made a sally to the woods, about fifty being slain in their attempt to escape.

The besiegers entered the castle and extinguished the fire. After making some necessary repairs Sir Charles left a garrison there and marched to Cork.

Upon the breaking out of the rebellion of 1641 it was again in Lord Muskerry's possession, and when the Papal Nunzio landed in the south of Ireland he visited many places and amongst them Macroom Castle. He was received at the great gate of the fortress by Lady Helena Butler, sister of Lord Ormond, and the wife of Donough, Lord Muskerry. The Nunzio stayed at Macroom for four days.

In 1650 the Bishop of Ross assembled an army in the park. Upon the approach of Lord Broghill with a body of horse, the garrison in the castle set fire to it and joined the main body encamped outside. Then followed the battle of Macroom, in which about seven hundred of the

MACROOM CASTLE

Irish troops were slain. The Bishop and the High Sheriff of Kerry were taken prisoners. The latter was shot, but the bishop was promised freedom if he induced the garrison of Carrigadrohid Castle to surrender. When brought to that fortress he, however, exhorted the besieged to hold out, and he was at once hanged with the reins of his own horse.

Later in the war General Ireton is said to have burned both the town and castle of Macroom.

During the Commonwealth the castle was granted to Admiral Sir William Penn, father of the founder of Pennsylvania.

Upon the restoration of Charles II. the stronghold was restored to the MacCarthys, and was enlarged and modernised by the Earl of Clancarty.

In 1691 it again fell into the hands of an English garrison. They were hard pressed by James's troops, until the approach of Major Kirk and three hundred dragoons raised the siege.

The estate of the 4th Earl of Clancarty was confiscated for his allegiance to King James, and the castle was sold by auction in 1703. It was bought by the Hollow Sword Blade Co., who resold it to Judge Bernard, ancestor to Lord Bandon.

After this it was occupied by the Hedges Eyre family, the Hon. Robert Hedges Eyre dying 1840.

Colonel White Hedges, brother of Lord Bantry, owned the castle in 1861, and it is now in the possession of Lord Ardilaun, whose wife is one of the Bantry family.

AUTHORITIES CONSULTED.

Smith, "State of County and City of Cork."
Bennett, "History of Bandon."
J. Windele, "Notices of the City of Cork," &c.
C. Gibson, "History of the County and City of Cork."
Meehan, "Confederation of Kilkenny."
Murphy, "Cromwell in Ireland."
Parliamentary Gazetteer.

MALAHIDE CASTLE

THE town of Malahide is situated in the Barony of Coolock, about seven miles north-north-east of the City of Dublin, and about half a mile distant stands the ancient seat of the Talbot family.

A number of suggestions have been put forward as to the derivation of the name Malahide, perhaps the most probable being that it comes from Baile-atha-id, signifying the "town of Id's ford."

The present castle is almost square in form, with a Gothic entrance on the south-east. This side of the fortress is flanked at each angle by a round tower, one of them at least having been added during the last century. The whole effect is much enhanced by the building being largely covered with ivy.

During the early part of the eighteenth century the stronghold was enlarged and modernised by its owner, Colonel Talbot. It had at that time lost its castellated character, which was restored, while the moat that surrounded it was filled in and planted.

The former entrance was by drawbridge, protected by a portcullis and barbican. The old tower of the barbican now gives entrance to the stable yard.

The hall is flagged and vaulted, and the walls are hung with interesting martial relics, while a handsomely-carved chair is said to have belonged to King Robert Bruce.

A circular flight of stairs leads to the next floor, which contains the famous "Oak Room." The timber for its ornamentation is said to have been brought from the "faire greene commune of Ostomanstoune," which was not so far away, and from which King William Rufus is said to have obtained the oak to roof Westminster Hall. The panels in Malahide Castle are of an ebony black, and are richly carved in relief with scriptural subjects. The ceiling is cross-beamed with oak, and a wide mullioned window gives light to this beautiful apartment. It is said to have once been the castle chapel, and that behind a double panel, carved with scenes from the Garden of Eden, is a recess still occupied by the altar.

Here amongst other interesting objects is the suit of armour traditionally supposed to have been worn by Sir Walter Hussey, who was the first husband of the Hon. Maud Plunkett, and was killed on his wedding day.

The dining hall is said to date from the Tudor period, and it has a pointed ceiling of stained wood with a gallery at one end. In this room is displayed a very fine collection of historical and family portraits by many celebrated artists, amongst whom are Lely, Titian, Reynolds, Kneller, and others.

The portraits include those of "Handsome Dick Talbot," Duke of Tyrconnel, favourite of Charles II. and James I., the Duchess of Portsmouth and her son the Duke of Richmond, the Earl of Lucan, Ireton, Myles Corbet, and several royal personages.

The "saloon" has also some art treasures, the chief being an altar-piece by Albert Durer, which once belonged to Mary Queen of Scots, and was purchased by Charles II. for the Duchess of Portsmouth for the then enormous sum of £2,000.

The lands of Malahide were granted to the Talbot family in 1174 by Henry II., in whose train was Chevalier Richard Talbot, when the king came to Ireland in 1172. This grant was confirmed to Sir Richard Talbot by Edward IV. in 1475.

The foundations of the castle were laid by the first Richard Talbot in Henry II.'s reign upon the gentle elevation of limestone rock where it stands to-day. It was enlarged during Edward IV.'s reign.

Sir Richard Edgecomb landed at Malahide in 1488 as Lord Justice, and writes that "there a gentlewoman called Talbot received and made me right good cheer," until the Bishop of Meath and others came later in the day to escort him to Dublin.

During the rebellion of Lord Offaly or the "Silken Thomas," the O'Tooles and O'Byrnes ravished the country north of Dublin, and having plundered Howth, they "went to Malahyde and burst open the gates till they came to the hall-doors, when as they were resisted with great difficulty," they returned homeward.

After the rising had been suppressed, the unfortunate young leader executed, and his family attainted, Gerald, afterwards 12th Earl of Kildare, only escaped from the English Government through the assistance of his aunt, the Lady "Aleanora" FitzGerald, and for the protection she had afforded her nephew she was detained at Malahide Castle awaiting the King's pleasure. From here, in 1545, was dated her petition for pardon to Henry VIII., which he granted.

Lord Strafford tried to gain some of the Talbot possessions and privileges in 1639, but without success.

John Talbot was banished to Connaught for taking part in the rebellion of 1641, and his castle and 500 acres were granted on a seven-year lease in 1653 to Miles Corbet, who was Chief Baron. His house in Dublin had been visited by plague, and he took up residence at Malahide about Christmas time. Here he lived until obliged to fly for his life, and he was afterwards executed as a regicide.

There is a tradition that Cromwell was his guest at Malahide during his tenancy.

A picture appearing on the Down Survey Map (1655-56)

represents the castle as having a large tower at one end, and the notes describe it as "a good stone house therein, with orchards and gardens and many ash-trees, with other outhouses in good repair."

Upon the Restoration the Talbot family came again into possession.

Close to the castle are the ruins of a church which was erected and endowed by the Talbot family, and where they were buried for many years. Here is the altar tomb of Maud Plunkett, "The Bride of Malahide," who was "maid, wife, and widow on one and the same day." Her third husband was Sir Richard Talbot. The tomb is particularly remarkable because of the effigy which represents Lady Talbot as wearing the "horned coif" of 1412, and it is the only representation of this fashion in Ireland.

It is said the church was unroofed by Corbet, either to make bullets of the lead or to cover a barn with the other material.

The history of the castle would be hardly complete without mention of the famous ghost "Puck," who has a fancy for roaming the grounds in the costume he wore when he was an inhabitant of the castle. There are many stories regarding his appearances, amongst which is the following authenticated account: Not so many years ago a naval officer who had just been appointed to the Coast Guard Station at Malahide received an invitation to dine at the castle. On his way up the avenue he met a strange figure in a fantastic costume whom he thought was some one masquerading. Not liking to be made the subject of a joke, he threatened to knock him down unless he told him what he wanted, and upon getting no reply he endeavoured to carry out his threat, but his arm passed through his adversary, and he thought it advisable to hasten his steps to the castle. It was not likely to improve his appetite, however, to find the portrait of the strange figure looking down upon him from the dining-room wall.

Richard Talbot was created Lord Talbot de Malahide in 1831, and the present peer is 5th Baron.

AUTHORITIES CONSULTED.

D'Alton, "History of County of Dublin."
Proceedings of Royal Society of Antiquaries.
Carew MSS., Book of Howth.
Brewer, "Beauties of Ireland."
Burke, "Visitation of Seats and Arms."
M'Mahon, "Malahide Castle" in "Historic Houses."
Burke's Peerage.
Parliamentary Gazetteer.
P., "Malahide Castle," in *Dublin Penny Journal*.
Prendergast, "The Plantation of the Barony of Idrone," in *Journal of Kilkenny Archæological Society*.

MALLOW CASTLE

THE town of Mallow is situated on the River Blackwater, seventeen miles north-north-west of Cork, in the Barony of Fermoy.

The ruins of the castle are to the south of the town upon rising ground commanding the river. They consist of a great rectangular building running north and south, and measuring about 80 feet in length and 30 in breadth on the inside. It has thirty-one Tudor windows, which are generally large and square, having two series of oblong lights, three or five in number, and a window on the north contains as many as eight.

The structure is unroofed, and the floors being of wood have almost entirely disappeared. It was defended by three towers on the western side. The round tower at the north-west angle contained a clock until the middle of the last century. The centre tower measures about 12 feet by 15, and its door-head is depressed. The south-west tower has a five-sided exterior, and inside the upper part is circular, and the lower portion pentagonal.

The eastern front of the castle has one tower, with a five-sided exterior likewise. In 1836 a portion of the east side of the castle fell. The whole of it is now extensively covered with ivy.

This building is supposed to be of the Tudor era, and it is likely to occupy the site of an older fortress, as there are still traces of foundations which do not seem to have been included in the plan of the present ruin.

The Manor of Mallow passed by exchange from the De Rupes or Roches into the hands of the Desmond Fitz-Geralds at the close of the thirteenth century.

Tradition states that the Tudor fortress was erected by the "Great Earl" of Desmond, as Garrett, the 15th Earl, who succeeded to the title in 1558, is usually styled. It seems, however, more probable that it was built by his even greater father, James, who was Lord High Treasurer of Ireland.

MALLOW CASTLE.

It remained in the Desmond possession until the forfeiture of their princely estates in 1584.

At this time it was in the hands of Sir John of Desmond, the Earl's son, who was overtaken near Castlelyons and killed by a former servant of his own. His body was hung over one of the gates of Cork for some years, and his head sent to Dublin Castle.

The following description of the stronghold is taken

from an inquisition held at this time on the Manor of Mallow :—

"One castle containing in itself two small courts and one great barbican, namely, where the howse standeth the enterance in is on the north side ffyrste into one of the said courts, and then turninge one the lefte hande ye enter by a doore, beinge in a highe wall into the Balne or Barbican, which is reasonable large, and then goinge a little way, turninge one the lefte hande, have ye enterance by an other stone wall, whereas the castell or howse standeth, the lower rooms whereof ar sellers vauled over. And in the wall one the lefte hande there be stayres of stone of xii stepps in heyght that leadeth one the right hande into the Hall, which is about lx foote longe and xxvi foot wyde, within the howse, and is deepe, with a highe roofe, the Tymber wereof seemeth to be sounde, and is covered with thacke, some thinge decayed at the north ende; towards the west corner there is a square buyldinge vaulted as thother is, but not so broade, and riseth somewhat higher than the roofe of the hall in which, over the sellor, ar fower strong roomes that may be made meete for lodgings: the uppermost, savinge one, is vaulted."

The siege during the Desmond rebellion must have caused the castle to need repair, and even at subsequent dates it seems to have been in a ruinous condition.

At first after this, the district of Mallow was assigned to Pelham, H.M. Attorney-General, and Sir Thomas Norreys, who was holding the place, writes to Burghley in 1587: "I understand Mallow (a place which I have hitherto had keeping of) is assigned to H.M. Attorney-General, who doth little esteem it. I crave to be admitted an associate in Co. Cork, and still keep that place, which I doubt not the Attorney-General will easily yield to. I affect not the place for any special goodness, but having held it so long am the more unwilling to leave it, and, if I may obtain it. will endeavour the best service I can."

The same year Sir John Norreys, President of Munster, writes from Utrecht complaining that the honour of his office brings little land with it, and asking that Mallow might be granted to him.

He it was who settled the crown of Portugal on the royal house of Braganza, and Edmund Spencer described him in some of the lines of his "Fairy Queen."

In 1588 Sir Thomas Norreys received a grant of the castle and lands from Elizabeth.

Here, in Sir Thomas's arms, died his brother, the great Sir John Norreys, in 1597, of old wounds which had been neglected and turned to gangrene. One of many fables told regarding his death is that the devil, dressed in black, appeared while he was playing cards, and claimed his soul on the spot in fulfilment of an old bargain.

During the Tyrone rebellion in 1598–99 Norreys had his English sheep stolen from Mallow, and his park wall broken down, so that the deer roamed loose.

Upon the restored young Earl of Desmond's returning to Ireland in 1599 he spent much of his time at Mallow, where he was said to be in love with Lady Norris, widow of Sir Thomas.

The Attorney-General writes in 1606: "The first night we lodged at Mallow, a house of my Lady Norries, which is a well-built house, and stands by a fair river in a fruitful soil, but it is yet much unrepaired and bears many marks of the late rebellion." At this time Elizabeth Norreys, heiress to the estate, was a king's ward, and resided with her mother in the castle.

In 1613 a fresh patent was granted to Dame Elizabeth Jephson, and her heirs for £50 paid by her husband, Sir John Jephson, Knight, she having inherited her father's estate. The grant included the castle, manor, and town of Mallow, Short Castle, *alias* Castle-Gar, &c.

In 1636 the Earl of Cork made an offer for the manor, but he did not come to terms with the owners.

MALLOW CASTLE

Short Castle, which was on the north side of the town, was in charge of Lieutenant Williamson in 1641, when Lord Mountgarret marched against Mallow, while the larger fortress was placed in charge of Arthur Bettesworth and two hundred men by Captain Jephson.

After many assaults and several breaches, Short Castle was forced to surrender, which its commander did on terms. There are several versions of the following story.

After the castle's fall its defender and his men were refreshing themselves in a public-house in the town, when an officer and man belonging to Mountgarret's force entered with a block and sword, stating they had come to behead them. Lieutenant Williamson caught the sword up with one hand and the officer's hair with the other, and dragged him to the walls of the larger stronghold, where, dismissing him with a kick, he and his men joined the other garrison.

The Castle of Mallow was taken by the Earl of Castlehaven in 1645, and almost reduced to ruins.

In 1666 there seems to have been an attempt made to restore it. Lord Orrery, writing to the Duke of Ormond in this year, says: "This bridge is at Mallow, where there is a castle of good strength if it had a little reparation, and is one of the greatest passes and thoroughfares in this province, and if seized on by any enemy would, in effect, divide the country into two parts."

During the scare of the French invasion the Grand Jury presented money to repair it, but the Judge seems to have reserved his decision on the matter.

Major-General Sgravenmore sent Colonel Doness to destroy the bridge and reconnoitre the castle in 1689.

Norreys was added to the family surname Jephson in 1838, and some years later Sir Denham Jephson Norreys erected a mansion in Elizabethan style close to the old fortress. Sir Bernard Burke remarks of it: "Here are mullioned windows, pointed gables, tall chimneys, and all those various intricacies of building which characterised our noblest seats in the days of the Virgin Queen; somewhat fantastic, it is true, but picturesque in the extreme."

The manor and castle are still in the possession of this family, Mrs. Atherton-Jephson-Norreys being the present representative.

AUTHORITIES CONSULTED.

H. F. Berry, "The Manor and Castle of Mallow," in *Journal of Cork Archæological Society.*
J. O'Flanagan, "The Blackwater in Munster."
Sir B. Burke, "The Seats and Arms of Noblemen and Gentlemen, &c."
Smith, "History of County and City of Cork."
R. Bagwell, "Ireland under the Tudors."
Parliamentary Gazetteer.
H. Berry, "Manor of Mallow in the Thirteenth Century," in *Journal of Royal Society of Antiquaries of Ireland.*

MAYNOOTH CASTLE

MAYNOOTH CASTLE

"Ye Geraldines! ye Geraldines! how royally ye reigned
  O'er Desmond broad, and rich Kildare, and English arts disdained,
  Your sword made knights, your banner waved, free was your bugle call,
  By Glyn's green slopes, and Dingle's tide, from Barrow's banks to Youghal.
  What gorgeous shrines, what Brehon lore, what minstrel feasts there were
  In and around Maynooth's strong keep and palace-filled Adare!
  But not for rite or feast ye stayed, when friend or kin were pressed;
  And foemen fled, when "Crom a boo" bespoke your lance in rest."

THOMAS DAVIS.

SITUATED about twelve miles west-by-north of Dublin, this ancient fortress of the Pale was the chief stronghold of the Kildare branch of the Geraldines. It was built by Maurice FitzGerald (the first of the great family to settle in Ireland) to protect the lands of Offaly, granted to him in 1176 by Strongbow in lieu of part of Wexford which King Henry wished to retain.

From the excellency of the twelfth-century masonry, the great keep, with walls some 8 feet in thickness, and the gate-house, are the best preserved parts of the ruin. The large corner tower and three round arches adjoining belong to the thirteenth century, while the fifteenth century is represented by an oblong tower, now used as the belfry of the Episcopalian Church. The rest of the buildings which connected these, now isolated, structures have almost entirely disappeared.

The fortress was surrounded on two sides by water, being at the junction of the River Lyreen, a tributary of the Liffey, and a smaller stream.

In 1248 we read that Luke, Archbishop of Dublin, erected the chapel of Maynooth into a prebend of St. Patrick's Cathedral at the request of Maurice, second Baron of Offaly. This building, which was once the castle chapel, is now the parish church.

At the beginning of the fourteenth century Maynooth seems to have been the favourite residence of the FitzGerald family. John, the 1st Earl of Kildare, and Thomas, the 2nd Earl, both died there (1316 and 1328). The latter bequeathed the castle to his wife. It is described as being "built of stone, with numerous offices partly of stone, and two gates, one leading to the town, and the other to the garden."

The castle was added to in 1426, and is said to have been "one of the largest and richest Earl's houses in Ireland."

In 1534 the Earl of Kildare, being Lord Deputy, was summoned to London, and appointed his son, Lord Offaly, Vice-Deputy in his absence. Upon a rumour that his father had been executed, Lord Thomas, who was very young, went into rebellion, and such nobles and chiefs as refused to join his standard he sent as prisoners to Maynooth.

A division of the English army, landing at Howth to raise the siege of Dublin Castle, was met by "Silken Thomas" with two hundred men. An engagement followed, in which Lord Offaly was victorious, and the survivors of the King's troops were sent captive to Maynooth.

At this time the castle was splendidly fortified with men and ordnance.

MAYNOOTH CASTLE

Hearing that the whole English army was about to arrive, Lord Offaly left Maynooth in command of Christopher Paris, his foster-brother, and went into Connaught to raise forces.

In January, 1535, seven hundred men were sent from Dublin to burn Maynooth Castle. A skirmish took place, and although some of the rebels were slain, the royal troops retired.

The Lord Deputy, Sir William Skeffington, now collected his forces, and marched in full strength against the stronghold. The siege began on the 14th of March, and was continued until the 23rd.

Upon arriving at Maynooth, Sir William demanded the surrender of the castle, and offered free pardon and reward to all the garrison.

To this he only received a jeering reply, so planting his cannon to the north of the building towards the park he opened fire. The attack was varied north-east and north-west, but though this continued for over a week little damage was done, save destroying the battlements.

Towards the close of this time a letter was shot out of the castle to the Lord Deputy from Christopher Paris, offering to find means of letting the besiegers enter the castle for a certain sum of money and provision for the rest of his life.

Sir William Skeffington agreed to the terms, and upon the 22nd, a field-piece having been captured from the besiegers, the Governor made it an occasion for high revelry. Thus, while the men who guarded the outer battlements were sound asleep after their carouse, the King's troops easily entered the castle by scaling-ladders early on the morning of the 23rd.

Sir William Brereton led the attack, but the resistance was very feeble, the drunken soldiers believing that the cry of "St. George! St. George!" was but a dream. Sir

William hoisted his standard from the highest turret, so as to inform the Lord Deputy that the castle had been won.

Sir William Skeffington entered in the afternoon. The garrison consisted of thirty-seven persons. Two singers of the chapel were pardoned, at the intervention of Chief Justice Aylmer, on account of their sweet voices.

Twenty-five of the men were beheaded, and one hanged, outside the castle gate, and the principal heads placed upon the battlements. Amongst these was that of the Dean of Kildare. Paris was paid the sum stipulated for his treachery, but as he had forgotten to make his safety a condition, he was executed with the rest.

The Lord Deputy left a garrison in the castle and returned to Dublin.

Lord Offaly was marching to the relief of his stronghold with an army of seven thousand men when the news of its fall reached him. At this, most of his forces melted away, and the rebellion became rather a series of raids than regular warfare.

At last, Lord Thomas, tempted by a promise of pardon, surrendered himself, and was sent prisoner to England. Here, after some months of captivity, he and his five uncles were beheaded at Tyburn.

There is a tradition that the last evening "Silken Thomas" ever spent at Maynooth he played the harp under the venerable yew which is now enclosed in the grounds of St. Patrick's College.

A bill of attainder was passed in 1536 against the Earl of Kildare and his heirs; and Maynooth, being forfeited to the Crown, became a King's castle. It seems to have been a favourite residence of the Lords Deputy at this time.

In 1552 Edward VI. restored Gerald, 11th Earl of Kildare, to his title and estates. His widow lived at Maynooth until her death; and it was in the castle garden

MAYNOOTH CASTLE

that Lord Delvin was first approached by the Earls of Tyrone and Tyrconnell to join the insurrection in 1606. In a letter written by the Countess of Kildare she expresses her regret for such an occurrence.

After the death of the 14th Earl in 1612, Maynooth Castle seems to have fallen into a state of dilapidation on account of his son's minority. It was restored by his guardian, the great Earl of Cork, who placed an inscription over the gateway recording its restoration, and bearing the date 1630.

In 1629 we hear of the Earl's title deeds being preserved in the Council House, which was a stone building that stood on the site now occupied by the President's house of St. Patrick's College. It was removed about 1780. The doorway is still preserved in a school of the town, and the council table, bearing the date 1533, stands before the Duke of Leinster's residence at Carton.

The 12th Earl of Kildare lived at Maynooth until civil war broke out in 1641. Shortly after hostilities began the castle was plundered and the valuable library destroyed.

In 1643 Captain Michael Jones, under the Marquis of Ormond, held possession of the fortress; and in 1644 the Earl of Kildare asked for powder and men to increase its defence, he having taken down the spouts to make bullets.

In 1647 General Owen O'Neill sent a detachment from Trim, which carried the castle by assault. Twenty-six men of the garrison and some officers were hanged, and the fortress dismantled.

The next Earl lived chiefly at Kilkea Castle, and Maynooth gradually fell into decay.

In 1707 Robert, 19th Earl of Kildare, wished to restore the building, but finding it too dilapidated he decided to enlarge Carton House instead.

Houses were subsequently built among the castle ruins,

and these were removed by the Duke of Leinster in 1848 and the space round planted and enclosed.

AUTHORITIES CONSULTED.

Duke of Leinster, "Maynooth Castle." Addenda by Miss M. Stokes (*Kildare Archæological Society's Journal*).
Marquis of Kildare, "Earls of Kildare."
Most Rev. John Healy, D.D., "Maynooth College."

MONGEVLIN CASTLE

THIS castle is situated on the banks of the Foyle where it narrows inland, somewhat over a mile south of Saint Johnstown and seven miles from the City of Londonderry.

Only the keep now remains, but during the last century the walls of the courtyard which lay between the Foyle and the fortress were still standing, and over the arch of the gateway was a small stone engraved with the initials "I.S.E.S.T." and the date 1619. This has, however, now disappeared. Another inscribed stone bears the following: "The Hon. Elizabeth Hamilton, daughter of John Lord Culpeper, and widow of Colonel James Hamilton (who lost his life at sea in Spain, in the service of his king and country), purchased this manor, and annexed it to the opposite estate of the family, which paternal estate itself has improved by her prudent management to nearly the yearly income of the dower she received thereout. She has also settled her younger son, William Hamilton, Esq., in an estate acquired in England, of nearly equal value in the purchase to this, and given every one of her numerous offspring, descended from both branches, some considerable mark of her parental care. Her eldest son, James, Earl of Abercorn, and Viscount Strabane, hath caused this inscription to be placed here for the information of her posterity, Anno, 1704."

There are two incidents in the castle's history which are of particular interest. In the sixteenth century it was the chief residence of the beautiful "Ineen Dubh," daughter of Macdonnell, Lord of the Isles, and mother of the famous Red Hugh O'Donnell, Chief of Tyrconnell.

It was said of her that she was "excelling in all the qualities that become a woman, yet possessing the heart of a hero, and the soul of a soldier."

The State Paper recording her possession is as follows: "From Cul-Mac-Tryan runs a bogg three myles in length to the side of Lough Foyle—in the midst of the bog is a standing loughe called Bunaber—here at Bunaber dwells O'Donnell's mother (Ineen Dubh M'Donnell). Three miles above Cargan stands a fort called McGevyvelin (Mongivlin) upon the river of Lough Foyle—O'Donnell's mother's chief house."

The fortress is mentioned in 1619 in Captain Pynnar's Survey of the Escheated Counties of Ulster in the following manner: "Sir John Stewart hath 3,000 acres called Cashell Hetin and Littergull. Upon this proportion there is built, at Magevlin, a very strong castle, with a flanker at each corner."

James II. was the guest of Archdeacon Hamilton at Mongevlin during the siege of Derry. From there he sent proposals of surrender to the garrison by his host, which were rejected.

A sad incident occurred in connection with the castle last century. A servant lad being employed by the owner of the time was so terrified by the ghost stories he heard in connection with the building that he left his situation and went home. His friends persuaded him to return, but the matter so preyed upon his mind that he shortly after hanged himself.

AUTHORITIES CONSULTED.

"The Donegal Highlands."
J. A. H., "Mongevlin Castle," in *Dublin Penny Journal*,

MONKSTOWN CASTLE, COUNTY CORK

SITUATED at the western extremity of Cork Harbour, in the Barony of Kerricurrihy, is the now ruined castle of Monkstown. The name is derived from the Monastery Legan, belonging to the Benedictine Monks, which was formerly established here, it being a cell of Bath Abbey.

The castle consists of a quadrangular building, flanked by four square towers, having machicolated defences projecting from their angles. The windows are in excellent preservation, being of square Tudor style, divided by strong stone mullions, with horizontal weather cornices. The moulding of the door displays excellent workmanship.

The estate belonged to the Archdeacons, who changed their name to MacOdo, or Cody.

The castle was erected in 1636 by Anastasia Archdeacon, *nee* Gould, who intended it as a pleasant surprise for her husband, who was a naval officer, and away on a voyage at the time.

Tradition says that it only cost the thrifty lady a groat. At first she found that the builders objected to go to so out-of-the-way a situation, as provisions were difficult to procure. Nothing daunted by such an excuse the lady offered to supply the workmen with provisions at the ordinary retail rate. This she did, but as she purchased her goods at wholesale prices she found when she came to balance her accounts that she was only 4d. out of pocket.

The castle was erected in a twelvemonth and a day, and the date 1636 appears on one of the mantelpieces.

Smith states that the fortress was originally styled Castle Mahon or O'Mahony's Castle, and in an ancient MS. document (probably now in the possession of Captain Shaw, late of the London Fire Brigade) it is described as being "remade" at the above date, so that it may occupy the site of an older stronghold.

The following interesting extracts are taken from the manuscript alluded to, which has been preserved in the Shaw family, they having at one time leased the castle: "A.D. 1636, Monkstown Castle and court were remade. Reader, you are to observe that it was not John Archdeacon, but his wife, Anastatia Gould, who built the four castles of Monkstown, and the court, in his absence, as he was from home. On his return he did not like the building, and said that a building near a harbour was a building of sedition, which, alas! turned out so."

"A.D. 1660.—Archdeacon died, as when Cromwell came to Ireland he was deprived of his castle, lands, &c., but not his life, which they did not covet."

In 1612 the wardship of the son of the late John Archdeacon, of Monkstown, was given to Sir John Jephson Knt., and it was this ward's wife who afterwards built the castle.

He died in 1660, and both he and his wife are buried in the disused graveyard of Teampul Oen Bryn, west of the castle. Upon his tomb appears a long Latin inscription which, among other things, states that—"Here lies the body of that most noble man, John Archdeacon."

Colonel Hunks, one of the three deputed to execute the death warrant of Charles I., was granted the lands of Monkstown by the Commonwealth before the demise of John Archdeacon, who lost his estate on account of loyalty to the Stewarts. Hunks sold it to Primate Boyle, brother of the Earl of Cork, for £400.

MONKSTOWN CASTLE, COUNTY CORK

But it evidently returned to the Archdeacon family upon the Restoration, for it was again confiscated in 1688 on account of the family's loyalty to King James.

It then passed again into the hands of the Boyles, and through two granddaughters of the Primate it descended to the present owners, the Lords De Vesci and Longford.

In 1700 Dive Downes writes: " Mr. O'Callaghan, a Protestant, lives in Monkstown, in a good square castle with flankers."

Later in this century it was rented by the Government as a barrack.

Lord De Vesci leased the castle to Bernard Shaw in 1861.

AUTHORITIES CONSULTED.

Smith, " County and City of Cork."
Gibson, " History of Cork."
J. Windele, " Historical Notices of City of Cork," &c.
Proceedings of Royal Society of Antiquaries.
Parliamentary Gazetteer.

PORTUMNA CASTLE

THERE have been three consecutive castles at Portumna, which is situated in the Barony of Longford, Co. Galway. The town stands at the head of Lough Derg, about eleven miles west of Birr. The name signifies "the bank of the oak."

The territory formerly belonged to the O'Maddens, and was included in the grant to De Burgo 1226.

Soon after this the first castle was erected close to the River Shannon. The ruins were removed some years ago, but its position can still be traced.

The second fortress, which was an imposing castellated building of the Tudor period, was burnt in 1826. The chief apartments were the great hall, handsome state drawing-room, and library—a beautiful long room in the upper storey. They were all completely destroyed, only the walls being left.

Some of the out-offices were fitted up as a residence for the Dowager Countess of Clanricard shortly afterwards.

Since then the Earl of Clanricard has erected a magnificent modern residence in the demesne, but on a different site.

The manor passed, by the marriage of Elizabeth, daughter of William de Burgo, Earl of Ulster, to Lionel, Duke of Clarence, through whom it passed to the Mortimers, and later to the Earls of Clanricard.

In 1582 it was held by Ulick Burke, Earl of Clanricard,

PORTUMNA CASTLE

to whom Portumna and the earldom were confirmed, as his brother John disputed his right.

In 1608 it was granted to the Earl, with other houses, to be held by knight's service *in capite*.

The Earl of Strafford held a council in the castle in 1634 to establish the King's title in Connaught. The jury, however, negatived the matter, whereupon the Earl arrested them and the sheriff, and sent them prisoners to Dublin.

In 1641, Ulic, 5th Earl of Clanricard, was at Portumna upon the breaking out of hostilities. He fortified the castle and proceeded to Galway, of which city he was governor. He used every effort to maintain peace, and in 1650 was appointed Lord Deputy in place of Ormond. At this time he made Portumna his chief place of residence.

In 1659 General Ludlow laid siege to the fortress.

In the struggle between James and William it was garrisoned for James, but surrendered to Brigadier-General Eppinger, who, with one thousand two hundred horse and dragoons, arrived to reduce it.

Authorities Consulted.

Hardiman, "History of Galway."
State Papers.
Lewis, "Topographical Dictionary of Ireland."
Parliamentary Gazetteer.
Carew MSS.
MS. Ordnance Survey.

ROSCOMMON CASTLE

In the Barony of South Ballintobber, County Roscommon, seventy-five miles west-by-north of Dublin, stands the now ruined fortress of Roscommon. Joyce says the name signifies "Coman's wood," from St. Comas, who founded a monastery there about the year 746, but O'Donovan traces its derivation from "crooked stick."

The plan of the castle consists of a quadrangular space enclosed by curtain walls flanked at the angles by towers rounded on the outside. The whole measures about 223 feet in length and 173 in breadth. On the east side the entrance, under a pointed arch, was also protected by two towers, which were connected by a rectangular building inside that probably contained the state rooms.

The lower storeys of the towers were vaulted, although some of them are now broken. The upper floors have larger windows, and also the remains of fireplaces. Most of the windows contain four lights, but some have Elizabethan mullions.

The north-west tower has a winding stair, which leads to the top of the curtain wall. On the western side of the stronghold is a small rectangular tower, which contained a little entrance.

There is now no trace of the moat, but a few remains of earth outworks are visible.

On the east is a long enclosure surrounded by walls and flanked by bastions, which is known as the orchard, although at present it contains no trees.

The north and south walls of the castle, which had been

broken down, have been again raised for farming purposes. The inside of the walls exhibit traces of blasting. The castle was built of blue limestone, and much of the stone has been used elsewhere.

Weld considers it likely that the fortress was built from an English plan, and remarks on the apparent absence of patching, it all seeming to date from the same period.

Robert d'Ufford, Lord Justice of Ireland, began to erect the castle in 1268, while Hugh, King of Connaught, was too ill to prevent such encroachment on his territory. Some authorities state a fortress existed here prior to this time. During 1270–72 there are numerous accounts of payments for building and fortifying the stronghold.

In 1275–76 is an entry of payment to Brother Maurice, Bishop of Elphin, for the site that had been used, and which appears to have been Church property.

The castle is said to have been razed by O'Conor in 1272, but the word "broken" used in the Book of Howth seems to be nearer the truth, as four years later the Irish again seized it by scaling ladders and overthrew the English garrison.

In Weld's Statistical Survey he gives an amusing account of the contradictions which obscure the early history of the stronghold, and from which it appears impossible to gather the true facts at this distant period.

In 1277 Sir Robert d'Ufford was again Lord Juctice, and with Thomas de Clare, Maurice Fitz-Maurice and all their forces was hemmed in by the Irish in the Slievebawn Mountains. They were only released on the condition that Roscommon Castle was surrendered to the O'Conors.

It is also chronicled that Hugh O'Conor destroyed it in this year and that it was rebuilt by Maurice Fitz-Maurice.

At any rate it seems again to have been in English possession in 1282–83, as there are entries regarding payment for its fortifications, and a grant to the Prior and Convent of St. Coman of a right to water their animals for ever at the lake under the castle. This sheet of water, which was called Loch-na-nean, or "the lake of birds," has now entirely disappeared.

The names of numerous constables of the castle are mentioned in the State Documents.

In 1290 the castle was garrisoned by Welshmen, and the townspeople were in great distress because of the constables and bailiffs preying upon them. The King issued an order that nothing must be taken without consent and payment.

There was a long trial in 1292 of William de Prene, a carpenter in charge of works at Roscommon Castle, who was accused of various frauds in connection with his contract.

A very interesting account of repairs is recorded in 1304 which gives a fair idea of the extent of the fortress. An artilleryman was paid for repairing war engines, and the well was enclosed by a wall 3 feet thick. It was 5 feet across and 32 feet deep, with a wooden cover. Three drawbridges and two portcullisses are also mentioned. The postern was closed with masonry 7 feet thick. The step of the hall repaired, and the tower near it vaulted with two arches. Also St. Bridget's well was drained into the lake.

Somewhere about this time Felim O'Conor is said to have laid low the castle, while in 1341 his son Hugh was taken prisoner by the King of Connaught and imprisoned in the stronghold, but was released for a ransom the following year.

Roderic O'Conor occupied the castle in 1375.

While in possession of the O'Conors it was a constant source of dispute between O'Conor Don and O'Conor Roe. In 1409, being in the former's possession, it was besieged by the latter, but the garrison was relieved by Brian O'Conor Sligo, who managed to get provisions into the fortress.

ROSCOMMON CASTLE

Rory O'Conor died there in 1453. Tadhg O'Conor was treacherously killed by his own people in 1476, and they took the castle of Roscommon, but did not keep it long.

In 1499 the Earl of Kildare led his forces into Connaught, dislodged O'Conor Roe and installed O'Conor Don. In 1512 the Earl of Kildare again took the fortress, and this time he garrisoned it with his own warders. It, however, immediately reverted to the O'Conors, and remained with them until 1566, when it was taken for Queen Elizabeth.

It had been granted to M'William Bourke in 1544, but as he would have had to drive out the occupiers, it is not to be wondered at that he never took possession.

It was restored by the O'Conor Don, and Sir Thomas L'Estrange made constable in 1569. The O'Conor Roe, having a spite against the constable, attacked and burned the castle in 1573, and L'Estrange claimed compensation to the amount of £1,000.

Sir Henry Sydney lodged a night in the castle in 1576, and complained of having no cheer. The O'Conor Don visited him at this time.

Sir Nicholas Maltbie, to whom the castle was leased in 1577, asked to be made Seneschal of Roscommon in 1580 as compensation for rebuilding the fortress.

Captain Brabazon, Governor of Connaught, summoned a meeting of the chiefs in the castle in 1582. It was held in the "Tower of the Narrow Passages," and the joistings giving way the whole meeting, including the Governor, was precipitated to the bottom. Chief O'Flanagan died from the fall.

After this the English constable was murdered, and Sir Henry Sydney left a garrison in the castle.

Sir Nicholas Malbie died in 1584, and the castle remained in his family's possession for some years afterwards. In 1609 Lady Sydley, widow of Henry Malby, Esq., asked allowance for the repairs of the castles of Roscommon and Longford, both of which she rented from the Crown. Roscommon had been ruined by various garrisons which had been placed there by Sir John Norris and others.

One of the charges against the northern Earls was their intention to seize Roscommon Castle amongst others.

The garrison made a brave defence against the Irish in 1642. The castle was chiefly defended by Scotch warders. It is quaintly noted that at the beginning of these "commotions" it had belonged to Lord Grandesson.

Three years later General Preston arrived and laid siege to it, opening fire on both town and castle.

On the ninth day of the siege the garrison offered to make honourable terms, which were accepted. The same day the besieging party had a sharp encounter with a relieving force, who were, however, defeated, and the castle surrendered. Captain Leicester was left in command.

It remained in the possession of the Irish forces until 1652, when it was delivered on articles to Commissary-General Reynolds, of the Parliamentary troops, by Captain Daly.

It is probable that it was demolished at this time. Tradition states it was burned by fugitive Irish after the battle of Aughrim, and some blackened joists are pointed out in corroboration.

It is now leased to a farmer by the Earl of Essex.

AUTHORITIES CONSULTED.

Weld, "Statistical Survey of County Roscommon."
O'Conor Don, " O'Conors of Connaught."
Meehan, "Irish Franciscan Monasteries."
Joyce, "Irish Names of Places."
State Documents.
State Papers.
Carew MSS., including Book of Howth.
Parliamentary Gazetteer.
MS. Ordnance Survey.
Murphy, "The Castle of Roscommon," in *Journal of Royal Society of Antiquaries, Ireland.*

ROSS CASTLE

ROSS CASTLE

> "Its embers smouldering here and there,
>   Unfed, the civil war-flame dies;
> But still defiant on the air,
>   O'er Rosse the green flag proudly flies.
>
> *   *   *   *   *
>
> "'Till Birnam wood meets Dunsinane,'
>   Macbeth before no foe shall quail,
> And Rosse may all assaults disdain,
>   'Till on Lough Lein strange ship shall sail.' "
>
> A. B. ROWAN.

THIS castle is situated on what is now known as the Island of Ross, on the east shore of Lough Lene, or the Lower Lake of Killarney, about a mile and three-quarters south of the town.

The island has been artificially formed by cutting across the peninsula or *ros* on which the fortress is built and from which it takes its name.

The channel, which is flooded by the waters of the lake, is crossed by a bridge, although it is usually dry during the summer months.

This bridge was formerly protected by a guard house and gates, which were closed every night, sentinels being posted at the entrance when the castle was garrisoned in later times.

The present ruins consist of a keep, with the remains of the surrounding bawn wall, which was flanked by semi-circular towers at the corners. A spiral stone stair leads to the top of the keep, with doorways opening at the various floors.

The fortress is based on a limestone rock, and sustained on the land side by a buttress of masonry.

The peninsula contains 158 acres, and copper mines were opened on it in 1804, which were worked for four years, in which time £80,000 worth of ore was extracted. Water getting in stopped further work. It was clearly proved that the mines had been worked many centuries before, and a number of stone implements, locally called "Danes' hammers," have been found on the island.

The castle is supposed to have been built towards the close of the fourteenth century by the family of O'Donoghue-Ross, who added the appellation of their home to distinguish them from the family of O'Donoghue-More.

A modern barrack capable of holding some two hundred men and officers was erected against the keep, but when it ceased to be used Lord Kenmare had the unsightly erection removed.

There is a legend regarding a great and wise Prince O'Donoghue who possessed the secret of eternal youth, and under whose rule the land prospered greatly. It is related how that during a splendid feast at Ross Castle he rose up amongst the company and made a prophetic oration, recounting accurately all that the future years would bring. In the midst of speaking he walked over to a window (which is still shown) and through it he passed out over the lake. Upon nearing the centre he turned round and waved his hand in farewell to those behind, and, the waters opening, he disappeared beneath them.

On May morning he is said to rise from his watery grave and ride over the lake on a white steed, surrounded by beautiful women and youths. His appearance is looked upon as a sign of a bountiful harvest.

It is also related how a young maiden imagining herself

in love with the phantom prince, cast herself into the lake on a May morning and was drowned.

The O'Donoghues were succeeded at Ross by the M'Carthy Mores, through whom the castle passed in 1588 to Sir Valentine Browne, ancestor to the present house of Kenmare.

In 1651 Lord Muskerry was guardian to his nephew Sir Valentine Browne, who was then a minor of about twelve years old. Hence it was that after his defeat by the Parliamentary forces at Knockniclashy on the 5th of July he retired with his army, numbering some one thousand five hundred men, to Ross.

Ludlow, accompanied by Lord Broghill and Sir Hardress Waller, followed with four thousand horse and two thousand foot.

Lord Muskerry was the last Royalist commander in arms, and his submission was a matter of great moment.

Ludlow reports that the castle was only accessible by the causeway which the besieged had fortified, being otherwise surrounded by water and bog.

Finding that this made the reduction of the fortress a matter of difficulty, and probably hearing of the tradition which stated Ross Castle could not fall until a ship should sail on the lake, Ludlow asked for a small fleet of boats to be prepared for transport at Kinsale.

In the meantime he found that the besieged were obtaining supplies through the thick woods surrounding the island. A force of two thousand foot were, therefore, despatched to clear the thickets. Some of the enemy were killed, some taken prisoners, and the rest saved themselves "by their good footmanship."

The rest of Ludlow's forces were employed in fortifying the peninsular so that a few men could keep the besieged in, while a large company was despatched to Killorgan, on Castlemain Bay, to receive the boats and supplies.

The preparation for the expedition was undertaken by

the Rev. Dr. Jones, and the command was given to Captain Chudleigh.

The vessels were sent in pieces, so that the workmen who accompanied them could put them together in a few days. Two pinnaces carrying ordnance, and capable of holding fifty (or Ludlow says a hundred and fifty) men, were forwarded so as to be ready for use in two days. Also five or six boats to hold fifty men each, and material to make more.

Great has been the controversy as to what route was followed in conveying these vessels to Killarney. The River Laune, which drains the lakes, is not navigable above the place where Ludlow's force was to receive the goods.

Tradition asserts that they were conveyed by the mountain road, and in Ware's Annals it is recorded that a ship was "carried over the mountains." On the other hand, Smith distinctly says they were "brought up by the River Lane, by strength of men's hands." He also relates how a recent sexton of Swords, called Hopkins (who had died at the age of 115), had been one of those who "assisted in drawing the above-mentioned vessel into the lake." It is, therefore, likely that Smith's informant on the matter had received the correct impression from an eye witness.

On Captain Chudleigh's tomb at St. Multon's, Kinsale, the fact is recorded of his having constructed a ship to sail on land for the reduction of Ross.

Some naval men are said to have drawn a vessel up the Laune in later years.

It is on the whole most likely that the hulls of the pinnaces were brought up by the river bed, while the lighter craft were conveyed by road. At any rate the transport and preparation occupied only the short period of four days, at the end of which time the terrified garrison perceived a warship being rowed upon the lake.

ROSS CASTLE

It is not unlikely that pressure was put on Lord Muskerry by his superstitious garrison, for no sooner had the vessel appeared than he notified to Ludlow that he was willing to treat.

Commissioners were appointed on both sides, and after a fortnight spent in debating the terms the treaty of Ross was signed. Lord Muskerry's son and Sir Daniel O'Brien were delivered as hostages.

Fair terms were granted to the Royalist Army, and five thousand horse and foot laid down their arms.

For a long time Ross Castle gave rank and emolument to a governor. One of these owed his position to the confusion of names between New Ross, County Wexford, and the Ross of Killarney, for having rendered valuable service at the former during the rebellion of 1798, the governorship of the latter becoming vacant he was at once appointed.

AUTHORITIES CONSULTED.

M. F. Cusack, "History of Kerry."
I. Weld, "Illustrations of Killarney."
J. Savage, "Picturesque Ireland."
C. Smith, "State of County Kerry."
J. Cook, "Murray's Handbook for Ireland."
Mr. and Mrs. Hall, "Ireland."
Parliamentary Gazetteer.
Proceedings of Royal Society of Antiquaries of Ireland.
J. Prendergast, "Surrender of Ross Castle"; A. B. Rowan, Notes on same, *Journal of Kilkenny Archæological Society*.

ROSSCLOGHER CASTLE

THE shores of Lough Melvin comprise part of Leitrim, Fermanagh and Donegal. The lake is about six miles long and a mile and a half at its greatest width. The castle of Rossclogher is situated on an artificial island to the south, near the Leitrim shore, and it gives its name to the Barony of Rossclogher in that county.

The Four Masters record the miraculous formation of the lake in 4694 B.C., while during the preparation of the grave of Melghe Molbhthach the waters gushed forth. He had been King of Ireland for fourteen years and was killed in battle. The lake was then called Lough Melghe, from which comes the modern Melvin.

The castle belonged to the M'Clancys, who were chiefs of Dartraigh in 1241 according to the Irish annals. They were a subordinate sept to the O'Rourkes and the name is variously spelt Glannaghie, M'Glannough, M'Glanna, M'Glanathie, M'Glanchie, Maglanshie, &c.

The lake fortress of Rossclogher was built by one of this family before the reign of Henry VIII., but the exact date is unknown.

It is interesting to note that the island next it, to the east, is called Inisheher (Inis Siar), meaning western island, having evidently received its name long before the foundations of the castle were laid, which at the present time form the most western land in the lake.

The structure upon which the fortress is built is like that of the Hag's Castle in Lough Mask, and Cloughoghter

Castle in Cavan. It consists of a foundation of heavy stones laid in the lake and filled in with smaller stones and earth so as to form an island.

The castle consists of a circular tower surrounded by a wall about five feet in height. It is built of freestone taken from the mainland near, cemented together with lime and coarse gravel. The walls, which are very thick, were coated outside with rough cast, which is unusual in the ancient buildings of the neighbourhood. On the side nearest the land are the ruins of a bastion with holes for musketry. The water is very deep between the fortress and the land, which is about 100 yards distant.

On the mainland opposite the stronghold are the remains of earthworks which would seem to have been formed by some attacking party possessing military skill. On a hill above this is situated the ancient "cattle-booley" of the MacClancy clan. It is a circular enclosure of earth, faced with stone, and is about 220 feet in circumference.

The ruins of a church are also on the mainland, within hailing distance of the castle.

The Four Masters record a night attack made by the O'Rourks in 1421, by which they took MacClancy Oge prisoner, and became possessed of "Lough Melvin and its castle." The attack, however, is said to have been made on the island of Inisheen, in consequence of the guards of the lake giving up the boats to the attackers. It was on this island the MacClancy's wooden crannog was situated, and its plundering again in 1455 by Maguire is recorded.

In 1588 three ships belonging to the Spanish Armada were wrecked on Streedagh Strand.

In one of these was Captain Cuellar, whose graphic narrative of his adventures in Ireland, when he had escaped with his life from the sea, have been published of recent years.

After various wanderings, sufferings and ill-treatment in the neighbourhood, he met a priest who directed him, in

Latin, to a castle six leagues off. "It was very strong, and belonged to a savage gentleman, a very brave soldier and great enemy of the Queen of England and of her affairs, a man who had never cared to obey her or pay tribute, attending only to his mountains, which made it strong."

On the road he fell in with a blacksmith who forced him to work at his forge until the same clergyman, passing that way, promised to ask the chief to send an escort for him.

The following day MacClancy despatched four of his own people and a Spanish soldier to fetch him. He states they were much grieved at his sore state and assisted him in every way, and he adds: "I remained there three months, acting as a real savage like themselves."

He describes his hostess as "beautiful in the extreme," and very kind to him. One day while sitting with her and some of her women friends he began to tell their fortunes by palmistry, and "to say to them a hundred thousand absurdities." Soon this got abroad, with the result that hundreds of people flocked to him to have their hands told. At length he said he would have to leave, and then MacClancy ordered that no one should molest him in future.

While Captain Cuellar was thus spending his time at Lough Melvin, news arrived that the Lord Deputy, Fitzwilliam, had marched from Dublin with a great force, and was hanging all the Spaniards he could find and punishing those who had succoured them.

MacClancy (Cuellar calls him Manglana) decided to fly to the mountains with his people, most likely by a bridle-path still to be traced from the "cattle-booley." It was two feet wide, and the paving was enclosed by a kerb. He asked Cuellar and eight other Spaniards what they wished to do. After a conference they offered to defend the castle against the Lord Deputy. MacClancy was delighted, and at once made all provision. They then

ROSSCLOGHER CASTLE

retired to the castle, taking with them the church valuables, three or four boat-loads of stones, six muskets, six crossbows, and other arms.

Captain Cuellar describes the stronghold thus: "The castle is very strong, and very difficult to take if they do not (even though they should) attack it with artillery, for it is founded in a lake of very deep water which is more than a league wide at some parts, and three or four leagues long, and has an outlet to the sea; and, besides, with the rise of spring tides it is not possible to enter it, for which reason the castle could not be taken by water nor by the shore of the land that is nearest to it. Neither could injury be done it, because (for) a league round the town, which is established on the mainland, it is marshy, breast-deep, so that even the inhabitants (natives) could not get to it except by paths."

As the Spanish captain never mentions the name of the fortress, its identification with Rossclogher has been called in question, chiefly because the measurements are much greater than those of Lough Melvin (a league equalling 3·66 miles), but all the distances in the narrative are greatly overstated. Again, Lough Melvin has not been open to the sea within the historic period. A map, however, of 1609 in the British Museum represents the river which drains it as being nearly as wide as the Erne, and we do not read that Cuellar personally explored its outlet.

In all other matters the castle accurately answers to his description, and no other building has ever been put forward as the probable scene of the siege.

When the Lord Deputy appeared upon the shore (with, Cuellar says, one thousand eight hundred men) he could not get nearer than a mile and a half on account of the marshy ground. From this it would seem that he arrived at the point of Rossfriar on the north-west shore of the lough. He then hanged two Spaniards as a warning, and demanded by a trumpeter the surrender of the castle, promising the garrison a free pass to Spain. This they pretended not to understand.

The siege lasted seventeen days, when a great snowstorm obliged the Deputy to return south.

Upon this episode the State Papers are silent; the Lord Deputy merely giving the following account of his northern expedition. "First, therefore, it may please your lordships, I undertook the journey the 4th November, and finished the same the 23rd of this instant, December, being seven weeks and one day, returning without loss of any one of Her Majesty's army."

When the English forces had retired MacClancy returned in great delight and fêted the Spaniards. He offered his sister to Cuellar in marriage, but this was declined. The chief decided to keep the foreigners as his guard, by force if necessary, but they hearing this left secretly. After much hardship Cuellar eventually crossed to Scotland from Dunluce, and from thence to Antwerp.

In 1590 MacClancy's death is officially recorded as follows: "M'Glannaghe ran for a lough which was near, and tried to save himself by swimming, but a shot broke his arm, and a gallowglass brought him ashore. He was the best killed man in Connaught a long time. He was the most barbarous creature in Ireland, and had always 100 knaves about him. He would never come before any officer. His country extended from Grange beyond Sligo till you come to Ballyshannon. He was O'Rourke's right hand. He had some 14 Spaniards, some of whom were taken alive."

Thus in trying to reach Rossclogher fortress MacClancy lost his life, his head being exhibited in triumph.

The estates of the sept were forfeited in 1641, and the island fortress now belongs to St. George Robert Johnston, Esq., of Kinlough House, the village of Kinlough being near the ruins.

Upon approaching Lough Melvin from one direction at

# ROSSCLOGHER CASTLE

about a mile distant the castle of Rossclogher bears a most remarkable resemblance to a ship in full sail upon the lake.

AUTHORITIES CONSULTED.

H. Allingham, "Captain Cuellar's Adventures in Connaught and Ulster," with Translation of Narrative, by R. Crawford.
Donovan, "Annals of the Four Masters."
O'Reilly, "Remarks on Captain Cuellar's Narrative," in Proceedings of Royal Irish Academy.

SHANE'S CASTLE

"In th' historic pages of Erin's green isle
How bright shines the name of old Phelim the brave,
Who lived where the groves of Shane's Castle now smile,
And Neagh's crystal waters the green meadows lave."

J. S. M. C.

THE ancient name of this fortress was Edan-dubh-Cairrge, meaning "the front or brow of the black rock."

It is situated near the village of Randalstown, about two miles and a quarter north-west of Antrim. The present demesne, which extends for two miles along the northern shore of Lough Neagh, is bisected by the river Main.

The castle has not been inhabited since it was burnt down on the 15th of May, 1816. A large addition was being erected at the time, and it as well as the older buildings were all consumed. Only the beautiful conservatory and the fortified terrace escaped uninjured. Several turrets and towers still stand to indicate its former extent and grandeur.

A passage about a hundred yards in length runs underground from the castle to the adjacent graveyard, and was the servants' entrance to the mansion. Connected with this are great vaults which were built at the same time as the conservatory and the rooms near, so as to raise the addition above the level of the Lough, and give the building a better frontage.

An old safe is still to be seen in one of the castle walls, and not far from it a curious figure-head, supposed by

SHANE'S CASTLE

some to have been brought from the East and to belong to a much earlier date than the ruins among which it stands. Tradition states that when it falls the family of O'Neill will come to an end.

It is recorded that in 1490 Edan-dubh-Cairrge, the castle of Niale, the son of Con, son of Hugh Boy, was taken and demolished by Felim, grandson of Niale Boy. It is probable that the present ruins are the remains of a castle which was erected in the sixteenth century upon the site of an older fortress, though the exact date of building is uncertain.

Edenduffcarrick belonged to the O'Neills of Clandaboy, and a younger branch of the great Tyrone family.

They were descendants of Hugh O'Neill, surnamed *buide* or *boy*—yellow-haired, from which fact the district got its name.

In Queen Elizabeth's reign Sir Brian MacPhelim O'Neill usurped the O'Neill estates with the help of the English, but they were shortly afterwards confiscated and bestowed by the Crown on Sir Thomas Smith.

In 1573 there is a memorandum by Secretary Smith offering to give up to the Earl of Essex upon certain conditions "Belfast, Massareen, Castle Mowbray *alias* Eden Doucarg (now Edenduffcarrick or Shane's castle, in the county of Antrim) and Castle Toome."

After the treacherous seizing and execution of Sir Brian in 1574 a fierce struggle for possession of Clandaboy began between his son Shane MacBrian and a cousin, Neal Oge. In 1583 Captain Thomas Norreys captured the castle of Edenduffcarrick from Hugh Oge and handed it over to Shane as Captain of Lower Clandaboy.

A writer about 1586, describing Antrim, states that Edenduffcarrig and Belfast were the only wardable castles at that time.

In 1588–89 Lower Clandaboy was divided between Shane M'Brian M'Felim O'Neill, and Neale M'Hue, son of Hue

M'Felim. The latter was granted the castle with a fourth of the country and followers, but as he was unable to provide the pledges required for the safe delivery of the castle and the payment of rent, he was imprisoned in Dublin Castle until he could find them. In the meantime his men garrisoned Edenduffcarrick.

Shane M'Brian O'Neill endeavoured to get possession of North Clandaboy in 1591 for himself and his heirs, and the Government received warning that it would be best for them to keep Shane's Castle in their own hands, especially as it could be used to guard the fisheries of Lough Neagh, where a "civil English plantation" might be formed.

The same year Shane and his cousin Neale agreed to submit to arbitration regarding the division of North Clandaboy. Commissioners were, therefore, appointed by the Lord Deputy, and Shane's Castle was reserved to the Crown according to advice.

The Earl of Tyrone formed a camp near the castle in 1593-94, and the Sheriff of Antrim appealed to the Lord Deputy for a guard to be put in Edenduffcarrick, saying that otherwise the country was unprotected, and that it "is the only mark that these fellows shoot at."

After this the castle seems to have been allowed to fall into decay, for in 1596 Mr. Francis Shane, discoursing about the rebellion in Ulster, states that upon the edge of Lough Neagh "standeth a ruinated pile called Edendowcarrick," which being made wardable could be converted into a store for provisioning Blackwater and Coleraine in case of sea storms.

Later it was evidently taken possession of by Shane M'Brian O'Neill, who had joined with his great namesake and kinsman, the Earl of Tyrone, for in 1597 Sir John Chichester, with the help of Neale M'Haghe (the other claimant to Clandaboy) took the castle from him. It was a somewhat unexpected victory, as Sir John did not at first intend the capture. He had divided his forces into three companies of a hundred men each. One party he sent to seize some horses of the enemy, the second was detailed to harass the rebels, and the third, which he himself commanded, was intended to prevent a sally from the castle. The garrison did make an attempt to issue forth, and he presently came up "pell mell with them," and entered the bawn.

After two assaults the English came so near that they set the building on fire. It was said to have contained large stores, and that its loss was a great bridle to the Earl of Tyrone.

After this the chieftains of both the Clandaboys laid down their arms and gave hostages.

The castle had not long been in Government hands when the warders, although well provisioned by the help of Shane M'Brian (now siding with the English), made a raid upon the country people, and carried off a number of horses.

Neill M'Hugh M'Phelim, having escaped from prison, took up the people's cause and assaulted the castle. They broke the bawn and burned the door of the main keep, whereupon the garrison killed their prey in the cellar, and as it is reported, "by this wilful accident put the house in danger."

A new door was ordered, and also a more plentiful stock of provisions for the garrison.

In 1598 Sir Hugh O'Neill resided at Edenduffcarrick, it having passed again out of the hands of the Government.

In 1607 King James I. finally settled the castle and estate upon the descendants of Shane MacBrian O'Neill. It is most likely that the present name of Shane's Castle is derived from this man. Richard Dobbs uses this designation in 1683, so that the popular belief that the name was altered by French John who came into possession in 1716 is clearly erroneous. He was called "French" John because, being of a younger branch, he had made his own way in the world engaged in the wool trade abroad. When he came into possession of the estate he displayed in the castle hall the very wool-cards he had used in his poorer days to show he was not ashamed of his calling. It was he who built the family vault in the adjacent graveyard in 1722.

In 1798 the first Viscount O'Neill, who was then the family representative, rode into Antrim on the day of the battle of that town. He received a mortal wound from a pike in his side, and being conveyed by boat to Shane's Castle, he lingered for a fortnight. It is supposed that it was at his wife's instigation that he enlarged the castle demesne and removed the ancient village of Edenduff-carrick.

A most interesting note from Mrs. Siddon's diary, mentioning her visit to the castle in 1783, is as follows:—

"When my Dublin engagement concluded I made a visit to Shane's Castle, the magnificent residence of Mr. and Mrs. O'Neill. I have not words to describe the beauty and splendour of this enchanting place, which, I am sorry to say, has since been destroyed by a tremendous fire. Here were often assembled the talent, and rank, and beauty of Ireland. Among the persons of the Leinster family whom I met here was poor Lord Edward Fitzgerald, the most amiable, honourable, though misguided, youth I ever knew. The luxury of this establishment almost inspired the recollections of an Arabian Night's entertainment. Six or eight carriages, with a numerous throng of lords and ladies on horseback, began the day by making excursions around this terrestrial paradise, returning home just in time to dress for dinner. The table was served with a profusion and elegance to which I have never seen anything comparable. The sideboards were decorated with adequate magnificence, on which appeared immense silver flagons containing claret. A fine band of musicians played during the whole of the repast. They were stationed in the corridors which led into a fine conservatory, where we plucked our dessert from numerous trees of the most exquisite fruits. The foot of the conservatory was washed by the waves of a superb lake, from which the cool and pleasant wind came to murmur in concert with the harmony from the corridor. The graces of the presiding genius, the lovely mistress of the mansion, seem to blend with the whole scene."

The great fire already alluded to occurred in 1816, and is supposed to have originated in a chimney where jackdaws were building. It quickly spread to the drawing-room, and nothing was saved except the family papers and plate. A most valuable library and many pictures were destroyed.

The sky was crimson for miles round, and people flocked to all the adjacent hills to witness the magnificent sight.

The present family residence is about a quarter of a mile from the old castle. The owner, Lord O'Neill, is the 2nd Baron, the former title having become extinct in 1855.

"The Rockery," formed from an ancient quarry and stocked with rare plants, is one of the attractions of the demesne.

Authorities Consulted.

Calendar of State Papers.
Calendar of Carew MSS.
G. Hill, "Macdonnells of Antrim."
W. S. Smith, "Shane's Castle."
Donovan, "Annals of the Four Masters."
Parliamentary Gazetteer.
W. S. Smith, "Memories of '98"; G. Hill, "Shane's Castle"; "Origin and Characteristics of the Population in the Counties of Down and Antrim," and Notes, all in *Ulster Journal of Archæology*.

SWORDS CASTLE

ABOUT seven miles from Dublin, on the chief highway to the North, is situated the town of Swords, Sword, Surd, or Swerdes, as it is variously termed in ancient manuscripts. From the earliest ages of Christianity the church founded by St. Columbkille, with its attendant offices and monastery, made the neighbourhood a powerful ecclesiastical centre; so that, when in later years the church lands of Swords became joined to the see of Dublin, they formed no inconsiderable part of the Archbishop's revenue.

In the Bull of Pope Alexander III. in 1179 to St. Laurence O'Toole, Archbishop of Dublin, confirming his archiepiscopal see, Sword is placed second on the list of churches in importance.

Therefore it is not surprising that the Englishmen who succeeded O'Toole in the see of Dublin should have erected their country residence in a town, from the surrounding lands of which they derived so much of their income.

The site for the castle or palace was chosen on the east bank of Swords River, and the area covered by the buildings was more extensive than is usual for a Norman fortress, while the defences were somewhat less, as we hear no mention, nor see any remains, of the keep, which forms so universal a feature of the chief baronial strongholds.

Authorities place the date of building variously between 1184 and 1282, which gives a somewhat wide margin, but its erection is most generally assigned to John Comyn, the

SWORDS CASTLE

first English Archbishop of Dublin, who was elected at Evesham, 1181, and who was one of those to welcome Prince John at Waterford in 1185. An inquisition of 1265 finds that there was a constable of the castle in this Archbishop's time.

The palace was built in castellated style, and the range of embattled walls flanked with towers is still complete. The warders' walk is yet easy to trace. Over the gateway were the apartments for the guard, and just below is still

SWORDS CASTLE.

visible the bakchouse chimney, of which mention will be made later.

Like so many of the castles of Leinster, Swords provided for years a convenient quarry for the neighbourhood, and what had once been corner stones of a palace went to support the thatched roofs of the surrounding cabins, so that few of the buildings which stood inside the battlements are now traceable.

In the line of walls is a large window which once

occupied the gable end of what is likely to have been the great hall. The mullions of this window, which remained intact until recently, were remarkable for being of red sandstone, which is unknown in the country.

The situation of the chapel may still be discerned by the remnants of some of the stone carving which once adorned its sacred walls.

In 1192 Archbishop Comyn obtained a patent authorising him to hold an annual fair in his manor of Swords, and in 1387 this privilege was confirmed to Robert de Wikeford.

King Henry III. enlarged the possessions and added new privileges to the manor, which he granted to Henry de Loundres in 1216, on condition that he should build and maintain Castlekevin, near Glendalough, County Wicklow, to defend the pale in that quarter from the invasions of the great Irish families of O'Toole and O'Byrne.

We read later (1380) that Sir Nicholas Daggeworth seized the manor of Swords as Commissioner of Forfeitures, on the plea that the conditions above stated had not been complied with. He, however, afterwards confessed that the charge had not been proved, and therefore a writ of restitution was issued by the Treasurers and Barons of the Exchequer to Robert de Wykeford, Archbishop of Dublin.

The great prelates seem to have lived in almost royal state within their manor of Swords. They had their own seneschal, who was exempt from the authority of the sheriff of the county, and the law courts. The archbishops could try every case except the four pleas of the Crown, and their gallows was erected near the town on an eminence since known as Gallows Hill. Every writ issued from the civil courts had to be transferred to the prelates' seneschal before it could be served.

The office of chief constable of the palace was a post of considerable importance, and survived the occupation of the castle for a considerable time. William Galrote held the position in 1220, Sampson de Crumba in 1240, and Thomas Fitzsimons in 1547.

In 1624 we read that Patrick Barnewell, of Grace Dieu, received pardon for alienation of certain interests, amongst which was the Constableship of Swords with ten acres in the Broad Meadow that belonged to the office.

It was most likely in connection with this post that the Lords of Kingsland were required to attend the Archbishop whenever he visited Swords, and to hold his stirrup as he mounted or dismounted, for which service they held lands to the value of some £300 a year.

It seems to be uncertain at what exact period the castle ceased to be used as a residence by the Archbishops, but in 1324 Alexander de Bicknor built the archiepiscopal palace of Tallaght, which was used as a country seat for the Archbishops for centuries, and only ceased to be considered as a palace in 1821.

It is most likely, therefore, that the invasion of Ireland by Edward Bruce, brother to the King of Scotland, rendered the position of Swords palace (which was not wholly built for defence) a somewhat dangerous one, as Bruce, having his headquarters at Dundalk, was in possession of the country almost up to the walls of Dublin.

In 1326 this same Alexander de Bicknor having displeased Edward II., and also being in arrears with his accounts as Lord Treasurer, the profits of his See were seized by the King to compensate for the deficiency, and in order to ascertain their real value inquisitions by jurors were held on the different manors.

The finding as regards the palace of Swords was as follows:—

"Who being sworn, say on oath, that there is in this place a hall, and the chamber adjoining said hall, the walls of which are of stone, crenelated after the manner of a castle, and covered with shingles.

"Further, there is a kitchen, together with a larder, the

walls of which are of stone, roofed with shingles. And there is in the same place a chapel, the walls of which are of stone, roofed with shingles. Also there was in the same a chamber for friars, with a cloister, which is now prostrate. Also, there are in the same place a chamber, or apartment, for the constables by the gate, and four chambers for soldiers and warders, roofed with shingles, under which are a stable and bake-house.

"Also, there were here a house for a dairy, and a workshop, which are now prostrate. Also, there is on the premises in the haggard a shed made of planks, and thatched with straw. Also, a granary, built with timber and roofed with boards. Also, a byre, for the housing of farm horses and bullocks.

"The profits of all the above-recited premises, they return as of no value, because nothing is to be derived from them, either in the letting of the houses, or in any other way. And they need thorough repair, inasmuch as they are badly roofed."

This gives some idea of the lost buildings, and also shows that even at this date the castle was beginning to decay.

Later the manor of Swords seems several times to have been granted to archbishops who wished during their lives to resign the arduous duties of the See. In 1484 we read that "Doctor Walton, Archbishop of Dublin, being blind and infirm, resigned his dignity, and reserved to himself for a maintenance the manor of Swords during his life, which reservation was confirmed to him by Act of Parliament during the following year." And again, in 1562, it is recorded that, by Act of Parliament, John, late Archbishop of Dublin, was assured the manor of Swords for his life in consideration of surrendering the bishopric to Walter FitzSymons.

There is no evidence to show that these aged prelates ever resided in the castle, and as the following extract, written in 1583, records its state of ruin, it is most likely they were content with the revenues alone.

Sir Henry Sydney, Lord Deputy in Queen Elizabeth's reign, when sending to Sir Francis Walsingham a summary of his services in Ireland, says: "I caused to plant and inhabit there about forty families of the reformed churches of the Low Countries, flying thence for religion's sake, in one ruinous town called Surds (Swords). And truly (Sir) it would have done any man good to have seen how diligently they wrought, how they re-edified the quite spoiled old castle of the same town and repaired almost all the same, and how godly and cleanly they, their wives and children lived. They made diaper and ticks for beds, and other good stuff for man's use, and excellent good leather of deer skins, goat and sheep fells, as is made at Southwark."

Upon the disestablishment of the Church of Ireland the castle ground was purchased by the late Charles Cobbe, Esq., who leased it to the late Henry Baker, Esq., whose successor still holds the land.

The ground enclosed by the walls is at present laid out as an orchard and garden, and the castellated battlements, which were built to protect the royal state of wealthy prelates, have now no sterner duty than to shelter the delicate apple blossoms from the harsh spring winds, and to catch the sun-rays for the ripening fruit.

Authorities Consulted.

Right Rev. W. Reeves, D.D., Pamphlet on "Antiquities of Swords."
Rev. Canon Twigg, MS. Paper read to Antiquarian Society.
Grose, "Antiquities of Ireland."
D'Alton, "History of County Dublin."
D'Alton, "Archbishops of Dublin."
Calendar of Carew MSS.

TILLYRA CASTLE

NOT far from Ardrahan, in the County Galway, stands this castle, which originally belonged to the Burkes or De Burgos. We read that Ulick, 3rd Earl of Clanricarde, married a daughter of Burke of Tullyra, but it seems to have passed to the Martyns during the sixteenth century. This is generally supposed to have been through marriage. Hogan mentions the Martins of Tillyra in 1598.

In one of the upper chambers is carved the date 1614, accompanied by the initials "S. B."

A somewhat modern doorway opening into the courtyard is surmounted by a stone shield bearing the Martyn arms. They are said to have been presented to the family by Richard I., who was accompanied by Oliver Martyn when he went to the Holy Land.

Underneath the arms on the right side are the letters "R.M.," and on the left "C. M."

In 1702 Oliver Martin of Tulliry, Esq., was allowed to retain his lands after the rebellion, because he had assisted so many Protestants during the insurrection. This was an almost unique concession at the time.

The present owner, Mr. Edward Martyn, of literary fame, has recently erected a beautiful modern mansion near the old fortress.

AUTHORITIES CONSULTED.

J. Fahey, "History and Antiquities of the Diocese of Kilmacduagh."
J. Hardiman, "History of Galway."
Hogan, "Description of Ireland, 1598."

TIMON CASTLE

THIS fortress was one of the castles of the Pale, and is situated in the County of Dublin on the right-hand side of the road which leads from Balrothery to Greenhills.

The name Timon or Timothan is derived from *Teach-Munna*, signifying "the house of St. Munna."

The stronghold is built upon an esker and is therefore conspicuous for a considerable distance round.

There seems to be no trace of outworks, which were probably unnecessary owing to the castle having formerly been surrounded by marshes. In recent years the land has been drained and the water carried off by a small stream which crosses the road near the castle and is a tributary of the Poddle.

The building consists of a square keep with a projecting stair tower adjoining the south-west angle, which is now covered with ivy. The main structure was formerly divided into two floors by an arched roof over the lower room. The battlement slightly projects. The east wall has been destroyed, while about two-thirds of the north wall and some of the south have gone. The western side is still perfect.

There is a narrow window splayed outwards on the ground floor, while several "slit" windows and larger openings are noticeable at different heights. There are a few recesses in the walls.

A flue projection resting on two corbels is to be seen near the summit, and also a walk inside the battlements at the top of the tower.

The entrance was in the west wall, and a small machicolation for pouring lead or water on an enemy was situated over the arched doorway. There were holes at each side of the entrance for securing it with wooden bars.

A great rent now runs from base to summit of the ruin.

A view of the castle as it was in 1770 is published in Handcock's "History of Tallaght."

The fortress is supposed to have been erected in the reign of King John, who granted the manor to Henry de Loundres for his expenses incurred in fortifying Dublin Castle. This grant was confirmed in 1231.

Timon was constituted a prebend of St. Patrick's in 1247, and it is so still, but without endowment, though in 1306 it was valued at £10 a year.

In an inquisition in 1547 it is described as a "ruinous fortress," and three years later being a suppressed prebend it was granted to Bartholomew Cusack for twenty-one years. Two or three years later the lands were granted to James Sedgrove, after which they were purchased by Sir Charles Wilmot, from whom they passed to the Loftus family.

Dudley Loftus was in possession of the castle when he died in 1616, and in 1618 the property was confirmed to Sir Adam Loftus.

William Conolly purchased the estate, which still remains in his family.

Some peasantry inhabited the castle towards the close of the eighteenth century.

There was once a village of Timon, of which no trace now remains.

Authorities Consulted.

D'Alton, "History of County Dublin."
Handcock, "History of Tallaght."
Joyce, "Rambles Around Dublin," in *Evening Telegraph* Reprints.
Dix, "Lesser Castles of the County Dublin," in *Irish Builder*.
Joyce, "Irish Names of Places."

TRALEE CASTLE

THE town of Tralee, formerly Traleigh, meaning the "strand of the River Leigh," is situated in the Barony of Trughenackmy, in the County Kerry. It is nearly two miles east-north-east of Tralee Harbour, and the Lee Rivulet, from which it takes its name, formerly filled the moat of the great castle. Sir Thomas Denny made it run along the Mall in the eighteenth century, and it is now covered over.

The town had originally four castles, only two of which were standing during the famous siege of 1641. Short Castle had disappeared in 1756, while the great castle was demolished in 1826 by consent of its owner, Sir Edward Denny, for the improvement of the town. Its former site, and that of the bowling green attached, is now occupied by the handsome thoroughfare known as Denny Street. The entrance to the castle demesne or 'green," is at the top of this street, and the public have always had access to it.

The great mahogany doors from the castle may still be seen, cut down to fit ordinary doorways, in the houses in Denny Street belonging to Sir John Neligan and Mr. Francis M'G. Denny. Mr. Denny also possesses some parts of a grey stone mantelpiece carved in high relief with the Denny arms, crest, and motto, which also came from the old fortress.

This last castle was a restoration of the chief seat of the Desmond FitzGeralds for close on four hundred years.

There are several versions of the legend which accounts for the crest and supporters of the Geraldines being represented by monkeys. One of these is that in 1261, after the battle of Callen, where MacCarthy Reigh slew the chief heads of the Munster FitzGeralds, only a little baby of eight months old, at nurse in Tralee, was left to represent the great family. Upon hearing the news of the disaster the child's attendants rushed into the streets, when to their horror they presently beheld their charge exhibited on the battlements of the castle in the arms of a pet ape. The animal, however, returned the baby unharmed to his cradle, and afterwards this Desmond was known as "Thomas a Nappagh" or "of the ape." Some authorities mention the abbey as the scene of the child's escape.

Sir Henry Sidney, in his report on Munster, declared that there would be "neither peace nor order in the South, until the palatine jurisdiction of both Ormond and Desmond (East and South Munster) were reduced."

Therefore, in 1576 Sir William Drury, Lord President of Munster, declared his intention of giving the Queen's writ currency in the palatinate.

At the Council the Earl of Desmond tried to dissuade him, but being unsuccessful he offered him hospitality during his visit.

Upon approaching Tralee the Lord President was met by seven or eight hundred armed men who emerged from the cover of the wood, and rushed towards him shouting and brandishing their weapons. Sir William, not knowing whether the display was friendly or otherwise, determined to be on the safe side, and gathering his body guard of a hundred and twenty men round him, he charged the on-coming troop, who did not wait for an attack, but withdrew as hastily as they had advanced.

The President rode on to the castle, where he demanded admittance and explanation, both of which were given to

TRALEE CASTLE

him by the Countess, who received him at the entrance, and assured him (or endeavoured to do so) that he had but received an Irish welcome, and that her husband had meant no harm, but awaited him in the fortress to go hunting.

In 1579 Sir William Drury, then Lord Deputy, sent Henry Danvers to the Desmonds to enlist their aid in repelling a threatened invasion of some foreign mercenaries. This he failed to do, and upon his return journey he slept a night in Tralee Castle, having formerly been a great friend of Sir John of Desmond, the Earl's brother. This friendship is said to have weakened Sir John's influence among his countrymen, and that in consequence he determined to show it had ceased to exist. Be that as it may, he demanded admittance to the castle during the night, and he and his followers murdered Sir Henry Danvers, the Justices Meade and Charters, and their servants, while they slept. It is said that Danvers awoke and seeing Sir John said, " My son, what is the matter?" But his murderer answered, " No more of son, no more of father, make thyself ready, for die thou shalt."

Tradition always pointed out a room in the castle as the scene of the murder, which had a small room off it in the thickness of the walls, from which access was obtained to a narrow stairway and postern. This was commonly called the " murdering hole," and regarded with great superstition.

A despatch to Cecil in 1580 states " all the houses in Trally burnte and the castles raised."

The Earl of Desmond's estate was forfeited in 1583.

" Traylye" was granted to Sir Edward Denny in 1587, and delivered to him by Mr. Thomas Norreys.

The castle was at this time in a ruined condition, and when the family came to Ireland they resided at Carrignafeely Manor until the close of James I.'s reign.

The " Sugan" Earl of Desmond seized the fortress in

1599 and employed a hundred and fifty men to undermine it. Sir Charles Wilmot surprised the rebels with fifty horse. He killed thirty-two, and seized the arms of about a hundred more while the rest escaped to the mountains.

In 1627 Edward Denny, grandson to the first grantee, began to rebuild the stronghold.

Upon the breaking out of the rebellion in 1641 Sir Edward Denny collected his English tenants and the loyal Irish, and they fortified themselves in the two castles. Lady Denny and her children went to England, while Sir Edward joined the President. His step-father, Sir Thomas Harris, took command of the Tralee garrisons, but it was not until early in the following year that the Irish laid siege to the town, under the command of Florence Carty with six hundred men.

The guns of Short Castle opened fire, but nevertheless the Irish raided the town. They stripped or murdered all the inhabitants they captured, and hundreds fled to the two strongholds for protection.

Upon the 10th of February a spy named Laurence gained admittance to the larger castle, on the plea of seeing the Governor, who was asleep. He carried a pass from the rebel poet, Pierce Ferriter, who commanded the Irish forces in the district. His movements at length awakening suspicion he was taken prisoner.

Shortly after this the Irish took possession of the town during the night. The guns of both castles played with little effect, and some of the inhabitants were drawn up into Short Castle by ropes. The Provost, who had left the town to see to some outlying property, was prevented returning, and Sir Thomas Harris had command of both castles, a line from the top of each conveying letters from one fortress to the other.

About four hundred persons fled to the strongholds, so that the provisions intended to last two years gave out in

TRALEE CASTLE

seven months. Water failed, and although thirteen wells were sunk twenty feet each, only thick black water could be procured.

Captain Ferriter and a townsman of Tralee demanded a parley with Sir Thomas and asked him to surrender, but he refused.

They then hauled "sow" engines against the strongholds. The one sent against the great castle was smashed by a small cannon ball, and a cooper in Short Castle dislodged a pinnacle of the building on the top of the other, which they afterwards burnt. The Irish lost about twenty men and their engines in the attack.

An effort was made to relieve the town by sea, but the small force sent for the purpose was entirely routed.

When the siege had lasted about six months Sir Thomas Harris fell ill and died through bad water and anxiety.

Immediately after the provisions giving out the garrisons capitulated, the terms being their lives and a suit of clothes each. Most of them joined Colonel Crosbie in Ballingarry fortress on an island in the Shannon.

Of the six hundred within the castles of Tralee three hundred died during the siege. They were reduced to eating bran, tallow, and raw hides.

The castles were burnt upon being surrendered.

The great castle was shortly afterwards restored, but in 1691 it was again burned, by Sir James Colter's orders, and when the Royalists were defeated at Lixnaw the two Irish officers who carried out the order would have been hanged but for the intervention of Colonel Edward Denny. The famous "Denny Bible" in which this conflagration is recorded belongs to Tralee church, to which it was presented by the Denny family.

In 1698 the House of Commons decided to help in the rebuilding of the castle.

This fortress was of an L shape, but Sir Edward Denny,

3rd baronet, who succeeded to the title in 1795, added another wing in 1804, which contained several fine saloons, a large hall with a handsome circular staircase and other apartments. Soon after 1820 Sir Edward went to live in England.

A black coach, with headless horses and coachman, was formerly said to drive through Tralee upon the death of one of the Denny family, and if any one looked out at it, a basin of blood was thrown in his face. Of later years a banshee is said to have taken its place.

AUTHORITIES CONSULTED.

C. Smith, "State of the County Kerry."
M. A. Hickson, "Old Kerry Records."
"The Antiquities of Tralee," in *Kerry Magazine*.
J. J. Howard, "Miscellanea Genealogica."
M. Hickson, "Ireland in the Seventeenth Century."
Gilbert, "The Castle of Dublin," in *Dublin University Magazine*.
Marquis of Kildare, "Earls of Kildare."
Carew MSS.
Parliamentary Gazetteer.

TRIM CASTLE

> "What! rate—rebuke—and roughly send to prison
> The immediate heir of England! Was this easy?
> May this be washed in Lethe—and forgotten?"
>
> SHAKESPEARE.

THE ancient name of Trim was Ath Truim, signifying "the ford of the boortrees" or elders, the latter half of which appellation alone remains. It is situated on the Boyne, twenty-two and a half miles north-west by west of Dublin on the Enniskillen road.

The castle lies east of the town, on the right bank of the river, and has been said to be the only castle in Ireland deserving the name. It is certainly the finest specimen of the Anglo-Norman fortress, and was one of the chief strongholds of the Pale. It occupies a sloping mound and its walls enclose a triangular area of about three acres, which measures 486 yards in circumference, and was protected by eight circular flanking towers at nearly equal distances and two gate towers.

The north-east side was formerly washed by the Boyne, but now a low meadow intervenes.

On the west or town side a gate-tower occupies the centre. The grooves for the portcullis are still perfect, and from abutting masonry it would appear that there had once been a drawbridge and barbican. The lower portion of the tower is rectangular and the upper part octagonal.

In the southern side is a circular gate tower of Gothic shape. Here also are the portcullis grooves visible and a recess for the windlass, as well as the remains of arches over the moat, and a barbican beyond.

A moat or ditch surrounded the fortress, on the two sides not washed by the Boyne, which was supplied with water by a small stream.

Where the town wall joined the castle at the south-west angle a mound of earth has been artificially raised to the height of the castle wall. This was probably done for the mounting of cannon when the castle was re-fortified in 1647.

One of the towers near this mound was cleared in 1836. It is of three storeys, and the upper part was found to be a pigeon-house, having holes for 60 or 80 pair, while the lower storey contained a postern leading to the level of the moat water. In 1425 it is recorded that the King granted the custody of the dove-cot to Thomas Brown, with pasture called the Castle Orchard.

The north angle of the bawn contains the ruins of several buildings, one being of three storeys with a high gable, and four large windows in the wall towards the river. The piers for the arched roof are still to be seen, and it is likely to have been the banqueting hall or chapel. A large vault extends under part of it. In one of the towers near this the mint is supposed to have been situated. Another tower contains the remains of a small chapel.

The keep consists of a rectangular figure, on each side of which a small square tower abuts, thus forming a twenty-sided figure from which missiles could be showered in all directions. The walls of the centre tower are twelve feet thick, while those of the adjoining ones measure from four to six feet. Winding stairways lead to the summit, at some 60 feet from the ground, while on each angle of the centre tower is a square turret nearly 17 feet in height.

After Hugh de Lacy had been granted Meath in 1173

TRIM CASTLE

he erected the castle of Trim to guard his possessions. He surrounded it with a moat, and furnished it with stores. He then entrusted its custody to Hugh Tyrrell and proceeded to England. No sooner had he left than Roderick O'Connor, King of Connaught, descended on Trim with a large army. Tyrrell sent messages to Strongbow for aid, but in the meantime, finding himself unable to hold the fortress, he evacuated and burnt it.

The news was brought to Strongbow as he marched

TRIM CASTLE.

to its relief, and upon his arrival finding the Irish had retreated, and having nowhere to lodge, he pursued them and killed a hundred and fifty.

Giraldus states that the castle was rebuilt by Raymond le Gros, who had marched to its relief with Strongbow, having joined the expedition on the day of his marriage.

King John stayed at Trim, but he did not lodge in the castle, although one of the towers is called after him, and his signet ring is said to have been found in the enclosure.

In 1215 letters were sent from the King to Thomas Fitzadam to surrender the castle, and five years later it was restored by William Peppard, Lord of Tabor.

At this time Meath was wasted by the quarrels between William, Earl Marshal, and Sir Hugh de Lacy, Earl of Ulster.

There was an order in 1224 from Henry III. to the Lord Justice to allow Walter de Lacy to occupy a hall, rooms, and chambers in the castle. The same year the fortress was besieged.

De Lacy died in 1241, and through the female line the castle passed into the hands of Roger Mortimer, who landed in Ireland in 1308 and took possession.

Upon the invasion of Edward Bruce, Mortimer fled to Dublin, and Lord Walter Cusacke occupied Trim.

Orders for repairing the great hall were issued in 1326, and it was most likely at this time that the two arches which formerly crossed the northern division of the keep were erected, for when they fell in 1820 the plaster showed they had been added after the walls were built.

In 1330 Edward III. granted to Roger Mortimer, Earl of March, the moiety of Meath and the privileges exercised in Trim Castle. He was hanged as a traitor the same year, but Trim was restored to his widow.

Roger, Earl of March, was killed by the Irish in 1398, and the next year Richard II. landed at Waterford to avenge his cousin's death, with Humphrey, son of the Duke of Gloucester and Henry (afterwards Henry V.), son of the Duke of Lancaster. The boys he brought with him as hostages, and upon returning to England he left them as prisoners in Trim Castle. A very small steel spur, inlaid with silver, was found in the castle yard in 1836, which may have belonged to one of the princes.

In 1400 Henry IV. appointed a custodian to the late Earl of March's records at Trim and elsewhere. At this time the castle was in his hands owing to the minority of the heir.

The Privy Council in England (1403) notified to the King that the castle was in a most dilapidated condition.

From this time forward Parliaments were continually held at Trim, while in 1418 the Earl of Kildare, Sir Christopher Preston, and John Bedlow were imprisoned in the castle.

Four years later Richard Talbot, Archbishop of Dublin, resided in the fortress, and in 1425 Edmund, Earl of March, died there while Lord Deputy.

But, perhaps, the most palmy days of Trim Castle were in 1449, when Richard, Duke of York, came to Ireland as Lord Lieutenant, and held his court there.

The mint was opened in 1460, and the following year Christopher Fox was appointed Comptroller.

A Parliament held at Trim in 1465 enacted that any one discovered robbing might be killed, and in Meath their heads were to be sent to the Portreffe of the town of Trim, to be put on the castle wall. Several skulls have been found in the moat.

In 1495 an Act of Parliament passed at Drogheda provided that only Englishmen should be constables of Trim and the other principal castles.

The liberty and lordship of Trim were at this time annexed to the Crown for ever.

In 1541 an order was issued to restore the castle, half the cost of which was to be paid by the country.

A grant was made to Sir James Carroll, Lord Mayor of Dublin, in 1610, to build upon the ruins of the castle a house for the King, and also a jail within the castle enclosure.

Colonel Fenwicke occupied the fortress with a regiment of foot and some troops of horse in 1647. It was in the Royalists' hands until the fall of Drogheda, in 1649, and the garrison disobeyed the Duke of Ormond's instructions to destroy the place before letting it fall into the hands of Sir Charles Coote and his army.

It is stated that the yellow steeple near having been treacherously delivered into the hands of the Cromwellians, was used as a vantage point to make the castle untenable, and that afterwards when the Governor of the castle was reinstated he had one side of the tower blown up. It was in a sally from the town of Trim that Sir Charles Coote lost his life.

It is reported Cromwell spent one night in the castle, but there is no evidence that this is the case.

Adam Loftus sold the castle to Sir James Shean in 1666, and it seems to have been in military occupation in 1690. The whole property was purchased by the Wellesleys, who afterwards sold it to Colonel Leslie.

It is now in Lord Dunsany's possession.

Authorities Consulted.

R. Butler, " Castle of Trim."
W. Wilde, " The Boyne and Blackwater."
E. Evans, " Trim."
P. Joyce, " Irish Place Names."